Contents

7   Preface

9   History of the Louvre as Palace and Museum

25   Near Eastern Antiquities and Islamic Arts

83   Egyptian Antiquities

139   Greek, Etruscan and Roman Antiquities

205   Decorative Arts

279   Sculpture

345   Paintings

451   Graphic Arts

477   Index of Artists

Note on Measurements

Sizes are given in meters and
centimeters with inch measurements to one
decimal place shown in parentheses.
The following abbreviations and symbols are used:
D: depth
H: height
Th: thickness
W: width
Ø: diameter

Preface

This is neither a guidebook, nor a catalogue, it is an anthology. The Louvre is rich in fine objects and masterpieces in their thousands. The constraint was to make a choice and limit ourselves to five hundred items which for a variety of reasons are particularly worthy of attention. It is very much a personal selection, one made by the curators, who treasure the collections in their care and are eager to share their pleasure and knowledge with the reader.

The selection draws on objects from all seven departments within the Louvre and covers a vast array of items both chronologically and geographically, from the civilizations of the ancient East and Egypt right up to the Western world in 1848. There are paintings, sculptures, drawings, engravings and *objets d'art* of all kinds and origins spread throughout the rooms of the museum. It would be difficult for a visitor to see them all on one stroll through the museum. This book enables you to set out on an imaginary tour, either making a preparatory trip in your mind's eye or else going back over a visit in your mind after an exhausting day at the Louvre.

After more than two centuries as a museum, the Louvre is now enjoying a new lease of life. The lengthy building project to create the "Grand Louvre," with its extra floors that formerly housed the Ministry of Finance, is not yet completed. Not all the works of art have found their permanent home. There will be more construction sites, but already the revamped areas and the new displays allow most departments to display their masterpieces in an exemplary manner.

It is to be hoped that this anthology, an indispensable complement to the numerous guidebooks published by the museum, will steer the visitor towards the pleasures and delights of discovery—or rediscovery—of a Louvre undergoing a metamorphosis.

Pierre Rosenberg
President and Director of the Louvre Museum

A History of the Louvre
as Palace and Museum

The King's Palace from the Middle Ages to the 18th Century

The Medieval Keep

At the end of the 12th century, King Philip Augustus built a powerful defense work on the westernmost edge of Paris, ever under threat from the wars with the English. A new fortress was built outside the city and girded with ramparts at the place known as Louvre. This vast quadrilateral, bounded by towers and flanked by lodges on two sides, framed a circular dungeon or great tower, which became the symbolic heart of the kingdom. It even became a prison where the vanquished Count Ferrand de Flandre was incarcerated after the Victory of Bouvines (1214). For the medieval king who moved from place to place, the Louvre was but one of a several abodes. Charles V (1364–80) set up a prestigious residence within the Louvre, entrusting his architect, Raymond du Temple, with the building of new lodges reached by an ornate stairway, the "great spiral," an architectural wonder of the period. It was in the Louvre that Charles V brought together his library of manuscripts.

The dungeon moat of the medieval Louvre

The Saint-Germain-des-Prés Pietà (detail), c. 1500. Inv 8561.

The Renaissance Palace

The Renaissance kings strengthened further the Louvre's pre-eminence.
Francis I, who razed the great tower in 1528, decided in 1546 to transform
the ancient keep into a luxurious residence. This work was undertaken
by Pierre Lescot in the reigns of Henry II and Charles IX. In the "Tuileries,"
named after the tilers' kilns that had been set up on the site, Catherine
de' Medici, the queen-mother, began building an enormous palace but did
not complete it. West of the palace an Italian garden was decorated with
an enameled terracotta grotto, the work of Bernard Palissy. Charles IX
eventually decided to join the two palaces together with galleries; these were
completed by Henry IV after the long religious wars whose nadir was the
bloody St. Bartholemew Massacre (1572) executed on orders from the palace.

The gallery in the Salle des Caryatides, 1550.

The Galerie d'Apollon, decor c. 1661.

"Grand Plan" of the Bourbons

After defeating Paris, Henry IV decided in 1595 to turn the Louvre and the
Tuileries into a giant palace. This "grand plan" was that of a new monarchy
who wished to ensure the Nation's unity around the king. Henry IV's important
works were taken up by Louis XIII, by the Regency government and
by Louis XIV, for the Louvre remained the royal residence, except during
period of the Fronde (the movement against the absolutism of the crown). The
architects, Le Mercier and later Le Vau, continued the grand plan, tore down
the remains of the medieval Louvre and built the Cour Carrée. On the east
side, facing the city, Le Brun and Perrault completed the Colonnade following
Bernini's failure to win the contract. Within, first Poussin (1642) and later
Romanelli (1655–1657) and le Brun worked on the decoration—witness
Anne of Austria's apartment and the Galerie d'Apollon. The Tuileries, to where
the court withdrew while the building works were going on, were refitted:
the palace now opened onto a garden laid out in the French style, devised
by Le Nôtre as the vantage point for the greatest view in Paris. The golden
age of the Louvre came to an end when Louis XIV chose Versailles as the seat
of power; the building works were halted. The Louvre with its twin palaces
standing unfinished and partly unroofed became Louis XV's abode until
he came of age. However, the idea of the grand plan was still alive in the
second half of his reign when Gabriel and Soufflot undertook further work.

The Artistic Mission of the Louvre

The Royal Collections

In the Middle Ages some of the collections were linked with the exaltation of the royal person. There was the Ménagerie, with its lions, first of all in the Louvre and later in the Tuileries gardens in the 17th century. There was also the Library. Installed in the Tour de la Librairie under Charles V, it did not survive the Middle Ages but later projects in the 18th century and a purpose-built installation in the 19th would suggest that it was probably substantial. Lastly there were the royal collections of works of art. The installing of these royal collections in systematic or almost museum-like manner goes back to Henry IV who set up in the Louvre, on the ground floor of the eastern end of the Grande Galerie (now the rooms housing the collection of Roman antiquities), a marble-lined "Antiques room" to display statues and busts, small bronzes and ancient marbles, as well as "modern" works commissioned by the Bâtiments du Roi. This room and its counterpart in the Tuileries palace formed the core of the sculpture collections. The Cabinet des Dessins du Roi was another field of interest for artlovers. The Cabinet des Tableaux was set up under Louis XIV by the Galerie d'Apollon.

Ann of Austria's apartments, 1655–1656.

Artists at the Louvre

In 1608 Henry IV housed artists and craftsmen in the lower part of the
Grande Galerie. Little by little, grants afforded them lodging and workshops
in outbuildings, then in the palace itself. The setting up of the carpet
workshop (out of which grew in 1671 the Gobelins manufactory) and of the
mint for coins and medals that functioned there until 1775 highlights
the creative life of the palace. In the 18th century, the Louvre was a hive
of artists and courtiers. Under the French Revolution, the artists remained
masters of the palace. David superintended from his workshops on the pre-
mises. In 1806, Napoleon I abolished this colony, which had been a veritable
focal point of artistic life.

Under Louis XIV, several academies were set up in the Louvre: the Académie
Française, the Académie des Inscriptions et Belles-Lettres, the Académie des
Sciences. The Académie de Peinture et de Sculpture, attracted by the royal
collections, was set up in the Louvre in 1692, with its courses, lectures, and
own collections. This academy inaugurated an annual, then biennial,
exhibition which later assumed the name of "Salon" after the Salon Carré
where it took place.

Hubert Robert, *La Salle des Saisons in le musée des Antiques*, 1802–1803. RF 1964–35.

Hubert Robert, *Projet d'aménagement de la Grande Galerie*, 1796. RF 1975–10.

The Museum

In this palace of the arts, the directors of the Bâtiments du Roi wished to create a muses' palace, a "museum." In 1750, an artlover, Lafont de Saint-Yenne, requested that the king's pictures in the Louvre should be put on show; in 1768, the director of the Bâtiments, the marquis of Marigny (brother of Mme de Pompadour), suggested that the library, the pictures, the prints, medals and curiosities should be brought together in the Louvre. From 1776 to the Revolution, his successor, the count of Angiviller, sought to create the Museum, for which he commissioned museum projects, ordered statues of "great men," and acquired and restored pictures. The Revolution was to complete the program of the men of the Enlightenment: a commission set up the Musée Central des Arts, which opened its doors to the public in November 1793. A considerable amount of work cataloguing and installing was accomplished. Meanwhile other museums such as the Musée des Monuments Français in Paris, the special museum of the French school at Versailles and museums in the provinces were also opening. The antiquities, especially those looted by revolutionary troops in Italy, were housed on the ground floor of the Grande Galerie for which new decor and appropriate lighting were installed. The painter Hubert Robert, keeper of pictures under the ancient régime, and member of the museum guild in 1795, provided a continuity between the plans of the monarchy and the success of the Revolution. Unstintingly, he undertook a survey of the Grande Galerie, painted the Louvre and dreamt of its transformation.

The Double Destiny of the Palace and Museum

From Bonaparte to Charles X

Systems of government followed one another, punctuated by revolutions always involving the seizure of the palace of the Tuileries, for that was where power resided. First there was Louis XVI constrained to leave Versailles, then followed the Convention, then the Council of the Five-Hundred (1795–1798), the first consul in 1800, who became emperor and lastly the kings of the Restoration. Armed revolutionaries attacked the royal residence three times: on 10 August 1792, in July 1830 and in 1848. The grand plan was reborn. Plans to join the two palaces together proliferated from the time of the Revolution and Napoleon I recommenced work in 1806. His architects, Percier and Fontaine began the colossal undertaking, with Fontaine continuing alone from 1812 to 1848. Standing beside the residence of the head of state, the museum acquired nationwide importance. In 1793, the Musée Central des Arts was crammed with the spoils of the revolutionary armies in Belgium, Italy and Germany. Inaugurated in 1800, the ground floor of the museum devoted to antiquities was redecorated. To enlarge the museum, renamed the Napoleon Museum in 1803, the emperor ousted the artists from their workshops inthe palace in 1806, and continued the decorating and fitting out of the rooms. In 1808 he bought the collection of antiquities belonging to his brother-in-law, Prince Borghese. In 1815 the return of works of art to the allies drastically depleted the royal museum of the Louvre but conversely new collections were added: sculpture from the Musée des Monuments Français (1824); the Egyptian works studied by Champollion who first deciphered hieroglyphics (1826); the Musée Naval (1827); the Spanish collection of Louis Philippe; the Assyrian antiquities (1847). The architectural work was carried on by Fontaine who set up the Musée Charles X. The Louvre also housed the Conseil d'Etat (1825) in rooms adorned with paintings and hosted the opening of parliament in the State Rooms.

The salles Percier and Fontaine, 1812.

François Heim, *Charles X awarding prices to artists at the 1824 Salon.* INV 5313.

François Biard, *Four O'clock at the Salon, "Closing Time"*, 1847 Salon. RF 2347.

Napoleon III's New Louvre

In 1848, the Republic decided to complete the Louvre, now a "People's Palace" and dubbed by Victor Hugo "the Mecca of intelligence."

The architect Duban completed a first stage of the works while the architect Visconti was preparing his plans to extend the palace. In 1852 they were taken on by the prince-president, who was soon to become emperor and move into the Tuileries. Duban resigned in 1853 and Visconti died the same year; the building work was then entrusted to Hector Lefuel who continued the work with inordinate perseverance. It was at that time that the living quarters which separated the two palaces were pulled down. While Visconti had wished that "the architectural character should be borrowed religiously from the old Louvre," Lefuel distorted this precept through a taste for opulence and indulged in a debauchery of decoration as much on the outside of the building as within. The "new Louvre" opened in 1857, accomplishing at last, according to the emperor, the "grand plan sustained by the country's instinct for more than three hundred years." From 1861, the demolition of the Pavillon de Flore and of part of the Grande Galerie followed by their rebuilding were a prelude to the Universal Exhibition of 1867. The fruits of such effort only lasted three years; the Tuileries and the Louvre Library went up in flames in 1871.

Eugène Delacroix, *Apollo vainqueur du serpent Python*, 1850–1851. INV 3818.

The Salon Carré, 1850–1851.

The grand stairway and the Victory of Samothrace.

The Museum of the Republics

In 1882, after twelve years of planning and equivocation, the demolition of the ruins of the Tuileries brought the palatial function of the complex to an end. But Lefuel, still in charge, rebuilt the Flore and Marsan lodges, as well as the north wing where the Ministry of Finance relocated, having also been dislodged by a fire in 1871. Thenceforward, the history of the Louvre merged with that of the museum. New decoration was undertaken; from the grand stairway to be watched over by the Victory of Samothrace, to the antechamber of Henry II whose Renaissance ceiling became the background for Braque's 1953 compositions. The Louvre's history is also one of prodigious growth in the collections and of how to show them to their best advantage.

The Present and Future of the Grand Louvre

With the continuous expansion of the collections, the constant progress
in the history of art and in museum techniques and the ever-growing number
of visitors, a major reshaping of the museum was required. The Grand Plan
and the New Louvre have been superseded by the Grand Louvre, born
of the decision to transfer to the museum the buildings used by the Ministry
of Finance (1981).

Archaeological Research

Before any building work began, archaeological excavations unearthed the
spectacular Louvre of the Middle Ages, the Louvre district from the Gallo-
Roman period to its destruction as well as the tileworks which gave their
name to Catherine de' Medici's palace. Numerous objects, architectural
remains of the medieval Louvre and the kiln-workshop of Bernard Palissy
bear witness still to the richness of these discoveries.

Georges Braque, *Birds*, 1953. INV 20378.

The Pyramid and Bernini's *Louis XIV*.

The Pyramid

The building of a vast reception hall under the Cour Napoléon has given
the Louvre a heart and lungs at last. The American-Chinese architect,
Ieoh Ming Pei, designed a structure well able to welcome visitors, but also
to provide the museum with new and better public and service access.
An auditorium, temporary exhibition rooms and rooms devoted to the history
of the Louvre, linked to an itinerary to the heart of the Louvre of the Middle
Ages, give the new space a museum-like dimension. The glass pyramid
is more than the light source for this underground world, it is the symbol
of the permanence of architectural creation.

The Stages in Rearranging the Collections (1990–1998)

The opening of the Napoleon Hall was the prelude to a total reorganization of the museum. It began with the rehanging of the French paintings on the second floor of the Cour Carrée. To mark its bicentenary in 1993, the Musée du Louvre opened the new spaces in the Richelieu Wing that had been restructured by Pei, in the former Ministry of Finance. Islamic arts (mezzanine), French sculpture and Near Eastern antiquities (ground floor), decorative arts (*objets d'art*) (first floor), north European and French paintings (second floor) have been rearranged around the three glass-covered courtyards. The apartments of the Ministry of State, magnificently decorated in the style of the Napoleon III period, are now open to the public. In 1994, Italian and north European sculpture was moved to the ground floor of the Denon Wing.

The year 1997 saw the opening of new spaces in the elegantly refitted old museum building. On the ground floor of the north wing of the Cour Carrée, the display of Near Eastern antiquities has been enhanced within a long succession of rooms renovated thanks to the sponsorship of Dr. and Mrs. Sackler. Egyptian antiquities now have much more display space, taking up the ground and first floors of the Colonnade Wing as well as a row of four rooms of the Musée Charles X, where two sequences, one chronological and the other thematic ensure the antiquities from the time of the pharoahs are properly displayed. Egyptian antiquities of the Roman period are housed under the Salle du Manège, and Coptic antiquities are in the former rooms of the Ecole du Louvre (now relocated in the Flore Wing). The Department of Greek, Etruscan and Roman Antiquities has seen the refitting of the Ancient Greek gallery, of the ancient glass and jewelry rooms, of the four rooms of the Musée Charles X devoted to terracotta and of the long Campana Gallery devoted to Greek ceramics. The tour of Italian paintings has been rearranged in the Salle des Sept Mètres, in the Salon Carré and in the Grande Galerie. The great cartoons from the Graphic Arts Department are on display in the Mollien Wing.

Yet the Grand Louvre is still not finished. Some collections have still to be rearranged, such as the *objets d'art* of the 18th and 19th centuries, Mediterranean antiquities, the state rooms, and the English paintings. Until the requisite refitting has taken place, some collections are shown only in part and in temporary displays.

Near Eastern Antiquities and Islamic Arts

Ancient Orient:
Mesopotamia, Anatolia, Iran, the Levant, Arabia

Islamic Arts

Introduction

The ancient Orient covered a vast geographical area, united only once under the Persian Empire and stretching from the Indus to the Mediterranean. For a long time the only knowledge of the Near and Middle East came from biblical accounts and Greek and Latin travelers and historians. Having fallen into almost complete oblivion, their civilization was brought to light during the 19th century thanks to archaeological research carried out by Europeans anxious to learn about the roots of their own civilization. This research was begun in 1842, when Paul-Emile Botta, French Consul in Mosul—now in northern Iraq—determined to unearth what were supposed to be the vestiges of ancient Nineveh. Thus it was at Khorsabad, in March 1843, that the palace of Sargon II of Assyria was discovered, decorated with colossal sculptures. A selection of these was immediately sent to France and housed in the Louvre in the "Department of Antiquities." Thirty years later another diplomat, Ernest de Sarzec, discovered in southern Mesopotamia, on the site of Telloh, traces of the much older civilization of Sumer, the very name of which had been forgotten. This discovery prompted the creation of the Near Eastern Antiquities Department in 1881, which functioned from then on as an institution closely linked to archaeological research and in consequence exhibited not just the works of art but all the remnants that form the archaeological context of ancient civilizations. At the same time, other scholars explored the countries of the Levant in search of "Judaic" antiquities, and in 1860 Napoleon III appointed Ernest Renan to head an archaeological expedition there. In this way the first collection with Phoenician elements came into being. 1884 saw the start of excavation work on the palace of Darius at Susa, originally located by an English expedition. The site, which was the capital of the kingdom of Elam, before being that of the Persians, is in western Iran. Exploration of this site, from 1896 down to our own times, yielded up a unique series of masterpieces from the Babylonian civilization, brought home as spoils of war by the Elamites in the 12th century B.C. These prestigious antiquities were found alongside remnants of the Elamite civilization, and were exhibited at the Louvre in their entirety, thanks to a special treaty ceding them to France.

After 1918, France was granted a mandate by the League of Nations over the states of the Levant, Syria and Lebanon; it organized the research and conservation of antiquities, which was shared between the Louvre and local museums. Two large sites in particular—both still being worked—have yielded collections of primary importance; Ras Shamra, formerly Ugarit, (Schaeffer Expedition) from 1929, and Mari (Parrot Expedition) from 1933. From the outset, acquisitions and gifts have complemented the series assembled from regular digs. Since the Second World War, the Near Eastern Antiquities Department has been enriched mainly in this way, with collections made in the past by enlightened amateurs such as Louis De Clercq and, more recently, P. and J. David-Weill. Antiquities that had once been dispersed were thus saved for the purposes of research to which the department is devoted.

The collections, in the Richelieu Wing and two wings of the Cour Carrée, are divided between three great cultural and geographical unities:

Mesopotamia, of great historical significance since it was there that writing was first disseminated; Anatolia and Iran, linked to the great Mesopotamian states; the Levant and Arabia at the periphery. The periods which follow the Islamic conquest of these regions are presented in a special section of the department devoted to the arts of Islam.

Mesopotamia

The rich plain of modern-day Iraq, irrigated by the Tigris and the Euphrates, saw the development of the oldest urban civilizations following a long period when the principle of irrigation in agriculture was steadily mastered. The Sumerians created their civilization, characterized by the invention of writing, within the framework of City-States governed by Priest-Kings. Emerging during the fourth millennium, this civilization developed throughout the long period of archaic dynasties during the third. We know about the Lagash dynasty from antiquities discovered at Telloh, the ancient town of Girsu. The same civilization is represented at Mari, a Semite city of the Middle Euphrates. Around 2340, King Sargon, of the Semite dynasty of Akkad, founded an expansionist empire which annexed the old cities of Sumerian style. He sponsored an art glorifying royalty and royal victory; the masterpiece in this genre is the stele of his grandson Naram-Sin (no. 10). After the fall of this empire, the Sumerian prince Gudea of Lagash was patron of the so-called neo-Sumerian renaissance, illustrated by the series of statues discovered at Telloh from 1877 on (nos. 11, 12). The kings of Ur were next to develop this renaissance creating in their turn a great empire. The destruction of the latter, around 2000 B.C., practically marks the end of the Sumerian people; their archaic language was maintained from then on only for religious and esoteric purposes.

The Amorites, Semite nomads from the west, invaded the country and adopted its civilization, founding a series of kingdoms. Babylon was one of them, and it re-united Mesopotamia under the great Hammurabi in the 8th century B.C. Another Amorite dynasty transformed Assyria into a great commercial power.

The First Babylonian Dynasty, destroyed at the beginning of the 6th century B.C., was replaced by that of the Kassites from Iran, over a long period which is often obscure. The Kassites were conquered by the kings of Elam who razed Babylonia and carried away the immense spoils discovered at Susa by the Delegation to Persia. After a dark age marked by the invasions of Aramaean nomads, the Assyrians arose again and subjugated the entire Orient from the 9th to the end of the 7th century, governing from their palaces of Calah (present-day Nimrud), Khorsabad and Nineveh.

The decoration of their palaces took the form of a royal propaganda campaign. Finally, the Chaldaean kings of Babylon conquered the Assyrians and were patrons to a late renaissance: Nebuchadnezzar II restored Babylon in grandiose style, with glazed-brick decoration, and completed the famous Tower of Babel, the ancient description of which is in the Louvre.

1. Neolothic Statuette
Tell es-Sawwan (Middle Tigris)
Beginning of the 6th millennium B.C.
Alabaster. H 5.4 cm (2.1 in.)
Loan from the Museum of Baghdad, 1981. AO 33

2. Sumerian Priest-King
Southern Mesopotamia
Uruk period c. 3300 B.C.
Statuette, limestone. H 25 cm (9.8 in.)
Early acquisition. AO 5718

This example from the oldest
Mesopotamian statuary was found
by Iraqi archaeologists in a tomb
that antedates the use of clay pottery.
It comes from a village whose
inhabitants had just mastered the
practice of irrigation.
The forms in general and especially
those of the face are deliberately
simplified, reflecting a fear of human
realism which characterizes
the Neolithic civilizations of the
Near East.

The creation of the first properly
administered states, which preceded
the historical states of Sumer,
stimulated the invention of writing
in Uruk. This metropolis gave its
name to the corresponding period.
It was an epoch marked by a cultural
"revolution" which led to the
elaboration of the classic forms
of Oriental art; sculpture in the
round, bas-relief, etc., and to the
abandonment of archaic forms of art
such as highly stylized vase painting.
The new art had realism, albeit
crude enough at first, as its ideal.
The priest-kings of each city-state,
recognizable from their headbands
and beards, are the ancestors of the
historical Sumerian kings who were
called upon to play the role of gods
to whom human form was attributed.

3. Prince Ginak
Mesopotamia
Early phase of the Early Dynastic period
c. 2700 B.C.

Gypsum. H 26 cm (10.2 in.); W 10.8 cm (4.2 in.)
Gift of the Société des Amis du Louvre, 1951.
AO 20146

The period of the first semi-legendary
dynasties recorded in Sumerian
literature, saw the development
of a new art, and particularly
of votive statuettes designed
to perpetuate the ritual prayers
offered by all classes of men and
women, on an egalitarian basis,
in the temples. To begin with, this
art affected an angular, geometric
stylization deliberately removed
from realism, with a striking
idealization of human forms. The
figure of Ginak, prince (in Sumerian:
ensi) from an unknown city-state,
is representative of this archaic art.

4. War-Mace of Mesalim
Telloh, formerly Girsu
c. 2600 B.C.

Limestone. H 19 cm (7.5 in.); Ø 16 cm (6.3 in.)
Gift of Sultan Abd-ul Hamid, 1986. AO 2349

Like the antiquities which follow,
this one was found by Ernest
de Sarzec at Telloh. It is a votive
weapon bearing a Sumerian
inscription which puts it among the
most ancient of historical documents.
It was dedicated by Mesalim, who
was king of the Semite town of Kish
to the north of Sumer and presented
later as the arbiter of wars between
the Sumerian states. The mace
is decorated in an archaic style with
the "arms" of the Sumerian state
of Lagash. There is a lion-headed
eagle, personifying the thundercloud, dominating other lions which
form a circle around the mace.
The eagle, called Anzu, personified
the realm of the thundercloud god,
Ningirsu, the patron divinity
of Lagash.

Side A.

5. Ur-Nanshe Relief
King of Lagash
Telloh, formerly Girsu
c. 2500 B.C.

Limestone. H 40 cm (15.7 in.); W 47 cm (18.5 in.)
E. de Sarzec excavations, 1888. AO 2344

Founder of the dynasty which
reigned for nearly two centuries over
Lagash, King Ur-Nanshe liked
to commemorate his constructions.
He had himself portrayed
as a simple bricklayer, carrying the
brick basket in front of his family,
then seated at banqueting table.
He wears the fur skirt—the so-called
kaunakes—with its traditional,
angular tongue-shaped hangings.
The inscription names each member
of his family, then lists the main
temples built under his supervision.

6. The Stele of the Vultures
Telloh, formerly Girsu
c. 2450 B.C.

Limestone, H 1.80 m (70.9 in.); W 1.30 m (51.1 in.)
E. de Sarzec excavations.
AO 50, 2346, 2347, 2348, 16109

This badly damaged stele carries
a long Sumerian text which is the
oldest known page of history, relating
the struggles between the state
of Lagash and its neighbors during
the reign of Eannatum, grandson
of Ur-Nanshe, and his forebears.
His victories are illustrated on both
sides, in register form.

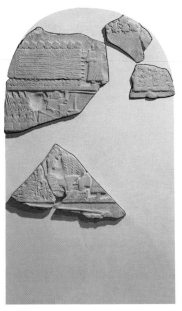

Side B.

Side A

The king in the role of his god Ningirsu has captured his enemies in a great net; the same symbolism is found in the Bible (Ezek. 12:13; Luke 21:35).
The king renders thanks for his victory to his goddess, of whom nothing remains but her head, recognizable by her horned tiara.

Side B

At the top, the vultures which tear at the bodies of the enemy gave the stele its name. Below, wearing the warrior's wig-headdress, the king leads the heavy infantry, which tramples the enemy corpses. Next, in his chariot, he leads his light infantry in the charge. Finally, at the bottom of the stele, the burial of the dead and a funerary sacrifice are depicted.

7. Vase of Entemena, Prince of Lagash

Telloh, formerly Girsu
c. 2400 B.C.

Silver and copper. H 35 cm (13.8 in.);
W 18 cm (7.1 in.)
E. de Sarzec excavations. Gift of the Sultan
Abd-ul Hamid, 1896. AO 2674

Entemena, nephew and second successor to Eannatum, bore only the title "prince" or "governor" (*ensi*) instead of king. He dedicated this vase as part of the "table service" of Ningirsu, patron-god of Lagash. The engraving depicts the lion-headed eagle, repeated four times, dominating various animals. Entemena was patron to a major literary flowering. One of his historical texts treats of the *liberty* given to his people; another, of the *fraternity*, which refers to the alliance he struck with the king of Uruk.

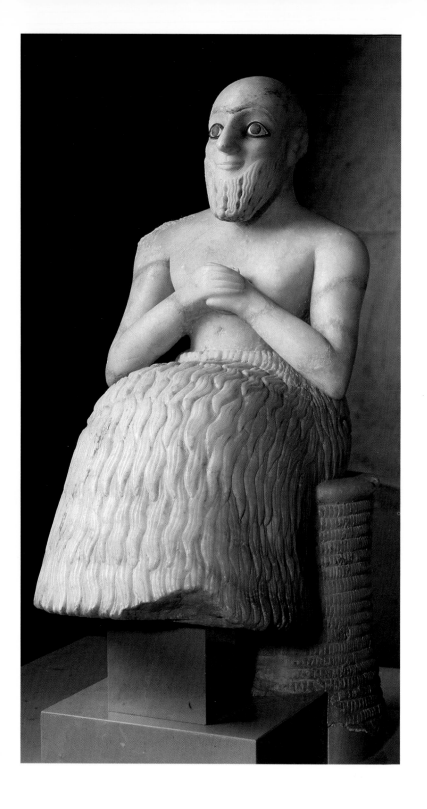

9. The Mari "Standard"
Mari (Middle Euphrates), temple
of Ishtar
c. 2400 B.C.

Shell mosaic.
A. Parrot excavations. AO 19820

8. Ebih-Il, the Superintendent of Mari
Mari (Middle Euphrates), temple
of Ishtar
c. 2400 B.C.

Statuette, alabaster. H 52 cm (20.5 in.)
A. Parrot excavations, 1934. AO 17551

Civilization of the Sumerian type
dominated the whole of Semite
Mesopotamia, particularly Mari,
modern day Tell Hariri in Syria,
explored from 1934 onwards
by André Parrot, and in our own
time by Jean Margueron. Here,
statuary developed rapidly from the
middle of the third millennium, and
with a marked originality in comparison with the South. A cheerful
optimism distinguishes it sharply
from the severe expressions connected
to the angular stylization of the
preceding epoch, as illustrated by the
statuette of Ginak (no. 3).
The "superintendent" was in fact
more the equivalent of a minister
of finance. He had himself portrayed
in the fur skirt, which is rendered
with remarkable realism revealing
the *kaunakes* in the style shown
for example on the Ur-Nanshe
relief (no. 5).

This picture was assembled from
scattered fragments found in the
temple of Ishtar and reconstituted
by comparing it with one found
intact at Ur. Traditionally known
as the "standard," it depicts a victory
in a style both freer and more
refined than that of the Stele of the
Vultures (no. 6). The conquering
dignitaries are protected by large
scarves worn over the shoulder and
they carry battle-axes. The defeated
foe was driven before them.

10. Victory Stele of Naram-Sin
Susa
Akkad period, c. 2230 B.C.
Pink sandstone. H 2 m (78.7 in.); W 1.05 m (41.3 in.)
J. de Morgan excavations, 1898. Sb 4

Originally this stele was erected
in the town of Sippar, center of the
cult of the Sun god, to the north
of Babylon. It was taken as plunder
to Susa by an Elamite king in the
12th century B.C. It illustrates the
victory over the mountain people
of western Iran by Naram-Sin,
4th king of the Semite dynasty
of Akkad, who claimed to be the
universal monarch and was deified

during his lifetime. He had himself
depicted climbing the mountain
at the head of his troops. His helmet
bears the horns emblematic of divine
power. Although the stone is worn,
his face is expressive of the ideal
human conqueror, a convention
imposed on artists by the monarchy.
The king tramples on the bodies
of his enemies at the foot of a peak;
above it the solar disk figures several
times, and the king pays homage
to it for his victory.

11. Gudea, Prince of Lagash
South Mesopotamia
Neo-Sumerian period, c. 2150 B.C.

Statue, diorite. H 70.5 cm (27.8 in.);
W 22.4 cm (8.8 in.)
Acq. 1987. AO 29155

After the fall of the Akkadian
Empire, Gudea, prince of Lagash,
instigated a Sumerian renaissance
marked by a literary flowering that
corresponded to Sumerian classicism,
and also by a courtly art devoted
to exalting an ideal of serene piety
and of a kind of humanism. This
independent prince, who was never
king, wears the turban-like headpiece
of sovereignty. His youthful face
may indicate that the statue was
executed at the beginning of his
reign.

12. Gudea, Prince of Lagash
Telloh, formerly Girsu
Neo-Sumerian period, c. 2150 B.C.

Head, diorite. H 23 cm (9.1 in.); W 11 cm (4.3 in.)
E. de Sarzec excavations, 1881. AO 13

This head, with the prince's
headpiece, wrongly taken
to be a "turban," was found at Telloh
at the same time as the votive
headless statues inscribed with
the name of Gudea and placed in the
temples the prince had built. These
statues were designed to perpetuate
the prayers he offered up in them.
The expression of confident piety
is characteristic of the human ideal
that inspired the neo-Sumerian
princes at the end of the third
millennium.

14. Bull with a Man's Head
Telloh, formerly Girsu
Neo-Sumerian period, c. 2150 B.C.
Soapstone. H 10 cm (3.9 in.); W 14 cm (5.5 in.)
Acq. 1898. AO 2752

13. Lady with a Scarf
Telloh, formerly Girsu
Neo-Sumerian period, c. 2150 B.C.
Statuette, chlorite. H 17 cm (6.7 in.);
W 9 cm (3.5 in.)
E. de Sarzec excavations, 1881. AO 295

There is every likelihood that this
statuette, dating from an epoch
when art was at the service of the
monarchy, portrays a princess
of Gudea's family. Léon Heuzey,
a Hellenist and the first curator
of the Near Eastern Antiquities
Department observed its "resemblance
to the Greek type" and added:
"There is no doubt that, from this
epoch onwards, the progress of taste
alone would have brought Chaldaean
sculpture, by the gradual attenuation
of a national type, to a conception
very close to that of the Hellenic
profile."

For temple decoration, Gudea and
his son commissioned a series
of statuettes of the bull with a human
head which was designed to hold
a little vase of offering. The androcephalus bull was called a *lama*,
or "protector god." It personified the
Eastern Mountain, from where the
sun rises in the morning; as such,
it was considered to be the animal-
attribute of the sun.
The neo-Sumerian artist has
succeeded in giving this monster,
which personifies a primal entity,
a serene expression in keeping with
the humanism which animated the
whole civilization of that period.

16. Sacrificial Scene
Mari (Middle Euphrates), palace
of Zimri-Lim
First half of the 18th century B.C.

Wall painting on dried mud plaster.
H 76 cm (29.9 in.); W 1.326 m (52.2 in.)
A. Parrot excavations, 1935–1936. AO 19825

The palace that king Zimri-Lim
of Mari completed before its
destruction by Hammurabi
of Babylon was decorated with
paintings of ceremonial inspiration.
This painting shows a very important
person, perhaps the king, dressed
in the rich fringed costume, leading
the lesser priests who are presenting
the bull prepared for the sacrifice.
This painting is a good illustration
of how Mari belonged as much
to the world of the Levant
as to Mesopotamia.

15. Stele of Gudea
Telloh, formerly Girsu
Neo-Sumerian period, c. 2150 B.C.
Limestone. H 1.25 m (49.2 in.); W 63 cm (24.8 in.)
E. de Sarzec excavations, 1881. AO 52

In the temples that he built, Gudea
erected a series of stelae commemorating the ceremonies of the cult, but
they were shattered in antiquity.
The largest fragment depicts
a musician playing a great lyre; its
sound box is supposed to represent
a bull, because a text by Gudea
explains that the sounds obtained
were compared poetically to its
bellow.

17. Temple Guardian Lion
Mari, temple of Dagan
19th century B.C.

Bronze with inlay. H 38 cm (15 in.);
W 70 cm (27.6 in.)
A. Parrot excavations, 1936–1937. AO 19824

Dagan was the great god of the
Semite Amorites; his temple was
built at Mari next to the royal palace
by the prince or independent
"governor" Ishtup-Ilum. Two lions
(the second is in the Museum
of Aleppo) stood guard over his door
to terrify potential enemies. They
are made of bronze plaques nailed
originally onto a wooden beam,
which has since disappeared. Eyes
of the same proportions, larger than
lifesize, were found nearby and
suggest that a "pack" of other wild
animals accompanied the two which
alone remained in place.

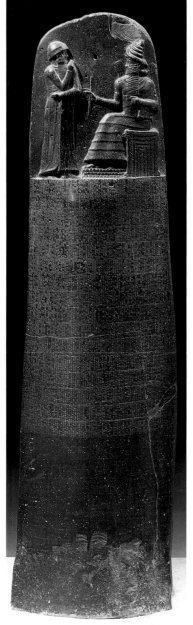

18. Legal Code of Hammurabi
Susa
First half of the 18th century B.C.
Basalt. H 2.25 m (88.6 in.)
J. de Morgan excavations, 1901–1902. Sb 8

Like a series of other remarkable
works from the Mesopotamian
civilization, this tall stele originally
stood in a town of Babylonia and
was taken as plunder to Susa by the
Elamites in the 12th century. It was
excavated by the de Morgan
expedition and the text written
on it was translated in six months
by Father Vincent Scheil. Hammurabi
was the sixth king of the first
Babylonian dynasty, and the first
to establish the supremacy of his city,
which had hitherto been of modest
standing only. What he had engraved
on this stele is not so much a "legal
code" as a collection of exemplary
royal pronouncements in keeping
with a tradition established by the
Sumerians. The bas-relief at the top
is a sober representation of the
meeting of king and god. The king
wears the royal headpiece like
Gudea; he holds his hand before his
face in the act of prayer. The sun-
god Shamash, patron of justice,
is recognizable from the flames
flaring on his shoulders. His crown,
with its four pairs of horns symbolic
of divinity, is indicative of his high
rank in the hierarchy of the gods.
He holds out but does not give to the
king the rod and the ring, also
denoting divine power.

19. Royal Head
Brought from Babylonia to Susa
First Babylonian Dynasty,
19th–18th century B.C.
Diorite. H 15 cm (5.9 in.); W 12.5 cm (4.9 in.)
J. de Morgan excavations. Sb 95

Like the stele of the "Codex," this
head was taken to Susa from
a Babylonian city as plunder. Often
thought to represent Hammurabi,
it remains anonymous, although
it certainly belonged to a statue
of the same epoch, and is stylized
according to the ideal image of the
king-lawmaker, as opposed to that
of the devout prince in the time
of Gudea or of the sovereign of the
universe in the Akkadian period.
This is not therefore a personal
portrait but an idealized effigy
of the king.

20. Worshipper of Larsa

Larsa (Babylonia)
First half of the 18th century B.C.
Statuette, bronze and gold. H 19 cm (7.5 in.);
W 15 cm (5.9 in.)
Acq. 1932. AO 15704

A dignitary named Awil-Nanna, from the ancient Sumerian city of Larsa, dedicated this little bronze "for the life of Hammurabi," king of Babylon, his sovereign. The dedication to Amurru, the patron-god of the Amorite nomads who had adopted Sumerian civilization, means that the bronze must have been kept in the temple of this god. It is possible that the kneeling figure wearing the royal headpiece is Hammurabi himself. He is depicted in bas-relief on the base, praying to the god before whom this object would thus have been placed; his prayer could then be perpetuated thanks to an offering placed in the little basin in front.

21. Kudurru of Melishipak

Brought from Babylonia to Susa
Beginning of the 12th century B.C.

Gray limestone. H 65 cm (25.6 in.);
W 30 cm (11.8 in.)
J. de Morgan excavations, 1898–1899. Sb 22

The kings of Babylon from the
Kassite dynasty made generous gifts
to their vassals. Record of this was,
in principle, kept on the boundary
stones—the *kudurrus*—of the lands
that had been made over. In actual
fact it was inscribed on great slabs,
or standing stones, kept in the
temples. These lists of donations were
placed under the protection of the
greatest possible number of gods,
most often represented in their
symbolic form and arranged
according to the hierarchy of the
pantheon. However, at the top, are
symbols of the three heavenly gods;
Sin (moon), Shamash (sun) and
Ishtar (the planet Venus), in order
of their position in the heavens,
rather than their importance. They
were surpassed by the supreme triad:
An (sky), Enlil (air) symbolized
by their horned crowns and
Ea (fresh water from the abyss),
symbolized by a kind of scepter
carried by a goat-fish. Below we find
the emblems of several other gods;
that of Marduk, patron-god
of Babylon, is identifiable as a pointed
hoe placed on a stand and the
serpent-dragon which guards
the underworld of the god. The same
dragon carries the scribe's stylet,
which is the emblem of Nabû,
Marduk's son. These emblems were
difficult to interpret, even for the
ancients who sometimes inscribed
the name of the gods symbolized
next to the symbols themselves.

22. Neo-Babylonian Kudurru
Uruk (southern Babylonia)
Middle of the 9ᵗʰ century B.C.
Limestone. H 32 cm (12.6 in.); W 15 cm (5.9 in.)
Acq. 1914. AO 6684

23. Dragon Head
Babylonia
Neo-Babylonian period
First half of the 1ˢᵗ millennium B.C.
Bronze. H 15 cm (5.9 in.)
Acq. 1903. AO 4106

King Marduk-Zakir-Shumi
of Babylon, who benefited from
Assyrian protection, gave land and
eight houses in the second year of his
reign (850 B.C.) to Ibni-Ishtar, a scribe
and priest in the temple of the great
goddess Ishtar. This high-ranking
dignitary is depicted greeting the
king who holds a small bunch
of flowers and is sniffing its scent.
Round about are the symbols
of gods, guarantors of the donation.
There is the great pointed hoe
of Marduk, patron-god of Babylon,
the double lightning of Adad the
storm god, the ram-headed scepter
of Ea, god of the freshwater deep,
and the lamp of Nusku, god of fire.

This dragon head belonged to the
cult of Marduk, patron-god
of Babylon, who was originally
a minor god in the pantheon. The
monster is linked to the formidable
horned serpent which symbolized
the underworld whence it emerges.
Thus the god Marduk was also
associated with vegetation, which
is why he also has a pointed hoe for
an emblem.

24. Door Guarded by Winged Assyrian Bulls
Khorsabad, palace of Sargon
of Assyria, 721–705 B.C.

Gypsum. H 4.20 m (165.3 in.); W 4.36 m (171.6 in.)
P.-E. Botta excavations, 1834–1844. AO 19857

King Sargon II built his palace in the citadel of the new city he founded near Nineveh, which Paul-Emile Botta unearthed in 1843.
The doors were guarded by pairs of androcephalus bulls. These benign spirits, known as *lamassu*, guarded the foundations of the world.
They performed the same service for the palace. The new presentation in the museum courtyard, known as the Khorsabad courtyard, recalls the monumentality of Assyrian palaces. It is complemented by a reproduction of a bull, cast from the original preserved in Chicago, the only survivor of its kind.
The inscription between its hooves reads: "Palace of Sargon, great king, mighty king, king of the universe, king of Assyria, razed Urartu… subjugated Samaria, captured Hanon king of Gaza…" It goes on to relate the building of the town, known as Dur-Sharrukin, in other words "Fort Sargon."

25. Medean Tribute-Bearers
Khorsabad (Assyria), palace of Sargon II
721–705 B.C.

Relief, gypsum. H 1.62 m (63.8 in.);
W 3.66 m (144.1 in.)
P.-E. Botta excavations, 1843–1844. AO 19887

The reliefs decorating the interior of the palace of Sargon were smaller than the colossal ones on the outside facades. They were arranged in two columns separated by an inscription describing the king's campaigns. This one shows the Medes surrendering their fortress symbolized by a model, and leading their magnificent horses as tribute. The sculptor is as gifted in rendering animals as he is ethnologically exact.

26. Assurbanipal in a Chariot
Nineveh, palace of Assurbanipal
668–630 B.C.

Relief, gypsum. H 1.62 m (63.8 in.);
W 77 cm (30.3 in.)
Gift of Rawlinson to the Place Expedition.
Entered the Louvre in 1856. AO 19904

Assurbanipal was the last of the great Assyrian kings; he patronized Assyrian palatial art at its apogee. In its upper columns the relief shown illustrates the deportation of the Elamites after the sack of Susa in 646. Below, the king advances in his chariot. He is sheltered by a parasol, wears the royal tiara and, like the king of Babylon (no. 22), holds a little bouquet which he is sniffing. Behind him, servants wave fly-swats and officials bear the king's arms.

27. Exorcism Plate
Assyria
End of 8ᵗʰ–7ᵗʰ century B.C.
Bronze. H 13.5 cm (5.3 in.); W 8.5 cm (3.3 in.)
Gift of H. de Boisgelin, 1967. AO 22205

This plate illustrates the rites
of exorcism; an explanatory text has
come down to us with variants.
The doctor's role was to expel demons
held to be the cause of diseases.
The plate hung above the patient
by means of the two rings at the top.
It is presided over by the demon
Pazuzu, charged with putting
the other demons to flight.
The decoration is divided into
columns: at the top are the symbols
of the gods invoked for the cure.
Next come the seven formidable
demons. Below there is the patient
on his bed, watched over by two
fish-genii—the "Sages" of the
Ea retinue, god of wisdom and the
deep. Finally, at the bottom, appears
the evil goddess Lamashtu who
torments the patient. She is carried
by a donkey whose duty is to take
her back into the desert; the donkey
stands on a boat floating on the river
of hell. Next to her are jewels and
other gifts offered to the goddess
to entice her back into the
underworld.

Anatolia

The Anatolian plateaux saw the growth of sedentary communities from the eighth millennium B.C. During the fourth millennium B.C., cultures closely akin to those of the Cyclades and the Balkans produced stone idols. Shortly after 2000 B.C. Assyrian merchants settled in Cappadocia to exchange textiles for precious metals: they imported the use of Mesopotamian cuneiform writing and cylinder seals. A new people, the Hittites, brought under their sway all the Anatolian princedoms from 1600 B.C. Their capital, Hattusha, present-day Bogazkoy, was administered by scribes educated in the skill of cuneiform writing. The urge to expand their empire brought the Hittites to the gates of Babylon in 1595 B.C. In the 14th and 13th centuries B.C., their hegemony spread over the Levant and brought them into headlong conflict with the Egypt of Ramesses II at the battle of Qadesh in 1285 B.C. The empire collapsed under the blows of the "Sea Peoples" around 1200 B.C. but witnessed a renaissance in the states of northern Syria and eastern Anatolia where the hieroglyphic Hittite writing survived.

28. Double Idol
Cappadocia
Ancient bronze, c. 2000 B.C.
Alabaster. H 12 cm (4.7 in.)
AO 8794

These extremely schematized images have some connection with sculptures from the Cyclades.

29. Hittite God
Yozgat, Bogazkoy region
Classic Hittite Empire, 1600–1400 B.C.
Gold. H 3.8 cm (1.5 in.)
Chantre coll. AO 9647

This pendent figurine is characteristic of Hittite art at its height. The dress, turned-up shoes and high conical crown are comparable with the reliefs of divine processions at Yazilikaya.

Iran

Dominating Eastern Mesopotamia, Iran covers a vast mountainous area, divided into several regions that for a long time remained lost in prehistory, except to the southwest where the kingdom of Elam was an organized, historical entity contemporary with those of Sumer and Babylon. Elam was a dual state consisting of the plain of Susa to the west, and the plateau of present-day Fars, with the city of Anshan to the east. Susa was founded around 4000 B.C. by a population linked to those of the plateau, as its magnificent painted ceramics indicate. They compare with those from Tepe Sialk in the center of the plateau. Susa and Elam were sometimes linked to Mesopotamian culture and sometimes to that of the Iranian plateau.

The third millennium saw the growth of nomad artisan cultures of Luristan, to the north of Susiana, with the first decorative bronzes, and to the east, in the province of Kerman, richly ornate vases cut from green stone (chlorite). At the end of the third millennium this civilization, known as the trans-Elamite, spread in a grand sweep to the boundaries of Central Asia, Bactria and as far as the gates of India.

Elamite power reached its zenith when, in the 13th century B.C., King Untash-Napirisha founded a new capital at Chogha Zanbil, not far from Susa. Dominating the site, was a tower with several stories which is remarkably preserved. Then, kings of a dynasty of the 12th century B.C., seized Babylonia and carried off to Susa as spoils such masterpieces as the stele of Naram-Sin (no. 10), the Hammurabi Code (no. 18), etc. At the same time, new peoples, possibly Iranian immigrants, settled in northern Iran and left precious vases in their tombs. The nomad civilization of Luristan, dormant since around the 18th century, re-emerged around the 12th century and created over a long span of time extraordinary bronzes in the prehistoric tradition which retain their appeal today.

The Elamites experienced a renaissance in the 8th and 7th centuries, before collapsing under the assaults of the Assyrians in 646. It was then that the Persians brought the whole of Iran together in one empire with two capitals: Persepolis and Susa. In the latter Darius built his Apadana palace with its rich glazed-brick decor excavated between 1884 and 1886 by Dieulafoy. With the fall of the Persian empire to Alexander the Great, Susa lost its importance as a political and cultural center. Iran was gradually hellenized, while retaining its originality, flourishing under the Sassanid dynasty from the 3rd to the 7th century A.D.

30. Goblet from Susa I
Susa: archaic necropolis
c. 4000 B.C.
Terracotta. H 28.5 cm (11.2 in.); L 16 cm (6.3 in.)
J. de Morgan excavations, 1907–1909. Sb 3174

The painted vases left in the tombs
of the first Susans illustrate, on the
eve of its extinction, the highest
point in the Neolithic tradition of the
mountain people who came down
to the plain. The forms are simple
and harmonious and the decoration
boldly stylized. At the top is a frieze
showing wader birds elongated
vertically; below, racing dogs
elongated horizontally while below
them is a large ibex, geometrical
in design, whose huge horns describe
an almost perfect ellipse. This
stylization is misleadingly reminiscent
of pictographic characters; it has,
in fact, a purely decorative function,
as its diversity from one vase
to another indicates. Along with
these vases, the dead were given
access to other objects, such as copper
axes, imported from central Iran.

31. Female Votary
Susa, Uruk period
c. 3200 B.C.
Statuette, alabaster. H 6.3 cm (2.5 in.);
W 3.8 cm (1.5 in.)
J. de Morgan, R. de Mecquenem, 1909. Sb 70

The adoption of the Sumerian-type
urban civilization encouraged the
Susans to create art that would
become classic. Breaking with the
purely decorative stylization
of prehistoric times, they adopted
realism as their ideal. The statuettes
of the devout were carved in this
vein; they are both delicate and full
of humor, kneeling under their
dresses in traditional Iranian manner.

32. Archaic Counting-Pieces
Susa, Uruk period
c. 3400–3300 B.C.

Light terracotta. Ø 6.5 cm (2.6 in.)
R. de Mecquenem excavations. Sb 1927

In order to manage the considerable wealth generated by urban-type development, the Susans created a system of book-keeping. They began by representing numbers with little clay objects rather like the *calculi* or pebbles used by other ancient civilizations which are at the origin of our word "calculation." They kept them in hollow clay balls to avoid their dispersal. The number symbolized could be represented by notches on the surface of the round container; the cylindrical seal of the scribe might be stamped on it as a guarantee of authenticity. These notches are the first true graphic symbols; they were soon transferred onto little clay slabs or "tablets" before their meaning was made more precise by conventional signs. The process that led to the invention of writing was thus started off by book-keeping.

33. Cultic Stand
Susa, early dynastic period
c. 2400 B.C.
Bitumen mastic. H 18.3 cm (7.2 in.);
Ø 11.5 cm (4.5 in.)
J. de Morgan excavations. Sb 2725

In the middle of the third millennium,
Susa became a city of the Sumerian
type, with an acropolis on which
stood a temple containing statuettes
of worshippers and cult objects
testifying to the originality of local
art. In cheap imitation of exotic
stones, artificially hardened bitumen
was used. It was carved into offering
stands with crudely stylized animal
motifs. The eagle protecting its
brood is less formidable here than
in Sumeria where it was given
a lion's head.

34. Elamite Goddess
Susa, c. 2100 B.C.
Statue, limestone. H 1.09 m (42.9 in.)
J. de Morgan excavations, 1907. Sb 54

The prince of Susa, Puzur-
Inshushinak, succeeded in creating
a dual empire, containing both the
Susan plain with its Semitic
language, and the plateau with its
Elamite language. He inscribed his
monuments in both languages:
Semite Akkadian and Elamite
written in a new linear writing that
has not yet been deciphered. The
statue with its bilingual inscription
representing the great goddess
portrays her as the Mesopotamian
Ishtar, enthroned above lions.
Her horned tiara is similar to that
of divinities at the time of Gudea,
prince of Lagash.

35. Trans-Elamite Pin-Head
South-eastern Iran
c. 2000 B.C.
Copper. Pin: L 24.8 cm (9.8 in.);
Head: H 5.85 cm (2.3 in.); W 5.1 cm (2 in.)
Gift of M. Foroughi, 1975. AO 26068

Semi-nomadic artisans settled at the eastern extremities of Iran, beyond Elam, in order to exploit the natural riches of the area. They established a trans-Elamite civilization which thrived from the middle of the third millennium to around the 17th century B.C. The stonecarvers produced richly decorated chlorite vases and the metalworkers cast real and ceremonial weapons and ornaments like this long pin. The openwork head depicts the intimate conversation of a couple in a dwelling, prefiguring a tradition that was to survive with surprising steadfastness in classical Persian art.

37. Ibex Cup
Susa
20th–19th century B.C.
Bitumen mastic. H 9 cm (3.5 in.): L 22 cm (8.7 in.)
R. de Mecquenem excavations, 1924. Sb 2740

The prosperity that Susa enjoyed at the beginning of the second millennium is evident from the wealth of objects left in tombs. As well as gold and silver jewelry, the dead were supplied with food left in ordinary dishes and in luxury vases carved from bitumen mastic in imitation of exotic stone. This cup is treated as a sculpture; the handle is an ibex head carved in high relief, renewing a tradition founded some thousand years earlier in Mesopotamia. Vases like this, so characteristic of Susan art, were exported to Babylonia in antiquity, where they were highly appreciated.

36. Composite Statuette
Bactria
Beginning of the 2nd millennium B.C.
Chlorite and limestone. H 18.3 cm (7.2 in.)
Acq. 1969. AO 22918

At the end of the third millennium and at the beginning of the second, trans-Elamite civilization spread beyond Iran to the boundaries of Central Asia, in Bactria (northern Afghanistan). The items left in tombs dug close to elaborate fortresses included everyday and luxury objects, and reveal a civilization similar to the Elamite. Next to ceremonial axes serving—as in Elam—to denote honors, composite statuettes of women were placed in the tombs. Their "crinoline" dress is like that of the queens of Elam. The dress here has been given the stylistic treatment of the *kaunakes* from the age of the archaic dynasties.

38. Elamite God
Susa
Beginning of the 2nd millennium B.C.
Copper and gold. H 17.5 cm (6.9 in.);
W 5.5 cm (2.2 in.)
Sb 2823

39. Funerary Head of an Elamite
Susa
15th–14th century B.C.
Painted unbaked clay. H 24 cm (9.4 in.);
W 15 cm (5.9 in.)
R. de Mecquenem excavations, 1926. Sb 2838

Susa's cultural dependence
on Babylonia remained great at the
beginning of the second millennium,
even though the town belonged
to the Elamite kingdom. Accordingly,
the gods were portrayed like those
of Mesopotamia, wearing the pleated
kaunakes dress and the many-horned
crown which signified divine power.
This one differs from Mesopotamian
idols because of its smile. One hand
still retains a layer of the gold
plating which originally covered the
whole statue.

In the middle of the second
millennium, the Susans buried
their dead in family vaults under
their houses. Next to the head of the
deceased, which was probably veiled,
they frequently placed a portrait,
executed at the moment of death.
It is the only kind of a genuinely
funerary art which aims at personal
likeness from the East. This one
shows the typical Elamite, with stern
expression characteristic of a tough
population with strong mountain
links.

40. Royal Axe
Chogha Zanbil, formerly Dur-Untash
c. 1250 B.C.

Silver, electrum. H 5.9 cm (2.3 in.);
W 12.5 cm (4.9 in.)
R. Girshman excavations, 1953. Sb 3973

King Untash-Napirisha of Elam
built a religious capital near Susa,
dominated by a storied tower
dedicated to the two patron-gods
of the two halves of the empire, the
highlands and the Susan plain. At its
foot, the goddess Kiririsha, wife
of the mountain god, had a richly
furnished temple. Notable among
the finds was this axe. The blade,
which issues from a lion's mouth,
has been inscribed with the words:
"I, Untash Napirisha," while the
handle is decorated with the figurine
of a young wild boar. This weapon
harks back to a specifically mountain
tradition created in Luristan in the
third millennium.

41. Elamite Worshipper
Susa
12th century B.C.

Statuette, gold and bronze. H 7.5 cm (2.9 in.);
W 2.4 cm (0.9 in.)
J. de Morgan excavations. 1904. Sb 2758

This statuette, like a similar one
in silver, depicts a devotee in prayer,
carrying a kid as an offering to the
divinity. It was designed to perpetuate
a ceremonial act in a temple.
This one, however, was added to the
funerary offerings found in a royal
tomb near the temple of Inshushinak,
patron god of Susa. It is a fine
example of the mastery of Susan
metalworkers who were capable
of casting a statue of a queen
weighing 1,750 kg (c. 3,855 lb)
without the head.

42. Model of an Elamite Cultic Site
Susa
c. 1150 B.C.

Bronze. H 60 cm (23.6 in.); W 40 cm (15.7 in.)
J. de Morgan excavations, 1904–1905. Sb 2743

This model carries a dedication from the greatest king of Elam, Shilhak-Inshushinak, who calls it a *Sit Shamshi*, "ceremony of the rising sun." Two naked priests officiate between two temples, next to ritual objects (raised stones, a water basin, a sacred clump of trees) which are akin to those of Canaanite holy places of the same period.
The model was not on display: it was enclosed in a block of chalk inserted into the masonry of a tomb.

43. Vase with Winged Monsters
Marlik region (northern Iran)
14th–13th century B.C.

Electrum. H 11 cm (4.3 in.); Ø 11.2 cm (4.4 in.)
Acq. 1956. AO 20281

The first Iranian immigrants seem to have settled during the second millennium to the north of the plateau to which they gave their name. Most probably nomads, they buried their dead in cemeteries like the one discovered at Marlik, not far from the village of Amlash.
Lacking any artistic tradition, they took inspiration from the art of the old traditions of western Asia in decorating their ornaments. This goblet, made of electrum—a natural alloy of gold and silver—is in a decorative style borrowed from the repertory of the middle empire in northern Mesopotamia: winged monsters with intertwined claws holding animals in their grip.

44. Pin Head from Luristan
Luristan (western Iran)
8th–7th century B.C.

Bronze. H 12.9 cm (5.1 in.); L 10.8 cm (4.2 in.)
Gift of P. and J. David-Weill, 1972. AO 25008

The mountain dwellers of Luristan created from the middle of the third millennium a rich tradition in metalwork which was eclipsed when they became sedentary in the second millennium. The tradition revived with the return to a nomadic way of life from the 12th to the 7th century. The mountain bronzeworkers adopted the same shapes as the urbanized peoples of the plains, but stylized them in a spirit appropriate to nomads who remained on the margins of history. A spirit master-of-animals, descended from prehistoric times, wears the pleated dress—an ancestor of the Persian type—and is depicted here with some realism.

45. The Archers of Darius
Susa
c. 500 B.C.
Relief, glazed bricks. H 2 m (78.7 in.)
M. Dieulafoy excavations, 1884–1886. AOD 488

Darius I (522–486 B.C.) made Susa
his administrative capital, building
his palace in the Babylonian tradition;
a throne room with columns in the
Iranian tradition was later added.
The glazed brick decor of this palace
focuses on images of the Persian
army. The archers are shown
in ceremonial dress, rather than
in fighting gear. Anxious to depict
this pleated dress in keeping with
the tradition of Luristan, the Susan
enamelers borrowed from the Greek
model, but stylized it in their own
characteristic way.

46. Achaemenid Vase Handle
5th–6th century B.C.

Silver and gold. H 27 cm (10.6 in.); L 15 cm (5.9 in.)
Formerly Tyzkiewicz coll. Acq. 1898. AO 2748

47. Sassanid Pitcher
Province of Dailaman (northern Iran)
5th–7th century A.D.

Silver-gilt. H 18.1 cm (7.1 in.); Ø 10.6 cm (4.2 in.)
Acq. 1966. MAO 426

In all probability, this zoomorphic parcel-gilt silver vase handle, and its twin in the Berlin Museum belonged to one of those wide-rimmed high-necked amphoras with the fluted ovoid bellies that are shown in the bas-reliefs of Persepolis and of which some examples in bronze or precious metal have come down to us. Like their nomadic ancestors from northern Iran, the great Persian kings greatly appreciated luxury tableware. Their gold and silversmiths were freely influenced by the art of peoples of the empire. Thus this winged ibex is markedly Iranian, but rests on a mask of Silenus, borrowed from the Ionian Greeks.

From the 3rd to the 7th century, the Sassanid Empire fostered a brilliant courtly art, reviving a tradition of ornate silverwork, which the early Iranians held dear. Despite a nationalist backlash against the Hellenism of the Parthians, the decoration on these precious vases is often Dionysiac in inspiration, and linked with Indian influences, recognizable in the dancers with their diaphanous veils. The design is in keeping with the atmosphere of drinking parties described by the Persian poets at the dawn of Islam.

The Levant

The term "Levant" encompasses those Mediterranean-facing countries of the Near East, aside from Egypt. Major collections from this region were assembled in the Louvre from the 1850s. They were enriched between the two world wars by scientific expeditions, which distributed the antiquities between Paris and the new museums founded at Aleppo, Damascus, Beirut, etc. Since the Second World War, archaeological finds have remained in the country of origin, but the Louvre pursues an active policy of on-site research, sometimes on the very sites which once contributed to the establishment of the museum collections: Mari and Ras Shamra.

Linking the Mediterranean to the Mesopotamian Orient, the Levant communicated with Babylonia, beyond the steppe where the nomads dwelt, via the Euphrates valley. The coastal plains separated from the hinterland by mountain ranges with numerous passes, and the courses of the Orontes and Jordan rivers have together shaped very diverse ecology. Doubtless this same geographical fragmentation has prevented the Levant from ever forming a political entity, and has often made the region a prey to its ambitious neighbors such as the Pharaohs of the 12th Dynasty (20th century B.C.) and the Assyrians (9th–7th century). From the seventh millennium, small settled communities gradually assumed mastery of their surroundings through livestock breeding and farming. These little settlements grew into cities. During the fourth millennium, urban communities, or Sumerian-style colonies established themselves along the Euphrates; in the Negev, villages specialized in the extraction of copper invite comparison with predynastic Egypt (Safadi, near Beersheba).

History begins with the third millennium and the first texts: hieroglyphic names of Pharaohs at Byblos, where the Egyptians came in search of building timber on the mountains of Lebanon; and cuneiform tablets at Ebla or Mari, where scribes adopted the Mesopotamian system of syllabic writing.

The first attempts which led to the invention of the alphabet, perfected by the Phoenicians, were made in the Levant around the middle of the second millennium.

Byblos and Ugarit, city ports and bridgeheads for the trade routes from the interior towards the Mediterranean prospered; the same is true of Cyprus, Enkomi, Paphos and Kition. Cultural and commercial relations developed with the great neighboring powers, Egypt, the Hittites and then the Assyrians. From the Mycenaean period (14th century) and throughout the first millennium, such exchanges also extended to the Greek world.

The Mediterranean of the first millennium was marked by major colonial exploits: while the Greeks settled on the shores of Anatolia, Sicily and Southern Italy, the Phoenicians spread to Cyprus and toward the west. The colony of Carthage founded its own satellite towns, in Sardinia, at Ibiza in Spain and all along the Maghrebi coast. There was more contact between Greek settlers and Phoenician and Punic merchants than the Latin historians admit to. The Roman conquest finally united these vast territories into one "mare nostrum."

48. Male Statuette
Safadi, Negev
Chalcolithic period
3500–3000 B.C.

Hippopotamus ivory. H 24 cm (9.4 in.)
J. Perrot excavations. AO 21406

49. Fertility Idol
Cyprus
Chalcolithic period,
end of the 3rd millennium

Painted and incised terracotta. H 12.9 cm (5.1 in.)
Couchoud expedition. AM 1176

Carved from a hippopotamus' horn,
this schematic image belongs to a set
of objects discovered at Safadi, near
Beersheba. It is characteristic of the
primitive culture of Sinai and
Negev, influenced by pre-Pharaonic
Egyptian art. The area around
Beersheba developed owing to the
mining in the region of copper and
turquoise for trade with Egypt.

This is one of the first images
related to fertility cults in Cyprus.
Goddess or woman, the figurine
is remarkable for evoking the stream
of milk—the source of life—collected
in a basin. The stylization of features
and the angle of the head are
comparable with other "primitive"
images from Greece, the Cyclades
and the Balkans.

50. Eyed Idol
Northern Syria
c. 3300–3000 B.C.
Terracotta. H 27 cm (10.6 in.)
Gift of the Société des Amis du Louvre, 1991.
AO 3002

These schematic idols are characteristic of the early stages of urban societies which developed in northern Syria and Anatolia at the dawn of the metal age (Chalcolithic Period). Through their extreme schematism, these anthropomorphic figures are comparable with contemporary works from the Cyclades and Troy and illustrate the links that existed between these early metalworking societies, from the Mediterranean to the Persian Gulf: similar idols, though in miniature, have been found in regions as distant as Sunna and southwest Iran.

51. Votive Statuettes
Byblos
19th–18th century B.C.

Bronze and gold. H 7 cm (2.8 in.)
Montet excavations. AO 10945, AO 14878 et seq.

Numerous figurines were given
as offerings in the "obelisk temple."
This building, notable for the
pyramidal steles which were

consecrated to it, was dedicated
to a storm god, most probably
Reshef, for it is he who is depicted
in these statuettes. They borrow the
garment and crown from Egyptian
art, while the molten bronze casting
covered with gold leaf is a strictly
local, Amorite technique.

52. Stele Showing the Storm God Baal
Ras Shamra, formerly Ugarit
14th–13th century B.C.

Sandstone. H 1.42 m (55.9 in.)
Schaeffer excavations. AO 15775

The god is shown brandishing
a mace and a spear, the tail of which
is tipped with vegetation; this
is an allusion to the beneficial effects
of the rain released by the storm.
A youthful and popular god,
celebrated in beautiful mythological
texts discovered at Ugarit, Baal
is also the tutelary god of the dynasty:
the king of Ugarit is shown in prayer
beneath the arms of Baal. The style
is both attentive to anatomical detail
and nobly hieratic. This stele of Baal
is one of the finest pieces of sculpture
that has come down to us from
Oriental antiquity.

53. Plate with Hunting Scene

Ras Shamra, formerly Ugarit
14th–12th century B.C.

Gold. Ø 18.8 cm (7.4 in.)
Schaeffer excavations. AO 17208

Found with another gold dish not far from Baal's sanctuary at Ugarit, this masterpiece is a royal offering to the patron-god of the dynasty. The dish in the Louvre shows the king out hunting gazelles and wild bulls. The fleeing animals are shown in the "flying gallop" attitude which was used by artists from Crete and the Levant during the Bronze Age. Hunting in chariots was the royal recreation *par excellence*, as Egyptian reliefs from the same epoch confirm.

54. The "Lady of the Animals"
Minet el Beida (port of old Ugarit)
tomb III
14th–13th century B.C.

Cosmetic box cover, elephant ivory.
H 13.7 cm (5.4 in.)
Schaeffer excavations. AO 11601

This sumptuous cosmetic box, designed for a high-ranking woman, is decorated in a hybrid style. The Aegean or Cretan style dress of the woman with the ibexes contrasts with the oriental style of composition and the symbolic imagery: a goddess or priestess taming wild animals. Precious ivory objects like this were common enough property among the rich merchants of Ugarit.

55. Goblet with Human Face
Minet el Beida (port of old Ugarit)
tomb VI
14th–13th century B.C.

Earthenware. H 16.2 cm (6.4 in.)
Schaeffer excavations. AO 15725

Objects like this belonged to women and were connected with fertility rites. A mask of a goddess, in "make-up," is depicted here, similar to the jewel-masks worn round the neck. The style is derived in part from Cretan art, and in part from Oriental and local traditions.

56. Model of a Sanctuary decorated with Nude Goddesses
Meskone (formerly Emar on the Euphrates)
12th century B.C.

Terracotta. H 44 cm (17.3 in.)
Margueron excavations. AO 27905

Exploration of the city of Emar, capital of a vassal Hittite kingdom established along the Euphrates, led to the discovery of a whole urban complex: palaces, temples and residential quarters yielded a rich hoard. The existence of household rites is confirmed by these "models" which were found in the houses. Adorned with symbolic images, they may have served as movable altars.

58. Lady at a Window
Arslan Tash, formerly Hadatu
8th century B.C.

Ivory, previously gilded. H 8 cm (3.1 in.)
Thurau-Dangin excavations. AO 11459

57. Stele of Si Gabbor, Priest
of the Moon God
Neirab, near Aleppo (northern Syria)
6th century B.C.

Basalt. H 95 cm (37.4 in.)
AO 3027

This monument, which bears
an epitaph, is highly representative
of the culture and religion at the
time when the Aramaean nomads
spread from the Syrian steppe
to Babylonia: the priest's garment
is very Babylonian in style.
Thenceforward the cult of the moon
god worshipped by the Aramaean
nomads, assumed a particular
importance.

This decorative motif belonged
to an item of furniture, a casket
or a seat. Produced in Phoenician
or Aramaean workshops, these
luxury pieces decorated royal
apartments, and most particularly
the gynaeceum (harem) in palaces
built by Syrian kings. They were
often taken as spoils of war
by Assyrian kings during their
conquest of the Levant.

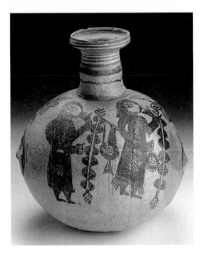

59. Vase Decorated with Gift-Bearers
Cyprus
c. 700–650 B.C.

Terracotta. H 25 cm (9.8 in.)
AM 1142

The richly imaginative style of the Cretan potters is employed here in the service of religious belief. The faithful bring vegetation to the divinity, symbolic of the power of fertility and fecundity.

61. Seven-Branched Chandelier, Palm and Trumpet
Oum Qeis, formerly Gadara, Jordan valley
6th century A.D.

Synagogue installation, basalt. H 38 cm (15 in.)
Gift of F. de Saulcy, 1852. AO 5042

This architectural item, possibly a lintel, well illustrates the development and expansion of primitive Judaism in the first centuries of our era.

60. Redoutable Mask
Carthage, Dormech Necropolis
End of 7th–early 6th century B.C.
Terracotta. H 19.5 cm (7.7 in.)
Delattre excavations. AO 3242

These objects, which were left in tombs, had a magical function to ward off evil spirits. Oriental in tradition, they are a good illustration of the cultural inter-dependency of the Punic world and Phoenicia in the western Mediterranean.

Arabia

Ancient Arabia encompassed a vast area stretching from the Yemen to the
shores of the Persian Gulf, from the Euphrates to the Red Sea. In these
steppe lands dotted with fertile oases, cultures, languages, indigenous forms
of writing evolved leading to the historic Arab world. The prosperity of this
region owes much to the domestication of the dromedary camel, which
enabled the oasis dwellers to undertake international trade over great
distances, bringing silks, spices, perfumes and precious stones from the Far
East to the shores of the Mediterranean. There they came into contact with
the Greek and later with the Roman worlds. At Petra, at Dura Europos
or Palmyra, great cities took on a Graeco-Roman appearance with colonnaded
streets and monumental facades. At Palmyra the great merchant families
built tombs for the effigies of their dead. In the Yemen, the "Arabia felix"
of the classical authors, kingdoms took shape; public monuments and tombs
were bedecked with sculptures in alabaster.

**62. Taime and his Mother
at a Banquet**
Palmyra
2nd–3rd century A.D.

Relief, limestone. H 43 cm (16.9 in.)
AO 2093

The Louvre possesses a fine set
of funerary sculptures from Palmyra,
a trading city and oasis in the Syrian
steppe. Rich merchants of Palmyra
erected public monuments and

tombs which show the cosmopolitan
character of their culture. Eastern
elements (language, writing,
ornament) combine with Western
ones such as Roman dress and the
naturalistic style.

Islamic Arts

After the Crusades, Christian Europe acquired various art objects from the Muslim world. Although eclipsed by the Western art, the old collections of the French crown did nevertheless boast some major pieces, such as the rock crystal ewer in the Saint-Denis treasure-house, the great brass bowl inlaid with silver called the "Saint Louis Baptistery"(no. 69) and a series of cups in jade of Turkish or Indian origin. But not until the middle of the 19th century, when the Louvre received some major gifts (1840: Despointes; 1856: Sauvageot), and more especially at the very end of the century, was any real interest taken in Islamic art. Bequests and private donations multiplied (1885: Davillier; 1892: Fouquet; 1893: Arconati Visconti). Thanks to the interest of certain curators of the decorative arts, a "Muslim art section" was finally put together and some significant purchases were made such as the "Barberini" Vase (no. 68) in 1899, one of the prize objects in the collection. A inaugural exhibition in 1903 showed more than a thousand pieces from private collections in the Pavillon de Marsan. A good many of these pieces were later donated to the Louvre, the collectors rivalling each other in their munificence: Doistau (who gave a rare, 16th-century "kilim" carpet from Iran woven in silk and metal thread and a Syrian bowl inscribed to the Sultan Ayyubid al-Malik al-Adil); Dru, Jeuniette and Marteau (who gave superb metalwork and miniatures), and Peytel among others. The scale of the exhibition and the quality of the pieces on show provided a perfect illustration of the temporal and spatial scope of the Islamic world and its works of art. At the time it included the Maghreb, a region later reserved for the Musée des Arts Africains et Océaniens.

In 1912 Baroness Delort de Gléon bequeathed a number of rare objects (Iranian and Syro-Egyptian woodwork, ivories and metals—all of the highest quality and including two signed and dated ewers). She also left the Louvre the sum of a hundred thousand francs to help pay for a larger room of Muslim art. A space was allotted for it on the second floor of the Pavillon de l'Horloge, and after a long delay caused by the First World War, the room was finally inaugurated in 1922. That same year the section was separated from the Decorative Arts Department and attached to the Asian Arts Department on which it depended until 1945. During this inter-war period, Gaston Migeon published two volumes in which the principal pieces in the collection were reproduced alongside his commentary; and Georges Salles brought out a small visitor's guide.

There were some especially rich legacies, among them from Baroness Salomon de Rothschild in 1922, from Mme Stern (rare Spanish metals: aquamanila peacock and lion), and from Raymond Koechlin, who left ceramics, including the famous peacock plate (no. 71), and metalwork.

For their part, the archaeologists began to explore the Islamic levels which had been neglected for so long. Archaeological treasures from the digs (the most famous being that of Susa in Iran) gradually entered the collection. After the Second World War, the section under the directorship of Jean David-Weill came once more under the aegis of the Near Eastern Antiquities Department.

63. Cup

Iraq
9th century

Clay ceramic with metal luster decoration in brown
and yellow on white opaque glaze.
H 6.3 cm (2.48 in.); Ø 22.3 cm (8.78 in.)
Vignier coll. Acq. 1931. 8179

Metal luster decoration was one
of the greatest glories of potters
working in the Abbasid caliphate
in Iraq and Iran during the 9th and
10th centuries. This costly and
complicated technique developed
to brilliant heights in the medieval
Islamic world before spreading
to the West, into Spain and Italy.

64. Panel

Egypt
End of the 9th century

Wood (Aleppo pine). H 73 cm (28.7 in.)
Fouquet donation, 1892–1893. 6023

Egyptian woodcarvings from the
Tulunid period reflect the influence
of the developed art of Baghdad and
Samarra. Vigorous beveled cuts
accentuate the play of light over the
supple curves of a motif that
is half-animal and half-vegetable,
depicting a bird in profile.

65. Pyxis of Al-Mughira
Cordoba, 968

Ivory. H 15 cm (5.9 in.)
Acq. 1898. 4068

During the period of the Cordoba Caliphate the workshops of Andalusia turned out masterpieces of sculpture on ivory one after the other. Most of these are rectangular or cylindrical boxes with curved lids as on this pyxis. Round the bottom of the lid is an inscription which gives the date, 968, and the name Al-Mughira, son of the caliph Abd al-Rahman III. The scenes depicted—fighting animals, princely recreations (hunting, music, drinking)—belong to an iconographic repertory common to the whole Muslim world.

Detail

66. Saint-Josse Shroud
Khurassan (eastern Iran)
Middle of the 10th century
Silk samite. H 52 cm (20.5 in.); W 94 cm (37 in.)
Commune of Saint-Josse. Acq. 1922. 7502

This cloth, which was almost
certainly brought home from the
First Crusade, was given to the
Abbey of Saint-Josse (Pas-de-Calais).
The very fine kufic inscription,
bearing the name of a Turkish
governor of Khurassan, put to death
in 961, confirms its provenance from
eastern Iran, which was at that time
a province independent on Baghdad.
The weaving technique as well
as the motifs—elephants meeting
head-on, a line of harnessed
camels—can be traced directly
to pre-Islamic Iran, though they are
treated with a new stylization.

67. Bowl
Iran
End of 12th–beginning of 13th century
Silicious ceramic with over-glaze painted
decoration embellished with gold and metal luster.
H 6.5 cm (2.6 in.); Ø 22 cm (8.7 in.)
Acq. 1970. MAO 440

For the sheer beauty of its forms and
decorations and for the variety
of techniques applied, the so-called
Seljuk period in Iran was a veritable
golden age for pottery. Long before
Europe, the over-glaze painted
decoration was perfected, enabling
a wide chromatic scale to be used.
On the most beautiful pieces, such
as this bowl showing a falconer
on horseback, finesse of line and
delicacy of color bring to mind the
art of the miniature.

68. "Barberini" Vase
Syria
Middle of the 13th century

Brass inlaid with silver. H 45.9 cm (18.1 in.);
Ø 37 cm (14.6 in.)
Barberini coll. Acq. 1899. 4090

The shape of this large vase which
belonged to the collection of the
Barberini Pope Urban VIII is more
frequently used for ceramic vessels
(spice or medicine jars).
It is decorated with inscriptions
bearing the name of an Ayyubid
Sultan of Aleppo, and with
medallions showing hunting scenes
of a rare finesse.

Detail

78

69. Bowl, known as the Baptistery of Saint Louis
Syria or Egypt
End of the 13th or beginning of the 14th century

Brass with gold and silver inlay,
signed Muhammed Ibn al-Zayn. H 23.2 cm (9.1 in.);
Ø 50.5 cm (19.9 in.)
Crown Collection in the Sainte-Chapelle
de Vincennes. Entered the Louvre in 1852. LP 16

This large bowl which was in the French Royal Collection was used for the baptism of certain princes in the 19th century, which explains the arms of France stamped on the interior. A masterpiece of Muslim brassware, it is of the highest standard of metalwork and a proof also of the wealth of the ruling Mamluk class. On the outside surface four circular medallions, each containing a prince on horseback, are set between a line of huntsmen and high officials with emblazoned boots. The decoration here is notable for the unusual height of the people and the absence of epigraphic inscriptions which are omnipresent on objects of this time.

70. Bottle
Syria
1342–1345

Gilt and enameled glass. H 50.5 cm (19.9 in.)
Spitzer coll. Acq. 1893. 3365

Drawing on a long tradition
of glass-work in the Near East,
Muslim artisans lent particular
brilliance to certain techniques such
as gilt and enamel decoration. Used
during the Ayyubid period, this
decoration was extremely popular
under the Mamluks, from the middle
of the 13th to the end of the
14th century. It appears on numerous
mosque lamps commissioned
by sovereigns or principal state
officials. Rarer in shape, this bottle
is decorated with a splendid blue
epigraphy, broken by the arms
of Tuqutzemur, viceroy of Syria
from 1342 to 1345 (a white eagle
over a white cup on a red shield).

71. Peacock Plate
Iznik, Turkey
Second quarter of the 16th century

Silicious ceramic with under-glaze painted
decoration. H 8 cm (3.1 in.); Ø 37.5 cm (14.8 in.)
K 3440

A peacock in profile can be seen
amidst a floral composition which
takes up the whole surface of the
plate. The tones used—a very delicate
palette based on blue, gray-mauve
and lime green—are typical of the
Iznik style during the second
quarter of the 16th century.

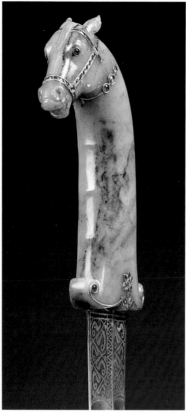

72. Portrait of Shah Abbas I
Isphahan
12 March 1627

Ink, color and goldleaf on paper, signed
Muhammed Oasim. H 27.5 cm (10.8 in.);
W 16.8 cm (6.6 in.)
Acq. 1975. MAO 494

73. Horse-Head Dagger
India
17th century

Gray-green jade, inlaid with gold, rubies
and emeralds; damascened steel blade.
L 50.5 cm (19.9 in.)
Salomon de Rothschild coll. Acq. 1927. 7891

This drawing is most probably the
only portrait in existence executed
during the Shah's lifetime.
Head shaved, and wearing a broad-
brimmed conical hat, he tenderly
embraces one of his pages who
is offering him a drink. The scene
set by a stream is pastoral. Under
the foliage is the name of the artist,
the date and a short poem: "May life
bring you all you desire from
the three lips: those of your lover,
the river and the cup."

Numerous objects, in gold, silver,
ivory or hard stones, often embellished
with enamel and precious stones
provide us with a glimpse of the
wealth of the court of the Great
Moghuls. White or gray-green jade
was highly prized and often used for
jewels, boxes or the handles
of ceremonial arms. The latter were
often delicately sculpted animal
heads of great expressiveness such
as this.

Egyptian Antiquities

The Nile
Writing
Materials and Techniques
Everyday Life
The Temple
Burials
Religion

Prehistory
and the First Two Dynasties
The Old Kingdom
The Middle Kingdom
The New Kingdom
The Third Intermediate Period,
the Saite Era
and the Last Indigenous Dynasties

Egypt under Greek Domination
Roman Egypt
Coptic Egypt

Introduction

The Department of Egyptian Antiquities displays the vestiges of cultures centered around the Nile from prehistoric to early Christian times—a period spanning 4,500 years of human history. The majority of objects in the collection have entered the Egyptian Department since it was set up in 1826. Champollion's recent deciphering of Egyptian hieroglyphs was having a wide cultural impact. After fifteen centuries the mystery of ancient Egyptian script had been unraveled at last and the history of Egypt under the pharaohs was rewritten. Meanwhile the English and French consuls in Egypt began disposing of collections they had acquired as investments. On Champollion's advice, Charles X of France acquired them, ordering the installation of new rooms for their display on the first floor of the Cour Carrée, the design of which was inspired in part by ancient Egyptian style. This was the world's first museum of egyptology. Around the middle of the nineteenth century, the collection grew with numerous finds unearthed by Mariette at the Serapeum, and with the purchase of the great collection of Dr. Clot. The end of the century saw the emergence of scientific archaeology and an excavation site was then seen to be as important as the objects it contained. With digs conducted by the Institut Français d'Archéologie Orientale at Cairo and by the Musée du Louvre, objects with a precise provenance and context came into the collection from sites such as Asyut, Deir el-Medineh, Medamud and Tod. Today the collection continues to grow with new acquisitions and gifts from collectors.

In December 1997, the department was expanded and completely refurbished on two floors of the Cour Carrée. The lower floor introduces you to the civilization of the Pharaohs in a thematic way with all the epochs jumbled together. After being welcomed by the great sphinx (room 1) and Nakhtorheb (room 2), you are taken into the Nile valley (room 3), and then introduced to different facets of the economy and of material life: farming and stockbreeding (rooms 4 and 5), writing (room 6), arts and crafts (room 7), and domestic life (rooms 8 to 10). In rooms 11 to 19 you discover aspects of religious life at the temple and the burial ground. On the upper floor, in rooms 20 to 30, a panorama unfolds of the history and art of Egypt from prehistory to the heritage of Alexander the Great. Artefacts from Roman and Coptic Egypt are now in newly fitted rooms in the Denon Wing as part of the display devoted to the east Mediterranean in the Roman and Byzantine periods.

74. The Great Sphinx
Tanis

Pink granite. H 1.83 m (72 in.); W 4.80 m (189 in.)
Salt coll. Acq. 1826. A 23

Carved from a single block of pink
granite, this large statue depicts
a pharaoh with a lion's body.
"Sphinx" comes from the Greek
word for a type of monster, and
in Egypt sphinxes served to indicate
and protect passages in religious
buildings. This is a particularly fine

specimen with a strong volumetric
sense and finely executed detail.
Several kings in turn inscribed their
names on it. The oldest inscription
reads Amenemhat II (1898–1866 B.C.)
and possibly the sphinx was sculpted
during his reign. However certain
details (like the headdress) might
suggest a much earlier dating, to the
beginning of the Old Kingdom
around 2620 B.C. If this were so, this
would be a rare example of royal
sculpture from that distant time.

75. Nakhthorheb
Reign of Psammetichus II
595–589 B.C. (26th Dynasty)
Statue, quartzite. H 1.48 m (58.3 in.);
W 46.5 cm (18.3 in.); D 70 cm (27.6 in.)
A 94

Nakhthorheb is kneeling in prayer and the text on the base of the statue informs us that he is appealing to the god Thoth, "lord of Dendera and Hermopolis." Leader of the officiating priests, he had some important religious duties and his family was recorded in many documents. The statue is in line with the archaizing tendency of the time with its simple costume; the smooth loincloth and hairstyle merge into and emphasize the lines of the body. The bare torso provided the sculptor with the chance to display his anatomical skills, though it is idealized like the characterless face. This is one of many statues which would have filled the courtyards of sanctuaries where worshippers of a god waited to receive some reward for their devotion: crumbs from the god's table.

The Nile

The long river that feeds the land of Egypt is evoked by model boats (no. 89), figurines of fish, crocodiles, hippotami (no. 105) or frogs. The Louvre mastaba (no. 76) gives a very complete picture of material life at a big country estate in the Old Kingdom, notably of hunting and fishing scenes. It serves as an introduction to the rooms devoted to an agriculture whose prosperity depended on the annual flooding of the Nile.

76. The Akhethotep Mastaba
Saqqara
c. 2400 B.C. (5th Dynasty)
Bas-relief, painted limestone
E 10958 A

This mastaba, reconstructed in the Louvre, is one of many funerary chapels of the great burial ground of Saqqara. Inside, family or funerary priests would make offerings of various goods before false doors which take up the back wall. Through these magic openings the dead person in his subterranean dwelling was expected to communi-cate with the living. Bas-reliefs in the chapel show all the activities and produce of a large estate such as the one here owned by the high official, Akhethotep. The main scene shows Akhethotep's funerary meal taking place to the accompaniment of music and dancing. Here we see a hunting scene on the banks of the Nile where birds are caught using a net affixed to a tree.

Writing

Alongside painted and sculpted hieroglyphs visible on temple walls, the Egyptians used a cursive script, in which the original hieroglyphs are more or less recognizable depending on the period, rapidity of execution and skill of the scribe. This is known as "hieratic script." From the 7th century B.C. this evolved into a form where the original signs are no longer recognizable. Known as "demotic script," it transcribed the language that was spoken rather than the classical language. In the last centuries of the pharaohs, scribes working on mural inscriptions in the temples toyed with the signs, inventing hundreds more which could only be interpreted by a few initiates. Invented around 3100 B.C., hieroglyphs were still in use at least until the 4th century A.D. As for the old Egyptian language, it survived the Arab invasion thanks to the Christian community. It was preserved in Coptic religious texts, written in Greek characters. It was his knowledge of Coptic that enabled Champollion to decipher hieroglyphs between 1824 and 1826, after fifteen centuries of oblivion.

77. Scribe's Palette
c. 1347–1337 B.C. (18th Dynasty)

Wood and reed. H 37 cm (14.6 in.);
W 5.5 cm (2.2 in.); D 1.3 cm (0.5 in.)
N 2241

The palette is formed of a strip of wood, hollowed at its center to hold reed sticks with chewed ends serving as brushes. Two hollows contain little cakes of red and black color. The red was used for chapter headings in texts such as the "Book of the Dead." The "cartouche" engraved on the object indicates that its owner lived under the reign of Tutankhamun.

Materials and Techniques

Arts and crafts are displayed according to the materials used: wood, stone, ceramics, metal. The displays show the techniques employed for each kind of material and the craftsmen who were pastmasters at using them. A bronze statue of the god Horus greets you with his hands outstretched in a gesture of libation.

78. The God Horus
Third Intermediate Period,
c. 1069–664 B.C.
Statue, bronze statue. H 95 cm (37.4 in.)
E 7703

Although metal statues were frequent in temples at all periods, bronzes reached the height of production during the Third Intermediate Period both in quality and sheer numbers. This great statue of Horus was part of a scene in which the two gods of royalty, Horus and Thoth, faced each other and sprinkled the king with water to purify him before ceremonials. To save metal, large statues were hollow, and made as follows according to the "lost-wax" process. A core of clay and sand is modeled to the required shape and coated with a layer of wax of the same thickness as the bronze is intended to be. It is covered in clay, then heated. The wax melts and runs out, leaving a space between the inner core and the clay mould, into which the molten metal is poured. After it is cooled the mould is broken; generally the core is left inside. This statue appears to be unfinished; the face has not been polished, and the tenons linking the arms (cast separately) to the body are still visible. It was probably covered with another layer of plaster or gold which has since disappeared.

Daily Life

The objects of Egyptian daily life, both humble and luxurious, are ours
to admire only because of the custom in the 18th Dynasty of placing articles
from everyday life into the crypt near the deceased to make their new life
as comfortable as possible. Of course an ordinary tomb with its carefully
selected collection of worn and humble articles such as wickerwork, headrests,
and cosmetics was a far cry from the tomb of a king like Tutankhamun
in which hundreds of objects of extraordinary refinement were found.
Most of the objects on display in the Louvre fall somewhere between these
two extremes. A large number were found in a burial ground on the west
bank at Thebes (now Luxor). Their middle-class owners had relatively
comfortable lives. Cosmetic articles such as mirrors, ointment jars, kohl
flasks, combs, hairpins, razors and tweezers are preponderant. Most are
decorated with designs inspired by animals or plants. Jewels, gold rings with
mobile settings of precious stones and ceramic, and polychrome ceramic bead
necklaces, were appreciated by men and women alike. Tools and weapons,
games and musical instruments have also been found.

79. Chair

c. 1500–1200 B.C. (18th–19th Dynasty)

Wood, inlaid with ivory (or bone); the leather strips
are modern. H 91 cm (35.8 in.);
W 47.5 cm (18.7 in.); D 59 cm (23.2 in.)
N 2950

The origins of this chair, which
found its way into the Louvre collection before the mid-19th century, are
unclear. Undoubtedly it came from
a well-furnished tomb, judging
from the quality of the woodwork.
The curvature of the various sections
of the backrest, the carved lion's paw
feet and the use of different woods
and inlay are all worthy of note.
As always the sections are assembled
with mortise and tenon joints,
reinforced with dowels. The feline
fore and hind paw motif can be traced
back to the time of the Pyramids,
but the inclined backrest was
fashionable during the New
Kingdom. The original caning was
in twine.

80. Spoon with a Swimmer

c. 1400–1350 B.C. (18th Dynasty)

Wood and ivory (or bone). H 29 cm (11.4 in.);
W 5.5 cm (2.2 in.)
E 218

The 18th Dynasty saw the development of a new genre of decorative
spoons with refined forms; handles
in the shape of duck's necks
or bunches of flowers, etc. They
were long thought to be cosmetic
spoons. However, the study of certain
inscriptions and of pictures featuring
these spoons has left some doubt.
Perhaps their purpose was to toss
myrrh onto the fire as an offering
to the gods or to the dead. Notable
for their grace and inventiveness,
these "swimmer" spoons doubtless
fall into the same category of utensil.
Here a young slender girl lies holding
a duck at arm's length, the duck's
wings forming the lid of the spoon.

The Temple

For anyone fortunate enough to have visited Egypt and its great temples
it is easy to visualize the many architectural fragments the Louvre contains
(columns and capitals, bas-reliefs, etc.) in their original setting. The layout
of the sacred dwelling, a stone palace designed for daily communication with
the god on earth, did not change. First came an open courtyard to which
worshippers had access, then a room with columns casting soft shadows
serving as a transition into the semi-darkness of the private sanctuary
beyond. Only officiating priests were allowed there, for this was the dwelling
of the god in statue form within a tabernacle.

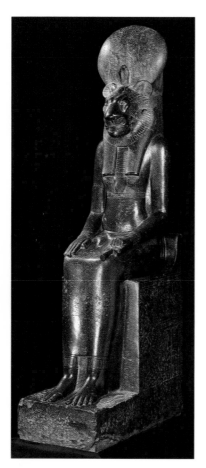

81. The Goddess Sakhmet
From the Mut temple at Karnak,
transported from its place of origin
on the left bank at Thebes.
Reign of Amenophis III,
c. 1391–1353 B.C. (18th Dynasty)
Statue, diorite. H 1.78 m (70.1 in.) (without
restored sundisk); W 55 cm (21.6 in.);
D 95 cm (37.4 in.)
A 8

The goddess Sakhmet has the head
of a lioness and the body of a young
woman; her schematic headdress
cleverly masks the change in form.
Volumes are well-balanced and
details are finely carved. None of the
eight statues of Sakhmet in the
Louvre is alike either in size or detail.
Originally there were a considerable
number of them, placed in the
temple of the ruler Amenophis III
at Thebes, a lost temple which
is marked now by the colossus
of Memnon. Each statue represented
a daily appeal to Sakhmet, the
combative goddess, to chase all evil
away from the temple throughout
the year.

82. Naos
Reign of Amasis, 570–526 B.C.
(26th Dynasty)
Pink granite. H 2.55 m (100.4 in.);
W 1.61 m (63.4 in.); D 1.50 m (59 in.)
Drovetti donation. D 29

Cut from one block of granite this
chapel once had a door to hide its
precious contents: the statue in which
the god was thought to dwell. Placed
at the end of the temple, where
processions culminated, the naos was
opened every day by priests; the statue
or god was offered libations, incense,
food and prayers as appeasements.
This naos from an unknown temple
to Osiris in the region of Lake
Mariut, near Alexandria, derived its
form from Archaic sanctuaries
of northern Egypt. A multitude
of divinities are carved on the outside,
a veritable Egyptian pantheon,
which protect and accompany the
god. The refined style of the
bas-relief, showing complete mastery
of working hard stone, is proof
of the high quality of contemporary
craftsmanship.

83. The Tod Treasure
Amenemhat II, 1898–1866 B.C.
(12th Dynasty)
Bronze, silver, lapis-lazuli, gold.
Large coffer: H 20.5 cm (8.1 in.); W 45 cm (17.7 in.);
D 28.5 cm (11.2 in.)
Tod Temple excavations. E 15128 to E 15328

While excavating the foundations
of the Middle Kingdom temple
at Tod, south of Luxor, the
archaeologist Fernand Bisson
de la Roque discovered four bronze
coffers buried in the floor of the
temple. They contained a large
number of silver bowls, most
of which were folded up, gold chains
and ingots, and lapis-lazuli in its
natural state or worked into
cylindrical seals. Both the raw
materials and finished products were
foreign in origin; for example, the
bowls are Aegean in style.
This precious hoard brought into
Egypt for political or commercial
reasons was dedicated to the god
Montu, lord of Tod, by the King
Amenemhat II.

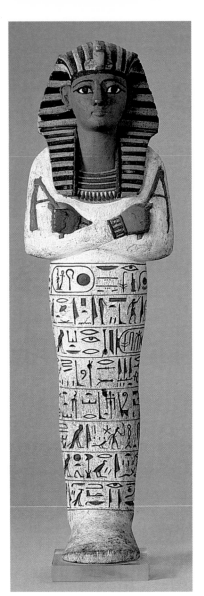

84. Funerary Servant of King Ramesses IV
c. 1153–1147 B.C. (20th Dynasty)
Statuette, painted wood. H 32.5 cm (12.8 in.)
N 438

The successors of Seti I and of Ramesses II (including many Ramesses from III to XI) also had deep tombs cut into the Valley of the Kings. The single unviolated example of Tutankhamun's tomb shows what treasures such underground chambers may have contained. Unfortunately most were pillaged as early as antiquity. Some objects have nevertheless come down to us, this funerary servant of Ramesses IV among them. Placed in the tomb with hundreds of his kin, all in the king's image, his function is inscribed on his body: he must stand in for the king "when his duty is to undertake any work in the necropolis, look after the fields, irrigate the banks, transport sand from east to west…" Clearly the afterlife, even for royalty, was not without its obligations.

Burials

The Egyptians were certainly not the only peoples to attend meticulously to funerary rituals. However, the exceptional condition of preservation of bodies and objects found in tombs and the sheer variety of furnishings and funereal iconography have encouraged the false notion that Egyptians were obsessed above all else with the day of their burial and their afterlife. Still, we do have precise information about the burial ceremony from tombs or from illustrations at the beginning of the "Book of the Dead." Aside from the procession of furnishings and the sarcophagus to the burial ground, an important moment was the reanimation ritual performed over the mummy or the sarcophagus before its descent into the tomb.

85. Sarcophagus of Madja
c. 1490–1470 B.C. (18th Dynasty)

Painted wood. H 62 cm (24.4 in.);
W 1.84 m (72.4 in.)
Gournet Mourraï excavations. E 14543

The sarcophagus of the lady Madja reflects the sobriety of middle-class funerary furnishing. The bier matches the shape of the mummy and the white background accentuates the composition. On one side men are bringing water and meat for the dead; on the other the sarcophagus is being towed to the tomb.

86. Lid of the Sarcophagus of Soutymes
c. 1000 B.C. (21st Dynasty)

Stuccoed and painted wood. H 2.10 m (82.7 in.);
W 79 cm (31.1 in.)
N 2609

Soutymes belonged to the highest class of officials in the powerful temple of Amun, a class gradually closing ranks at that period to form a sort of clergy. His power was principally temporal, in that he was in charge of finances in the temple. The body of this important man was protected by no less than three successive covers, each of which depict him as a mummy, with open eyes. The inside and outside of each case were painted with pictures of the great gods of the dead, Osiris and Re, in all their manifestations, accompanied by winged goddesses.

87. Burial Scene from the "Book of the Dead" of Nebqued
c. 1400 B.C. (18th Dynasty)

Painted papyrus. H about 30 cm (11.8 in.)
N 3068

Egyptian books were written on strips of papyrus which could extend to several yards in length, and could be rolled and unrolled as they were read. The writing is divided into columns or pages of lines. Funerary books such as this fine example of the "Book of the Dead" tended to be illustrated. The burial scene is shown at the beginning of the papyrus but given its format, it can be unrolled lengthways to show the funeral march and various stages of the ceremony.

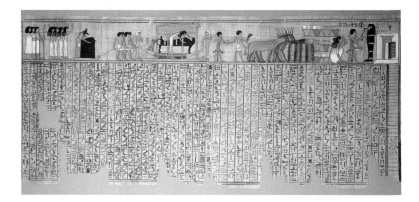

88. Jug and Basin
c. 2300 B.C. (6th Dynasty)

Copper, Jug: H 19.9 cm (7.8 in.); W 31.5 cm (12.4 in.);
basin: H 15 cm (5.9 in.);W 32 cm (12.6 in.)
E 3912 A and B

In the third millennium Egyptians
were as yet unaware that copper and
tin could be combined to make
bronze, but they were able to work
in copper with great success, and
even made statues larger than life
size. Copper vessels were common
and jugs and basins such as these
were set beside the dead in the
vaults, indispensable as they were
at mealtimes. Hammered and riveted
together, this particular set
is engraved with the name of its
owner, a priestess of Hathor known
as Pes.

89. Model of a boat
c. 1900 B.C. (12th Dynasty)

Painted wood. L 81 cm (31.9 in.);
H of hull 38.5 cm (15.2 in.)
Asyut burial ground excavations, tomb of the
chancellor Nakhti. E 12027

Within the tomb, this boat and crew
were to be of everlasting service
to the deceased for all river journeys
and would in particular have served
on his pilgrimage to Abydos and
to the god of the dead, Osiris. A cox
standing at the prow led eight
oarsmen and also had to keep testing
the depth of the water with his pole
so as not to run aground on one
of the many shifting sandbanks
beneath the river Nile. The two-
bladed rudder at the stern was
steered by the helmsman using
wooden interstices now lost.

90. Mummy of a Man
3rd or 2nd century B.C.
L 1.67 m (65.7 in.);
N 2627

During the Ptolemaic period, mummification became more artistic in
nature. Having been disembowelled
and dried in natron salt, the body
was skillfully swathed in a mesh
of linen. Then the mummy was
covered with a coating of plastered
old papyrus or cloth. A mask was
laid on the face, a case on the feet
and a large necklace on the chest.
The usual winged goddesses and
funereal spirits are depicted over the
legs along with a picture of the
mummy on its embalming bed.

Religion

The last two rooms on the lower floor (rooms 18 and 19) are devoted to the Egyptian pantheon with each god identifiable by character and attributes, and also to magic with magic steles, figurines, execratory texts and healing statues. One of the rooms is devoted to representations of the animals of the gods: Amun's goose, Montu's bull, Bastet's cat, Sebek's crocodile and so forth. Statuettes and mummies of animals are near by, including a magnificent statue of the bull Apis, worshipped at the Serapeum of Saqqara.

91. Healing Statue of Padimahes
4th century B.C.

Grauwacke (schist). H 67.7 cm (26.6 in.)
E 10777

This statue is representative of artistic tendencies in the 4th century B.C. and reveals the growing interest in witchcraft. The fine, smiling face stems from the idealizing line of Saite sculpture. Smooth, simplified volumes for the costume serve as a base for magic invocations designed to heal snake and scorpion bites. The text is formal; the bitten man must drink water which has run over the text of the statue and become infused with its magical powers. The stele the man is holding shows the young god Horus standing on some crocodiles. This type of stele is common as an independent sculpture and served the same purpose.

92. Seated Cat
c. 700–600 B.C.

Statuette, bronze; eyes ringed in blue glass.
H 33 cm (13 in.); W 25 cm (9.8 in.)
N 4538

Bronze ex-voto statuettes offered by devotees in the temples proliferated during the Late period. Bronzes of cats, for the most part representing the goddess Bastet, have been found in large numbers. They indicate the popularity of this goddess not only in her town of Bubastis, but in many other large cities such as Memphis, Thebes and Esna. The Egyptians also depicted her with her kittens or in the form of a woman with a cat's head.

Prehistory and the First Two Dynasties
(Thinite Period, c. 3100–2700 B.C.)

As elsewhere, Neolithic communities in Egypt are characterized by the beginnings of agriculture. It took man thousands of years to develop from the nomadic life of hunting and gathering of the Paleolithic era and evolve into the sedentary life of the Neolithic. Excavations in numerous fourth-millennium burial grounds in the Nile valley in Upper Egypt have uncovered objects bearing witness to belief in life after death and to a developed craft industry, which produced stone vases, ceramics decorated with stylized paintings, small ivory and stone sculptures and plaques. At the end of this period, around 3200 B.C., there are the first signs of Pharaonic civilization in bas-reliefs on schist plaques and in early picture-writing. According to an historical tradition of the ancient Egyptians the valley peoples were then united under a single authority, the first pharaoh. Excavations of the great burial grounds of these ancient kings and their courts at Abydos and at Saqqara give an indication of the high level of craftsmanship attained in the production of luxury goods such as ivory furniture legs, game pieces, statuettes, jewelry and precious vases. On steles found in the tombs, names of the deceased are written in primitive hieroglyphs.

93. Vase
c. 4000–3500 B.C. (Naqada I civilization)

Basalt. H. 42.8 cm (16.8 in.)
Gift of L. I. and A. Curtis. E 23175

Even from an early date Egyptian craftsmen worked with the hardest stones such as basalt, and hollowed them out to make containers. Lacking good metal tools they worked with stones, aided by abrasive agents such as quartz and emery. Both the technical mastery of this vase and the astonishing beauty of its form deserve our admiration.

94. Vase
c. 3500–3200 B.C. (Naqada II civilization)

Painted terracotta. H. 20.5 cm (8.1 in.);
W. 15.5 cm (6.1 in.)
AF 6851

At the end of the prehistoric period
Egyptians painted vessels with
stylized figurative motifs. On such
egg-shaped vases in beige clay they
would often depict large rowing
boats on which stand cabins bearing
various emblems. On this vase
a figure appears to be dancing with
his arms raised and joined above his
head. In the absence of a script, the
significance of such a scene remains
a mystery.

95. Plaque Framed with Quadrupeds, Hyenas or Lycaons
c. 3200 B.C. (late Naqada II period)

Grauwacke (schist). H 32 cm (12.6 in.);
W 17.7 cm (7 in.)
E 11052

From the end of the prehistoric
period, plaques or "palettes" carved
from schist and used for the grinding
of kohl, were laid beside the deceased.
Some of the later versions are much
larger and decorated with what are
among the first examples of Egyptian
bas-relief. This one uses relief and
silhouette carving for the four
mastiffs around the edges. On one
side a creature with an elongated
neck recalls similar animals found
in Mesopotamian art. On the other,
two giraffes serve as a reminder that
at one time the lower valley of the
Nile was savannah grassland.

96. Gebel el-Arak dagger

c. 3300–3200 B.C. (end of Naqada II
civilization)

Flint blade and ivory handle (hippopotamus tooth).
H 25.5 cm (10 in.); H of handle 4.5 cm (1.8 in.)
Probably from Gebel el-Arak, south of Abydos.
E 11517

Similar daggers to this with finely
carved handles may be found
elsewhere, but the scenes depicted
here are unique. On one side there
is a battle scene on land and water;
the other side depicts animals such
as lions, ibexes and dogs. At the top,
above the knop, a man in the robes
of a Sumerian priest-king
is restraining two rampant lions.
The piece raises questions about
artistic contacts with Mesopotamia.
It could depict a battle between

communities whose differences can
be seen in the design of their boats.
What is certain is that it is an early
example of Egyptian bas-relief and
is carved with great mastery. On one
side of the polished flint blade
narrow parallel flakes have been
chipped away; this is carving at its
most refined, characteristic of this
period of Egyptian civilization.

97. Stele of the "Serpent King"
c. 3000 B.C. (1st Dynasty)

Limestone, H 1.43 m (56.3 in.); W 55.5 cm (21.8 in.)
Abydos excavations, tomb of the Serpent King.
E 11007

Found in the tomb of the third king
of the 1st Dynasty, in the burial
ground of the Pharaohs of the first
two dynasties at Abydos, this large
stele is without doubt the finest
example of monumental sculpture
of its period. The slender pillar,
arched at the top and slightly convex,
is carved away in the upper section
to leave a crisp hieroglyph
of the king's name and his incarnation
as Horus, the falcon god of Egyptian
royalty. The motif is off-center
to create a harmonious composition.

The Old Kingdom (c. 2700–2200 B.C.)

The Old Kingdom was the period of the great pyramids at Giza and Saqqara near Cairo. Although we still have their gigantic monuments, our knowledge of 4th Dynasty sovereigns and even their successors in the 5th and 6th Dynasties is scant. Nearly all our knowledge of these centuries is based on discoveries made in the burial grounds near the capital, Memphis, and in the provinces. In underground chambers, furnishings for the deceased, consisting of domestic and funerary objects, have been found. Tomb chapels provide inscriptions describing the careers of high-ranking officials who are also depicted in steles and statues. People of humbler status can be seen working in the fields or in workshops in scenes decorating chapel walls. Altogether, such documents reflect a rigid hierarchical society dominated by the king.

The pattern appears to disintegrate around the end of the Old Kingdom and, after its demise, Egypt was divided up into several parallel dynasties in a period of relative obscurity, while the foundations of the old society were shaken by social and economic disturbances. This period, known as the First Intermediate Period (c. 2200–2033 B.C.), has left us with very few works of art.

98. Sepa and Nesa
c. 2700–2620 B.C. (3rd Dynasty)

Statues, painted limestone. A 36: H 1.65 m (65 in.);
W 40 cm (15.7 in.); D 55 cm (21.6 in.)
A 36 and A 37

These are among the first examples of large statues of private individuals from the Old Kingdom. Their solid forms are indicative of their archaism; it is as if the sculptor did not dare stray too far from the stone. Their rigid postures and smooth, serene faces remind us of their function, for within the tomb they served as durable stone reminders of the earthly form of the deceased. Inscriptions on the pediments identify them as Sepa, an important official, and his wife Nesa.

99. Head of King Radjedef

Abu Rawash
c. 2570 B.C. (4th Dynasty)

Red sandstone. H 26 cm (10.2 in.);
W 33.5 cm (13.2 in.); D 28.8 cm (11.3 in.)
Abu Roach excavations. E 12626

The head of King Radjedef, successor
to Cheops, is very different from the
faces of the Great Sphinx (no. 74)
or of Sepa and Nesa (no. 98); it quite
clearly depicts a particular individual
with a slightly receding jaw and
high cheek bones. The particular
beauty of this fragment lies in its
delicate mix of realism and idealism.
Cut in a crystal sandstone, it still has
traces of red paint on it. The set

of the head suggests that it was part
of a sphinx. It was found near the
remains of the funerary temple
beneath the king's pyramid at Abu
Rawash, north of Giza.

100. Stele of Nefertiabet

Giza
c. 2590 B.C. (4th Dynasty)

Painted limestone. H 37.5 cm (14.8 in.);
W 52.5 cm (20.7 in.)
From Giza. Gift of L., I. and A. Curtis. E 15591

The freshness of the colors and clear
composition delight the eye although
this stele was intended to be hidden
for all time, immured between the
funerary chapel and the superstruc-
ture or "mastaba" which would have
covered the tomb. Its function was
magical: to perpetuate through

a picture the receipt by the deceased
of the offerings essential for her
survival. The lady extends her hand
toward a tray full of slices of bread.
Hieroglyphs of different dishes
surround the table: chops, legs
of meat, poultry. Above and to the
right are other useful consumer goods
such as oil, make-up and linens.
Above her head hieroglyphs designate
the dead lady as "daughter of the
king, Nefertiabet" ("the beautiful
Oriental"), a princess from the time
of the great King Cheops.

101. The Seated Scribe
c. 2600–2350 B.C. (4ᵗʰ or 5ᵗʰ Dynasty)

Statue, painted limestone; eyes inlaid with rock
crystal and circled with copper. H 53.7 cm (21.1 in.);
W 44 cm (17.3 in.); D 35 cm (13.8 in.)
Saqqara excavations. E 3023

This famous statue was found
in the Old Kingdom burial ground
at Saqqara, but the identity of the
person is lost to us. Doubtless he was
someone of importance, judging
from the exceptional quality of this
statue, remarkable for its treatment
of face and body and for the attention
given to the eyes inset into copper.

We should not be misled by the
poised hands. This is not a humble
clerk preparing to write. The oldest
statues of scribes in fact depict
princes with high political respon-
sibilities. This statue has a particularly
striking presence with its original
colors, sharp eyes and intelligent
expression.

102. Raherka and Merseankh

c. 2350 B.C. (4th or 5th Dynasty)

Group, painted limestone. H 52.8 cm (20.8 in.);
D 21.3 cm (8.4 in)
Gift of L., I. and A. Curtis. E 15592

Statues of interlocked couples are
not uncommon in Egyptian tombs
during the Old Kingdom. This
is a particularly striking example.
The lady, known as Merseankh,
seems both to be nudging her husband
Raherka forward and relying on his
momentum as he alone is walking.
It is a refined piece of work and her
arm and his leg are clearly and
independently articulated. Their
round, smiling faces have a calm
confidence about them which
is typical of the period.

Middle Kingdom (2033–1710 B.C.)

Following the demise of the 1st Intermediate Period (c. 2200–2033 B.C.), Egypt was united again by another king, Mentuhotpe the Great. Originating from Thebes, the kings of the 11th Dynasty and their successors in the 12th Dynasty paid tribute to their god Montu, adorning shrines at Tod and at Medamud. French excavations have provided the Louvre with many fragments of the temples there. Royal statues of this period are often impressive. Official sculptors developed an art of portraiture based on the facial features of the great kings Sesostris III and Amenemhat III. Private statues also appropriated royal features and moved towards more geometric volumes, enveloping figures in tent-like robes. Goldwork also flourished during the Middle Kingdom, along with literature and the sciences. Fine examples of painted wooden sarcophagi have been found in tombs along with small wood carvings of groups of people at work. These help to give us a striking picture of the everyday life of the Egyptians.

103. Large Statue of Nakhti
c. 1900 B.C. (early 12th Dynasty)

Acacia wood. H 1.785 m (70.3 in.);
W of base 49.5 cm (19.5 in.); D 1.10 m (43.3 in.)
Asyut burial ground excavations. E 11937

The tomb of the chancellor Nakhti was undisturbed for nearly 4,000 years. In the entrance chapel two large wooden statues were found; both depict the deceased and are lifesize. Other smaller representations of Nakhti such as this were laid around the sarcophagus in the tomb. This is the most striking of all the statues; the quality of the wood, its carving and the facial expression are all remarkable. The collection of relics from this tomb are divided between Paris and Cairo; together they give us a good picture of the funerary possessions of a member of the privileged class of that time. Alongside painted wooden sarcophagi, models of scenes of life along the Nile, gift bearers and imitation weapons and tools surrounded the dead man.

104. Gift Bearer
c. 1950 B.C. (early 12th Dynasty)

Statuette, painted wood. H 1.085 m (42.7 in.);
D of base 32.7 cm (12.9 in.)
E 10781

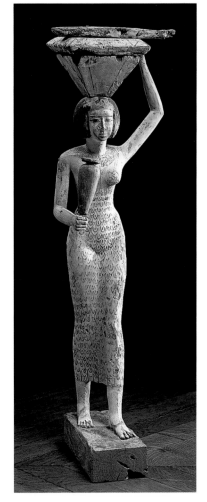

This attractive Egyptian lady
is not the owner of the tomb where
she was found. She is simply
an anonymous servant placed there
to bring her dead master an ox's foot
and a jar of water for all time. While
statues of gift bearers are common
at this period, the beauty of this one
is exceptional, with her slender body,
elegant bearing and refined,
attentive face.

105. Hippopotamus
c. 2000–1800 B.C. (Middle Kingdom)

Silicious faience. H 12.7 cm (5 in.);
W 20.5 cm (8.1 in.); D 8.1 cm (3.2 in.)
E 7709

If pictures in Old Kingdom mastabas
are anything to go by, it appears that
the hunting of hippopotami in the
Nile marshes was a sport for
noblemen. Hippopotami were placed
in tombs at the beginning of the
Middle Kingdom so that the sport
(which probably had symbolic
connotations) could be continued
in the afterlife. On the surface of the
animal are decorations derived from
its natural habitat; blue suggesting
river water and aquatic plants such
as the waterlily. The chubby outline
is rendered with a skill which
characterizes Egyptian depictions
of animals.

106. Lintel of Sesostris III
1862–1843 B.C. (12th Dynasty)

Bas-relief, limestone. H 1.065 m (41.9 in.);
W 2.21 m (87 in.)

Medamud temple excavations. E 13983

The subject-matter of reliefs carved
on architectural elements in Egyptian
temples bore some relationship
to the room's function. This is the
lintel to the door of the room storing
offerings. King Sesostris III appears

in two parallel scenes, making
offerings of bread to the god Montu,
the lord of Medamud. On the left
the king is shown in his youth, while
on the right his face is thin. The
drawn features are familiar from
other three-dimensional busts of him.
These two stages of the king's life
are possibly shown together to express
the idea of the cycle of life.

107. King Amenemhat III
1843–1798 B.C. (12th Dynasty)

Statuette, grauwacke (schist). H 21.4 cm (8.4 in.);
W 10 cm (3.9 in.)

N 464

Although its inscription is missing,
the identity of this statue is not
in doubt; the features, the large
mouth and aquiline nose of King
Amenemhat III are boldly delineated.
The exaggerated size of the ears
is characteristic of the period.
The idealized body co-exists with
a markedly realistic facial portrait,
a feature typical of royal statuary
at the end of the 12th Dynasty.

The New Kingdom (c. 1550–1069 B.C.)

The New Kingdom followed the expulsion of the Hyksos, a Near Eastern people who had invaded 150 years earlier under a politically weak late Middle Kingdom. Pharaohs of the 18th Dynasty (c. 1555–1305), the Tuthmosis, and Amenophis ruled over a huge empire stretching from the Sudan to Syria. The resulting prosperity led to the architectural flowering of great temples at Thebes, Karnak, and Luxor, and palaces, the splendor of which is hinted at in the luxurious furniture of Tutankhamun's tomb. Cultural contacts multiplied, availability of raw materials and wealth increased, and the whole of Egyptian society benefited, as is apparent from the increasing refinement and enrichment of the arts.

The ruler Amenophis IV-Akhenaten harnessed the economic strength and great creative energies of his time to his revolutionary ideas, doing away with many artistic conventions and constructing a new capital. The Ramesside period (19th and 20th Dynasties) saw a return to the old order. The rulers Seti I and Ramesses II made prestigious additions to the large sanctuaries. By the end of the second millennium Egypt had to defend itself against the first waves of displaced populations which shook the Mediterranean world. The rulers moved their residences to the north, leaving the south in the hands of the powerful priesthood of Thebes. A page of Egyptian history had been turned.

108. Head of a King, Amenophis II?
c. 1427–1401 B.C. (18th Dynasty)

Quartzite. H 21 cm (8.3 in.)
E 10896

This fine head belongs to a sphinx because the headdress (the royal "nemes") is raised up at the back. Over the forehead an erect cobra ("uraeus") symbolizes the pharaoh's powers to destroy the enemies of Egypt. Although the inscription is lost, the style of the face and particularly the eyes link it to artistic developments in royal sculpture around the first half of the 18th Dynasty.

109. Patera of General Djehuty
Reign of Tuthmosis III, c. 1479–1425
(18th Dynasty)
Gold. Ø 17.9 cm (7 in.); H 2.2 cm (0.9 in.)
N 713

The patera is made of hammered
gold with an embossed and chased
pattern. At the center is a flower,
a waterlily, seen from above; around
it are stylized fish and papyrus,
themes also found on contemporary
blue ceramic bowls. An inscription
engraved around the edge explains
that this magnificent gold piece was
offered by the ruler Tuthmosis III
to General Djehuty for his faithful
services abroad.

110. A Couple: Senynefer and Hatchepsut
c. 1410 B.C. (18th Dynasty)

Group, painted sandstone. H 62 cm (24.4 in.);
W 82 cm (32.3 in.)
E 27161

This lifesize couple, with colors as fresh as when they were first painted, are strikingly present. They are a good illustration of the purpose of Egyptian sculpture: to duplicate the body, serving as its earthly record. For once the faces are authentic likenesses; only the skin coloring is conventional; yellow for the woman and red ocher for the man. The couple would have been holding each other about the waist and seated against a backrest which served as a stele; a prayer is carved on it, for the offering that would ensure food for their eternal life.

111. King Amenophis III
c. 1391–1353 B.C. (18th Dynasty)

Head, diorite. H 32.5 cm (12.8 in.)
A 25

This fragment has lost its identifying inscription. However there can be no doubt that it is the ruler Amenophis III whose round cheeks, small, flattened chin, full lips, short nose and almond eyes are so recognizable. His helmet is in a royal style which emerged under the New Kingdom; the body of the "uraeus", a royal cobra, coils majestically over it.

112. Paser's Stele
c. 1410–1350 B.C. (18th Dynasty)

Limestone. H 98.5 cm (38.8 in.); L 77 cm (30.3 in.)
C 80

This form of stele served as
a funerary monument, designed
to be inset into the wall of the tomb
to perpetuate the cult of the deceased.
Here two offerings are shown;
above, the dead man called Paser
offers Osiris bouquets and food
saying: "I have come bearing you
gifts, all sorts of fine products from
the land of Egypt for you, O Osiris,
leader of Westerners (the Dead):
may you favor me, as the king
favored me on earth." In the lower
scene Paser himself receives
an offering made by his wife,
daughter and son. It was this very
son who had the stele made for him.

113. Touy
c. 1400–1350 B.C. (18th Dynasty)

Statuette in African red ebony. H 33.4 cm (13.1 in.),
W 7 cm (2.7 in.); D 17 cm (6.7 in.)
E 10655

The sculptor of this statuette
displays his craft both in the
perfection of volumes and treatment
of surfaces; the delicate engraving
on the braids of the wig encasing the
face contrasts with the fine polish
of the body in its tight-fitting robe.
On the base a prayer invokes Osiris
and then all the gods of the burial
ground so that Touy "may breathe
the soft Northern wind, that her
soul may enter the burial ground,
that she may be with the blessed
next to Osiris, that she may drink
water wherever she pleases." The
statuette was made for the tomb
of this society lady from the glorious
reign of King Amenophis III.

114. Flask
c. 1400–1300 B.C. (18th Dynasty)

Glass. H 10 cm (3.9 in.); W 7.2 cm (2.8 in.)
AF 2032

With increased foreign contacts
in the 18th Dynasty and a corresponding development of artistic
techniques, Egyptians manufactured
glass for the first time, concentrating
particularly on small containers
like this. Since glass-blowing was
unknown, a mould made
of compressed sand was dipped into
molten glass; colored glass strands
were applied onto the hot surfaces
and the garland effect obtained
by drawing lines across the still soft
surface with a pointed instrument.
When the glass cooled, the sand core
inside the bottle was removed.
The small size and narrow neck
of this jar suggest it was destined for
a precious liquid, probably a sweet-
smelling oil.

115. Ibex-Shaped Flask
c. 1470–1370 B.C. (18th Dynasty)

Painted terracotta. W 15 cm (5.9 in.);
H 10.2 cm (4 in.)
Dra Abul'Naggah excavations (western Thebes).
E 12659

During the 18th Dynasty the applied
arts, pottery among them, flourished.
Decorative containers like these,
in the form of women or animals,
were produced in abundance.
This represents an ibex lying down
with its kid; the aperture is in the
mother's mouth. In order to obtain
the fine red sheen, pottery was
coated in slip and the surface
carefully polished before firing.
A few black lines help define details
of forms.

Egyptians used kohl extensively, both to emphasize and protect their eyes. The wide rim of this small pot meant that small crumbs of this precious product, from distant Arabian mines by the Red Sea, were not wasted. It is made of Egyptian faience, a ceramic material made of quartz powder with a fine yellow glaze. The names of Amenophis III and Queen Tiy are inlaid in blue faience.

116. Kohl Pot
Reign of Amenhotep III,
c. 1391–1353 (18th Dynasty)
Silicious ceramic. H 8.4 cm (3.3 in.)
E 4877

117. Colossus of King Amenophis IV
Reign of Amenophis IV-Akhenaten,
c. 1353–1337 B.C. (18th Dynasty)

Painted sandstone. H 1.37 m (53.9 in.);
W 88 cm (34.6 in.); D 0.50 m (19,6 in.)
From a temple east of Karnak. Gift of Egyptian
government. E 27112

118. Body of Nefertiti?
Reign of Amenophis IV-Akhenaten
c. 1353–1337 B.C. (18th Dynasty)

Statuette, red quartzite. H 29 cm (11.4 in.)
E 25409

From the beginning of his reign Amenophis IV gave a new direction to art and religion, as is shown in remnants of a sanctuary he had built at the east of the Amun temple at Karnak. A large courtyard was lined with a pillared portico against which stood colossal statues in the ruler's image, his arms crossed over his chest like Osiris. This was a traditional form of architectural sculpture; the novelty resides in the extraordinary and unprecedented style of the statues. The king's body with its strangely feminine hips is crowned by an elongated head, its features heavily stylized like a mask. The coloring which by now has almost entirely vanished must have emphasized the extraordinary expression of this disturbing yet entrancing face.

Despite being damaged, this fragment is evidence of the mastery of certain artists during the revolutionary period of Pharaoh Amenophis IV, known as the "Amarna period." Remaining strictly within the canon imposed by the new official doctrine—slender arms and protuberant belly—the sculptor has created a new style of beauty. The ample but finely chiseled forms give it its originality; the generous proportions of the lower body are emphasized by the radiating folds of the costume, finely carved in red sandstone. Nefertiti, the celebrated queen of Amenophis IV-Akhenaten was most likely to be the inspiration behind this fulsome female body and not, as some have suggested, one of her daughters.

119. Head of a Princess
Reign of Amenophis IV-Akhenaten,
c. 1353–1337 B.C. (18ᵗʰ Dynasty)
Painted limestone. H 15.4 cm (6.1 in.);
W 10 cm (3.9 in.)
E 14715

120. Amun and Tutankhamen
Reign of Tutankhamun,
c. 1336–1327 B.C. (18ᵗʰ Dynasty)
Diorite group. H 2.14 m (84.2 in.);
W 44 cm (17.3 in.); D 78.5 cm (30.9 in.)
E 11609

Amenophis IV and Nefertiti had six
daughters. Their lives—and the
early death of one of them—can
be traced in the series of representations of the royal family which were
central to the official religious
imagery of the period. This
adolescent girl still with plump
cheeks has her hair styled like other
children of the time in a thick mass
of long braids, which fall down over
her right shoulder. The satisfying
combination of the "Amarna" style
with a certain realism, most apparent
in the treatment of the neck, mouth
and chin, is the mark of the finest
works of the end of this reign.

Many temple statues are groups
consisting of the ruler with one
or several gods. Here the god Amun
is recognizable from his two high
plumes. He was the great god of the
temple at Karnak who according
to official doctrine gave victory
to the great conquering kings of the
18th Dynasty. Suppressed under
the religious revolution led by King
Amenophis IV-Akhenaten, his cult
re-emerged with renewed strength
under the young Tutankhamun.
As a testament of his faith,
Tutankhamun had many images
of Amun made similar to this, with
the god protecting him. The almost
feminine body and the spiritual cast
of features nevertheless derive from
the art of Amenophis IV's time.

121. Wailing Women
Reign of Tutankhamun, c. 1330 B.C.
(18th Dynasty)

Bas-relief, limestone . H 75 cm (29.9 in.);
W 30 cm (14.2 in.)
From a tomb at Saqqara. B 57

In the reign of Tutankhamun people
of rank had fine tombs built for
themselves at Saqqara, the burial
ground for the town of Memphis.
By that time, the administrative
center of the country had moved
from Thebes to Memphis. The scene
of mourners at a burial, common
in 18th Dynasty tombs, takes
on a dramatic depth here, thanks
to the artistic innovations of the
"Amarna" period. Arms and hands
turn about, giving an impression
of movement and planes are treated
freely with incised and raised areas
suggesting a crowd.

**122. Piay, the Gatekeeper
of the Royal Palace**
c. 1300 B.C. (end of the 18th, early
19th Dynasty)

Statuette, karite wood (acacia base).
H 54.4 cm (21.4 in.); W 10.9 cm (4.3 in.);
D 31 cm (12.2 in.)
E 124

The statue of Piay is a good example
of artistic tendencies at the end
of the 18th Dynasty. Artists abandoned Amenophis IV-Akhenaten's
extraordinarily humane canon but
retained the new, milder approach
of his revolutionary art. Piay's gently
rounded belly, emphasized by the
pleated loincloth, derives from work
of the preceding period. The finely
detailed fuller costume lends further
elegance to the work and anticipates
the voluminous fashions of the next
Ramesside period.

123. King, Probably Seti I, Presenting the Goddess Maat

c. 1294–1279 B.C. (19th Dynasty)

Statuette, silver-gilt. H 19.5 cm (7.7 in.)
Ganay donation. E 27431

The silver statuette, covered with
gold leaf in some areas, was probably
part of a larger religious object,
possibly a ceremonial boat borne
by priests when sacred statues were
brought out on feast days. The king
is holding up a small seated woman,
Maat, goddess of world order. In this
way he shows his god that
he is maintaining divine order
on earth.

124. The Goddess Hathor and King Seti I

c. 1294–1279 B.C. (19th Dynasty)

Bas-relief, painted limestone. H 2.265 m (89.2 in.);
W 1.05 m (41.3 in.)
From the tomb of Seti I in the Valley of Kings,
brought back from Egypt by Champollion. B 7

This painted bas-relief once faced
a parallel scene (now in Florence),
half-way down the long corridor cut
into the mountain west of Thebes
(present-day Luxor). As always the
scene is closely connected to its
location; the goddess Hathor
is greeting the king who is leaving
the world of the living. She grasps
his hand and gives him a necklace,
her emblem, thereby placing him
under her protection. Particularly
venerated in western Thebes, burial
ground of the capital of the New
Kingdom, she assumed an important
role as receiver of the dead.
The bas-reliefs of the largest tomb
in the Valley of Kings combine
traditional hieraticism with the
softened approach of Amarna art in
an elegant classical form.

125. Pendant in the Shape of a Predatory Bird with a Ram's Head

c. 1264 B.C. (19th Dynasty)

Gold, turquoise, carnelian, lapis-lazuli.
Span 13.7 cm (5.4 in.); L 7.4 cm (2.9 in.)
From the Serapeum at Saqqara. E 80

At Memphis a sacred bull called Apis was venerated as the terrestrial incarnation of the god Ptah. At its death it was buried with the rites of somebody of rank, in a subterranean necropolis reserved for its kind. In 1851, Auguste Mariette found a beautiful ornament in cloisonné gold, inlaid with precious stones in the tomb of an Apis which died during the reign of Ramesses II. It is thought to represent one aspect of the sun god Re.

The Third Intermediate Period, the Saite Period and the Last Indigenous Dynasties
(c.1069–332 B.C.)

At the beginning of the first millennium B.C., the capital was at Tanis, in the delta, while the high-priests of Amun at Thebes enjoyed independence in the south of the country (21st Dynasty, c. 1069–945 B.C.). Political divisions widened; Libyan families seized the throne for a time (22nd and 23rd Dynasties). Then the kings of Sudan annexed Egypt (25th Dynasty), until they were overcome by the Assyrians (664 B.C.). Kings from the town of Sais, in the delta, subsequently reunited the country (26th or "Saite" Dynasty, 664–525 B.C.). But the Persians then conquered it for the first time (525–404). The 28th, 29th and 30th Dynasties saw the last pharaohs of Egyptian origin, before the Persians returned and made the country part of their great empire (340–332 B.C.).

126. Taperet's Stele
c. 900–700 B.C.

Painted wood. H 31 cm (12.2 in.); W 29 cm (11.4 in.)
Batissier donation. N 3663

At the beginning of the first millennium B.C. large funerary steles in stone were superseded by small wooden steles on which the dead were no longer shown seated at their funerary feast, but in adoration before the great gods of the hereafter. By the side of Osiris, different manifestations of the sun god are shown. The dead lady Taperet sends a prayer to Re-Harakhty (the sun at its zenith) on one side of the stele and to Atum (the setting sun) on the other. There are two different symbols for the universe surrounding these scenes; on one side the arched ribbon of sky is supported above the strip of black earth by heraldic plants of northern and southern Egypt. On the other, the sky is the goddess Nut, whose body is traversed by the sun. Every evening she swallows it and every morning she gives birth to it. The beneficial effects of sunlight are symbolized by lilies, another novelty in this richly colored and finely drawn stele.

127. Book of Mythological Pictures Belonging to Nespakachuty, Accountant of the Granaries of Amun
c. 1069–945 B.C. (21st Dynasty)

Painted papyrus. H 19.3 cm (7.6 in.);
W 270 cm (106.3 in.)
E 17401

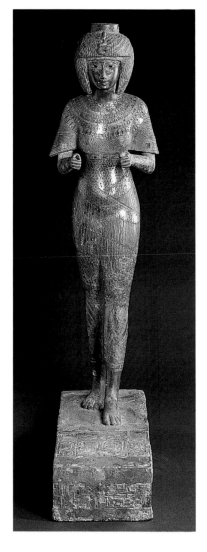

At the beginning of the first millennium new funerary books appeared, almost without text. They were compilations of mythological scenes in which the dead person regularly featured, rather like donors in church paintings. Most of the images are taken from the "Book of the Dead," which had already taken shape at the beginning of the 18th Dynasty: the weighing of the heart before Osiris, the fostering cows, the deceased being given water by the tree goddess. As on sarcophagi and painted wood steles of the period, there are the themes of homage to Re-Harakhty, the sun god with a falcon's head and of the separation of heaven and earth. The taste for symbolic images and displays of personal piety grew in importance from this time.

129. The Osorkon Group
Reign of Osorkon II, c. 874–850 B.C.
(22nd Dynasty)

Gold, lapis-lazuli, glass. H 9 cm (3.5 in.);
W 6.6 cm (2.6 in.)
E 6204

Osiris's family are represented here
in an original way. Isis, the mother
and Horus, the son with the falcon's
head, are shown at either side of the
god Osiris who is squatting on a pillar,
and they raise their hands over him
in a protective gesture. Legend had
it that Isis pieced together the severed
body of Osiris and breathed life into
him again for the time it took
to conceive a son by him, the god
Horus. The latter avenged his father,
challenging his murderer, the god
Seth, to a fight. The name of the
king, Osorkon II, is engraved
on the lapis pillar, thereby ensuring
assimilation with the great god
of the dead.

128. The "Divine Consort"
of Amun, Karomama
About 850 B.C. (22nd Dynasty)

Statuette, bronze inlaid with gold, silver and
electrum. H 59.5 cm (23.4 in.); W 12.5 cm (4.9 in.);
D 35 cm (13.8 in.)
Acq. in Egypt by Champollion. N 500

To strengthen links between the
powerful clergy of Amun dominating
the region of Thebes and the royal
family now governing from the
north, the pharaohs of the period
appointed one of their daughters
"divine consort" or "adoratress"
of Amun. As the "spouse" of the god
and of the god alone, she was invested
with great temporal power over the
region of Thebes. An unnamed
courtier to Karomama, one of these
consorts, dedicated this statuette
in the temple. It is one of the finest
Egyptian bronzes known to us.
Besides the beautiful modeling
of the statuette, a fine inlaywork
of precious metals makes her costume
into something quite sumptuous.
Two large wings, like those of queens
or goddesses, fold around her legs.
But above all there is a magnificent
necklace. On its weighty clasp,
which falls at her back, is inscribed
her name: "the beloved of Mut,
Karomama."

130. Bust of an Old Man
Saite period, c. 525 B.C. (26th Dynasty)

Peridotite. H 25.2 cm (9.9 in.); W 18.5 cm (7.3 in.)
N 2454

Unfortunately part of the inscription to this statue is missing; "under the protection of Ptah-Sokar, chancellor to the king of Lower Egypt…" Two tendencies merge in this fine piece of sculpture; a contemporary vogue for archaism discernible in the naked bust and sober hairstyle, and a concern for realism, confined to the face. The marks of age are minutely detailed, perhaps to indicate wisdom. With its smooth polished shapes and clear-cut modeling, the fine green stone gives the work a perfect finish. It is a remarkable portrait.

132. Man with a Shaven Head
4th century B.C. (30th Dynasty).

Grauwacke (schist). H 12.9 cm (5.1 in.)
Lami donation. E 25577

131. The Extraction of Lily Juice
4th century B.C. (30th Dynasty).

Bas-relief, limestone. W 37 cm (14.6 in.);
H 25.8 cm (10.2 in.); D 4 cm (1.6 in.)
E 11162

This fragment of a bas-relief comes
from a tomb dating from the last
indigenous dynasties. There are
several contemporary examples
of scenes like this. Lily flowers are
being gathered and their juice
extracted. The flowers are placed
in a cloth which is twisted with the
help of rods, to extract all the juice.
The liquid runs into a jar placed
on a low table or held upright
in a stand. More complete reliefs
show the juice being poured into
small jars given to the owner of the
tomb. The full figures of the working
women and their chubby faces
reveal the influence of Greek art
which, combined with the Egyptian
clarity of composition, gives this
work its peculiar charm.

Under the last Egyptian pharaohs,
men of note chose to be depicted
without wigs, their heads shaven,
as was the practice for priesthood
ceremonies at the temple. This work
is a fine example of the continuing
realistic tendency, showing a middle-
aged man, with full features, heavy
chin, and lined eyes. The sculptor's
skill is especially evident in the
closely observed anatomy
of the cranium.

Egypt under Greek Domination (332–30 B.C.)

The Greek, Alexander the Great, wrested Egypt from the Persians. After his death it was governed by one of his generals, Ptolemy. For three centuries Egypt was ruled by Greek "pharaohs" who descended from Ptolemy, with a Greek ruling class which, early on at least, did not mix with the indigenous population. In 30 B.C. the last of these Ptolomaic sovereigns, Cleopatra VII, fell to Octavius. Egypt remained part of the Roman world for several centuries.

134. Compartmented Box
Grecian Egypt, 3rd–2nd century B.C.

Silicious faience. H 5 cm (2 in.); W 12 cm (4.7 in.);
D 11.6 cm (4.6 in.)
E 11071

Pottery in Egypt under the Greeks provides a good example of a successful union between traditional Egyptian techniques and the repertoire of Greek forms and decorations. The hollow motifs are a deeper blue than the protruding areas, being more thickly glazed. One of the most important manufacturing centers was Memphis.

133. Body of Isis
Grecian Egypt, 3rd–1st century B.C.

Statuette, diorite . H 63 cm (24.8 in.)
Hoffmann donation. E 11197

Under Ptolemaic rule, Egyptian sculptors experimented to a limited degree with elements of Greek art. This body of a goddess in the traditional frontal position is dressed in a draped garment in the Greek fashion, though it has the symmetry beloved of the Egyptians. The knot of material between the breasts indicates this is a representation of Isis.

Roman Egypt (30 B.C.–4th Century A.D.)

Egypt remained under Rome rule until the 4th century B.C., during which time it came under the influence of Byzantium. While the emperors, made pharaohs, undertook construction work on the great Egyptian sanctuaries, they steered the economy of the country toward cereal production to feed the population of Rome. The funerary practice of embalming to deify the dead grew considerably at the time and endured even after the triumph of Christianity in the 4th century.

Appropriately enough, the new room devoted to this period is reminiscent of a crypt and the displays show the funerary material grouped by era, from the end of the Ptolomaic period to the 4th century. Some demonstrate the overcrowding in the sepultures.

Alongside works of art made according to the knowledge inherited from ancient Egypt, the portrait, of Graeco-Roman origin, was introduced in the 1st century A.D. Portraits were likenesses or realistic depictions, painted in encaustic on wood. In the 2nd century portraits were also executed using the Egyptian distemper technique and both were employed at the same time on the portrait shrouds of Antinoë; an illustration of the creative genius of the period. Items of batch production and masterpieces are displayed alongside each other and show the development from 1st century idealism to the realism of the 2nd and 3rd centuries, and, under the influence of the Near East, the culmination in the schematism of the 4th century.

Funerary iconography mirrors this double culture of Roman Egypt: the juxtaposition or co-existence of Greek culture and Egyptian religion. By way of example wooden tags to label mummies were produced. So on the one hand there was the deadman's "identification card" written in Greek and on the other a formulaic prayer in Demotic that his name might live forever.

135. Mortuary Mask of a Woman
Early 3rd century A.D.

Painted plaster. H 34 cm (13.4 in.);
W.62 cm (24.4 in.); D 26 cm (10.2 in.)
Antinoë excavations. E 21360

During both the Ptolemaic dynasty and the Roman Empire, Greek officials governed Egypt. Attracted to the Egyptian religion of the dead with its promise of eternal life, they adopted various practices such as mummification with the idea that the appearance of the terrestrial body should be preserved. However, their masks are very different from Egyptian "casings," being plaster busts, with realistic features and Roman hairstyles and embellishments.

136. Funerary Tapestry
End of 1ˢᵗ century A.D.

Encaustic and distemper on linen canvas.
H 175 cm (68.9 in.); W 125 cm (49.2 in.)
Saqqara. N 3076

Anubis, the god of embalmers,
embraces the deceased who is dressed
in clothes of the living and turns
him towards his double immortalized
in Osiris. On the right shoulder of the
deadman is a chadouf symbolizing
the water needed for his survival.
The portrait was painted separately
and applied to the tapestry.

137. Funerary Portrait of a Man
2nd century A.D.?

Encaustic paint on wood. H 38 cm (15 in.);
W 24 cm (9.4 in.)
AF 6883

Painted in encaustic on a thin
limewood board, this portrait was
inserted between the bands of the
mummy over the face. The three-
quarter view and the modeling
achieved through small parallel
brushstrokes lends a sculptural
quality to this man's face. The hair
and beard accentuate its elongation.

Coptic Egypt

The term "Copt" derives from the word "Algyptios," used by the Greeks
to refer to the inhabitants of the land of the pharaohs. By the time the Arabs
arrived in Egypt in 641 A.D., the whole country was Christian and the term
was used to designate not only the native group but their adherence
to Christianity as opposed to the Muslim faith of the invaders. Later it came
to refer also to the Christian practices of Egypt and by extension those
of Ethiopia.

The beginnings of Coptic script can be traced to the 2nd century B.C. and
it developed from the 3rd and 4th centuries A.D. Consisting of Greek letters
along with seven signs of pharaonic origin, it was superseded in official texts
by Arabic from the 8th century onward, and disappeared during the 11th.
It has survived only as a liturgical language in the church.

During the 4th century a stylistic change in Egyptian art took place giving
rise to an original style which lasted into the 12th century and beyond. When,
after the 9th century, the Copts were in a minority they gradually turned for
inspiration to the art of Byzantium and Islam. But Coptic art at its climax
(from the 5th to the 7th century) was strongly marked by Graeco-Roman,
Paleo-Christian and oriental influences.

Since 1997, Coptic antiquities have been exhibited in the new galleries and
the display retraces the history of art and civilization in Egypt from the
4th to 14th century. A "gallery of Coptic art" gives a full panorama through
displays that are either technical (ceramics, fabrics, painted woods…)
or thematic and iconographic (writing, mythological or Christian subjects…).
The "Salle de Baouit" (Bawit Room) takes its name from a Coptic monastery
in Middle Egypt from whence comes the church rebuilt in this second
display area.

138. Dionysus
4th century A.D.

High-relief, limestone. H 54.5 cm (21.5 in.);
W 52.7 cm (20.7 in.); D 17.5 cm (6.9 in.)
Acq. 1958. E 26106

A Dionysus emerges from a niche
lined with vine scrolls. This work
is in a new style that appeared
during the 4th century, which turned
resolutely away from Greek and
Roman styles. The disproportionate
body of the god is devoid of realistic
detail; the round, characterless face,
the large lined eyes with holes bored
for pupils, the beaded hair are all
signs of a new direction in Coptic
thought. Of all the pagan divinities,
Dionysus was particularly venerated
in Egypt. Assimilated with Osiris,
the god of wine, according to the
Texts of the Pyramids, he was
especially favored by the Ptolemaic
rulers. The theme of the vine, his
main attribute, also appears in the
Bible, evoking God the Father and
Christ, from whom the faithful
spread like branches.

139. Virgin Annunciate
Late 5th century A.D.

Bas-relief carving, fig wood . H 28.5 cm (11.2 in.);
W 14.2 cm (5.6 in.); D 2 cm (0.8 in.)
Acq. 1945. E 17118

Seated on a high stool, Mary is busy spinning the thread for the Veil of the Temple as described in the Apocrypha. The archangel Gabriel, of whom only a foot remains, would have faced her. This carving, which was once painted, probably belonged to a larger panel illustrating scenes from the life of the Virgin. Marian iconography spread throughout the Christian world after the Council of Ephesus in 431, which proclaimed Christ's mother to be the mother of God.

The woodcarving technique was always popular in Egypt despite the fact that there was an unquestionable lack of timber which often had to be imported from afar. Nevertheless, Coptic craftsmen and carvers were renowned for their skill and even in the middle of the Arab period they were brought in to work on the great constructions of the Near East.

140. Christat and the Abbot Mena
7th century A.D.

Distemper. H 57 cm (22.4 in.); W 57 cm (22.4 in.);
D 2 cm (0.8 in.)
IFAO excavations at the monastery of Bawit,
1901–2. E 11565

With a protective gesture Christ
is accompanying the abbot Mena,
head of the Bawit monastery. Both
figures are standing in strictly frontal
positions, against a background
of hills and red evening sky.
Destined probably to be inset into
a wall, the style of the panel matches
the numerous rows of saints
decorating niches and walls of chapels
at this monastery. Simplified and
boldly painted, the rounded folds
of the garments are typical of Coptic
painting. Byzantine influence shows
in the white highlights of the clothes
and the richly studded and bejewelled
binding of the Gospel that Christ
carries, which is offset by the
simplicity and sobriety of the rest
of the painting.

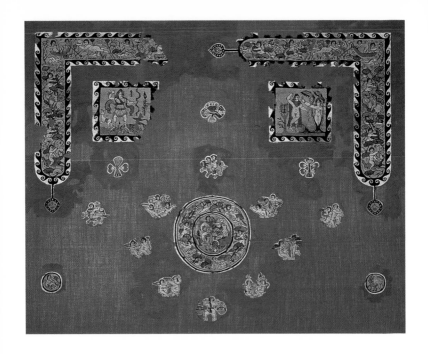

141. Sabine's Shawl
Antinoë, 6th century A.D.

Tapestry, wool . H 1.10 m (43.3 in.);
W 1.40 m (55.1 in.)
A. Gayet excavations, 1902–1903. E 29302

This garment was found
in an Antinoë tomb where it covered
the shoulders of a lady known as
Sabine. It is one of some 35,000 fabrics
recovered from Egyptian tombs.
Decorated with tapestries
on a canvas backing, the shawl
is composed of two squares framed
by right-angle bands, with a central
medallion. The iconography derives
from Graeco-Roman mythology:
Daphne and Apollo, Diana the
huntress, Bellerophon and the
chimaera. The Nilotic scenes of the
bands can be linked to subjects from
ancient Egypt which were adapted
to the taste of a wealthy Roman

clientele from the 1st century A.D.
The fashion for lavishly decorated
fabrics which started in the Orient,
with a few examples dating from the
New Kingdom, developed during
the 3rd century A.D. and spread
during the Christian era throughout
the Mediterranean world.

142. Censer with an Eagle
9th century A.D.

Perforated bronze, H 28 cm (11 in.);
Ø 20 cm (7.9 in.)
Acq. 1925. E 11708

This object, which probably had
a liturgical function, comprises
an incense burner with three feet
decorated with hares, and
a dome-shaped cover surmounted
by an eagle strangling a serpent. The
body of the censer is fretted with
elegant foliated scrollwork and the
brazier and lid are held together
with a pin. It is a fine example of the
consummate skill of Coptic bronze
founders; a skill which continued its
development well into the Arab era.
Hare and rabbit motifs are often
seen on monuments of the period.

Greek, Etruscan and Roman Antiquities

The Prehellenistic Age
and the Archaic Greek World

The Classical Greek World

The Hellenistic World

The Etruscans

The Roman World

Introduction

The Department of Greek, Etruscan and Roman Antiquities along with the Department of Paintings were among the first to be established in the Louvre. Antiquities from all three civilizations come in a wide range of materials including stone, bronze, terracotta, wood, glass, gold and silver, ivory, stucco and amber. They illustrate the artistic activities of a wide area centered principally around the Mediterranean, from the end of the Neolithic age (fourth millennium B.C.) to the 6th century A.D. Starting with the royal collection as a nucleus (begun during the reign of Francis I), and supplemented by the collections of Richelieu and Mazarin, the very extensive holdings have grown with new acquisitions over the years, principal among them being the Borghese (1808) and Campana (1863) collections.

Because of long-established tradition and the close historical links between certain objects and the palace itself, the department is located in some of the oldest areas of the building, such as the gallery formerly housing the queens' apartments and the Salle des Caryatides, which has witnessed many important events in French history since the 16th century. Owing to its weight and scale the sculpture is displayed on the ground floor. Here, strict chronological order has been observed wherever possible in both the Greek section, which contains original statues along with copies executed in Roman times, and the Roman section. On the same floor, however, large and small objects are arranged together in the rooms devoted to Etruscan art so as to make the transition from the Archaic style to the Classic and Hellenistic periods as apparent as possible.

The refurbishment work undertaken by the works department of the Grand Louvre has enabled the department's area to be extended and the rooms renovated. A new gallery, on the north side of the Cour Visconti now shows uninterruptedly objects from the Cycladic, Cretan and Mycenaean civilizations. This is followed by the artefacts of Greek archaism where several showcases of small objects echo the statues and reliefs. In tandem with this sequence is a space devoted to Greeks inscriptions on stone. Outside the gallery, a display on the landing brings together monuments of the Severe style period (480–450 B.C.). This is further illustrated in the next room on the ground floor: the Temple of Zeus at Olympia Room. On the same floor, the Salle de Diane, which offers information to the public, is used for small exhibitions designed to reflect aspects of the technical work of the department. The Roman gallery has been enlarged by one room and rearranged so that works from the Republican period are treated separately.

On the first floor, where Greek and Roman bronzes were already displayed, the Grand Louvre project has enriched the presentation of a room of glassware in the Cabinet du Roi with a new dispay of Roman silver in the Salle Henri II and enabled the terracotta statuettes to be rearranged in the first three rooms of the Charles X Gallery. Meanwhile the Campana Gallery has been overhauled and modernized. Six public rooms display masterpieces of Greek ceramics whereas the remaining three rooms have been turned into a study area.

The Prehellenistic Age and the Archaic Greek World

The Mediterranean basin area, settled in a series of invasions by what came to be known as the Greeks, was originally occupied by peoples of a non-Indo-European origin. The history of their art, from the Neolithic period to the end of the Middle Bronze Age, looks first to Thessaly, then to the Cyclades and finally to Crete. Each of these areas benefited in turn from the influence of the more advanced civilizations of the East. The flourishing of Minoan Crete in the first half of the second millennium was to have a profound effect on the early Greeks, the Mycenaeans, who were notable for their major artistic undertakings. Though centered principally in Argolis, the Mycenaean civilization had a powerful influence over the Aegean world in the Late Bronze Age. The Mycenaeans were the heirs to the art of Crete and they gave it a severity which quite possibly the Early Iron Age Greeks did not forget.

With the collapse of the Mycenaean world, Greek art re-emerged in the Geometric style. Here was an ever more learned asceticism that affected every form of decoration and sculpture. Within this common language of geometry each region had its own distinctive idiom, and Attica led the way. However, by the end of the 8th century, the system was on the wane. Oriental motifs flooded in, and the Greeks adopted them in their own unique way. Every city and province "orientalized" its art in a different manner during the 7th century, in a period which also saw the emergence of monumental sculpture. After exercises in the "Daedalic" style, the *kouroi* (naked men) at the end of the century marked an advance in the use of marble and in working on a giant scale. *Kouroi* and *korai* (artistically draped women) were reproduced on a humbler scale, within a conventional framework, right up to the Persian wars, and bear witness to an increasingly detailed observation of anatomy. The approach to relief sculpture became freer as did subjects which were less constrained by religious tradition.

The independent nature of the ancient cities favored the development of artistic centers, from which painted vases, bronze and terracotta statuettes emerged in profusion. For pottery Athens rivaled Corinth. The latter cornered the market especially with its small phials for sweet-smelling oils; but after adopting the black-figure technique from Corinth, Attic vases were in close competition and finally predominated. Remaining at the hub of this trade, Athens was by the middle of the 6th century B.C. the home of flourishing workshops which exported many objects to Etruria. Innovative artists revolutionized the technique of vase painting. Reversing the media, they painted the background and used the reserve red ground for the figures, thus bringing about the red-figure style. The greatest masterpieces of this genre were created at the turn of the 6th and 5th centuries B.C. A similar creative impetus can be seen in bronze figurines, and excavations in the great Pan-Hellenic sanctuaries have uncovered an astonishing variety of objects. Despite such diversity, however, the combination of religious function, use of myths and the increasing importance given to the human form, provide a strong sense of overall unity.

143. Female Head
Keros
c. 2700–2400 B.C.
Marble. H 27 cm (10.6 in.); W 14.5 cm (5.7 in.);
D 9.6 cm (3.8 in.)
Rayet donation, 1873. MNC 509 (Ma 2709)

This imposing, long head comes from a large family of figures and figurines which artists of the Cyclades produced during the Early Bronze Age (3200–2000 B.C.). In general they represent female nudes, though their size and shape may vary considerably. The Louvre marble is a fragment of a full-size statue, and the complete work must have been around 1.50 m (59 in.) in height.

Although the only detailed carving on this head is around the nose and ears, the sculptor's sensitivity to volumes is clear from the convex plane of the head and the depth of the profile. Similar heads can be seen on full-length figures represented standing, with tapering feet and forearms crossed at right-angles over their bodies. Belonging to what is known as the "cross-armed" type, these mark the culmination of the most classical version of the genre; the geometric treatment of form, evident in the construction of this head, is carried through to the body, in planes and volumes respecting consciously calculated laws of proportion.

The precise importance and function of such figures, which are generally found in excavations of necropolises and also occasionally in ordinary dwellings, are not yet clear, although there seems little reason to doubt their religious nature.

144. "Sauceboat"
Heraia of Arcadia (Peloponnese)?
c. mid-3rd millennium B.C.

Gold. H 17 cm (6.7 in.); W 10 cm (3.9 in.),
L 14.4 cm (5.7 in.)
Acq. 1887. Bj 1885

The high upright spout of this
receptacle has earned it the name
of "sauceboat." With the exception
of the solid handle decorated with
a herring-bone motif, it is made
from a single sheet of gold. Thus its
annular base was made by beating
out the wall of the bowl. Only one
other example is known to us and
the presumed origin of this precious
object, a site in the Peloponnese
called Heraia of Arcadia,
is an intriguing one. The shape,
however, was common to Early
Bronze Age potters in the Cyclades
as well as in areas on the Greek
mainland and to the northwest
of Anatolia. Its origin is now thought
to lie in the Cycladic archipelago
where the earliest examples are
to be found. A similar origin for this
Louvre vessel is possible, although
a Peloponnesian connection cannot
be excluded.

145. Geometric Crater (fragment)
Attic style, c. 750 B.C.

Terracotta. H 58 cm (22.8 in.); W 14 cm (5.5 in.);
Th 1.3 cm (0.5 in.)
Acq. 1884, A 517

After the destruction of Mycenaean
civilization, Greece seems to have
been submerged in the "Dark Ages."
However, an artistic revival took
place in the 10th century
characterized by decorative effects
derived from geometry. From
an early experimental phase
(Protogeometric style), it became
more assured, as can be seen from
the large funerary vases of the
middle of the 8th century B.C. found
at the Dipylon necropolis at Athens.
This vessel is an example, and boasts
a large number of decorative figures.
In the midst of ornamentation
dominated by the Greek key pattern,
we see a "prothesis" (a dead man
lying in state on his bier) with the
family gathered round his effects.
All are shown in lamentation with
arms raised in a distinctive
Geometrical manner. A chariot
procession and war boat point
to the heroic and noble lineage
of the deceased whose tomb was
marked by this great vase.
The extreme care given to the
execution is typical of painters
in Athens. The vase is no doubt the
work of one of the most proficient,
known as the "painter of Dipylon."

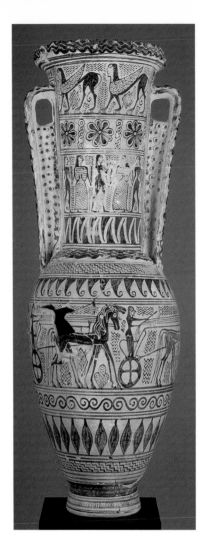

146. Amphora-Loutrophoros
Attributed to the "painter of Analatos"
Attica, c. 690 B.C.
Terracotta. H 81 cm (31.9 in.)
Acq. 1935. CA 2985

This vase, with its slender form recalling the amphora of the late Geometric style, must have served as a "loutrophoros", that is, a ritual vase used in wedding ceremonies or at funerals of unmarried people. But while the relief decoration applied around the mouth and handles, and the layout of motifs, conform to earlier designs, the motifs themselves generally break away from the Geometric register. The rosettes and braids around the neck, along with animated figures such as the sphinxes, the two couples dancing to the sound of pipes and the charioteers driving their chariots, herald the arrival of the orientalizing style in Athens.

By the early 7th century B.C., interest in the Geometric canon was waning and motifs from the East appeared increasingly in Greek decoration; with them, the outlines of human and animal figures regained their lithe and realistic proportions. Many cities produced painted vases in the new style. Though exporting little, Athens at that time manifested an inquiring spirit and an interest in the human figure, as is amply demonstrated in this vase.

147. Oinochoe
Miletus?
c. 650 B.C.

Terracotta. H 39.5 cm (15.6 in.)
Acq. 1891. CA 350 (E 658)

This terracotta wine jug, which was inspired by a metal receptacle as the form of the handle in particular indicates, has a trefoil lip to facilitate pouring. Bought by the painter E. Lévy in Rome in 1855, its origin is unknown, but the shape, technique and style of decoration, rank it with vases which the cities of Eastern Greece (whether on islands such as Rhodes or on the mainland such as Miletus) produced during the orientalizing period of the 7th century B.C. and after. Applied with a brush on top of a pale-toned slip, the decoration is arranged in superimposed bands. This design along with the abundance of motifs recalls embroidered fabrics we know about through contemporary texts. This highly orientalizing style is known as the "wild goat style" after the animal motif which recurs most frequently. The care taken in the detail of each outline around the deer and imaginary animals makes this a masterpiece of the genre. Here there is none of the monotony of kindred but looser compositions of a later date.

148. Aryballos
Corinth, c. 640 B.C.

Terracotta. H 6.3 cm (2.5 in.)
Acq. 1898. CA 931

Owing to its geographical location, Corinth was one of the first Greek cities to be affected by influences from the East from the end of the 8th century B.C. onward. Corinthian ware, an indication of the prosperity of this city on the Isthmus, dominated the market and was known throughout the Mediterranean. The small Louvre aryballos (scent bottle) is a good example of craftsmanship during the first phase of activity of the Corinthian artists known as the "Protocorinthian" style. Using the new black-figure technique, the artist has managed to give life to two parallel friezes, a combat and a hare-hunt, albeit within a confined area. The quality of this object is further enhanced by the modeling of the neck into the shape of a woman's head. The relationship between the face and hair and the composition of the latter link the vase with work such as the *Dame d'Auxerre* (no. 149). Corinth produced a considerable number of vases between the end of the 7th and the first half of the 6th century B.C., but they no longer came up to this quality.

150. Pendant
Rhodes (Camiros)
c. 630 B.C.

Electrum. H 8.5 cm (3.3 in.)
Salzmann coll. On loan from the Dept. of Near
Eastern Antiquities, 1949. Bj 2169

This pendant is a fine example of the
virtuosity of goldsmiths working
in Rhodes during the orientalizing
period. Its function is not certain,
although it is now believed to have
been worn at the neck or chest rather
than on a belt or over the forehead.
The techniques it uses such
as granulation and filigree, passed
down from Oriental jewellers,
clearly demonstrate the skills of their
Greek imitators. Motifs such as the
rosettes, griffon's protomes and
janiform heads (the Daedalic style
of which recalls the "Dame
d'Auxerre", no. 149), are also Eastern
in origin. On the plate bordered
with filigree, a lion and eagle are
depicted according to an Egyptian
tradition, here softened by Aegean
fantasy. The sheer luxury of this
ornament is a mark of the high level
of refinement attained by certain
Greeks in the 7th century B.C.

149. Female Statue,
known as the **"Dame d'Auxerre"**
Crete?
c. 630 B.C.

Limestone. H 75 cm (29.5 in.) incl. base
Exch. with Musée d'Auxerre, 1909.
Ma 3098

This small statue was discovered by
the archaeologist Maxime Collignon
in the reserve collection of the Musée
d'Auxerre. Its origin is unknown,
although the use of soft limestone
and its style link it closely to Cretan
sculpture of the 7th century B.C. The
style is known as "Daedalic" after
Daedalus, the inventor of Archaic
times. In contrast to the imaginative
contours of the Geometric style, the
"Dame d'Auxerre" is very solidly
constructed, her body sheathed
in a close-fitting costume, her right
hand across her chest and her left
hand flat against her thigh. There
is evidence that the costume was
probably painted as traces of pigment
remain: the incised designs would
have served as guidelines. Another
sylistic feature is the U-shaped face
set within a symmetrical Egyptian
hair style. Whether she does in fact
represent a goddess, or is simply
a priestess or worshipper, is open
to speculation. With a greater respect
for proportions and a sense
of volume, the "Dame d'Auxerre"
is a precursor of monumental Greek
statuary.

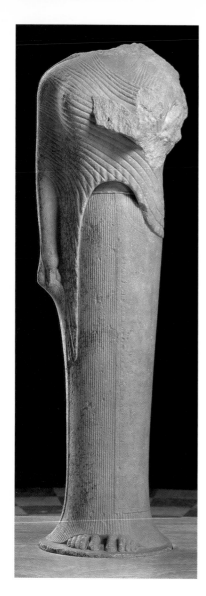

151. Female Statue
Samos
c. 570 B.C.

Marble. H 1.92 m (75.6 in.) with plinth
Acq. 1881. Ma 686

Found in 1875 in the sanctuary of Hera at Samos, this imposing female figure is one of the first *kore*, that is, one of the first Greek representations of a graceful woman shown at the peak of her beauty and offered as a gift to a god or goddess. She is the female counterpart of the male *kouros*, a young male nude shown at his athletic peak. *Korai* and *kouroi* mark the progress of the Archaic period from the origins of monumental sculpture to the Persian wars. A recent discovery in Samos has brought to light an identical statue with the same costume and the same dedicatory inscription: "I have been dedicated by Cheramyes to Hera as an offering." It is thus very likely that it was one of a group of at least two female figures. This is not an isolated example for we already know of a family group of six female figures from Samos. The statue here is dressed in a ceremonial garment combining tunic, mantle and veil. It was probably sculpted around 570 B.C. The legs are still joined and the right hand, seen under the veil, does not as yet alter the direction of folds in the tunic. It is possible the damaged left hand held some attribute. The quantity and similarity of sculptures discovered at Samos point to the existence of a local tradition which no doubt contributed greatly to the development of sculpture in Greece.

152. Kouros
Found in Actium
Naxian style, c. 560–550 B.C.
Marble. H 1 m (39.4 in.)
Acq. 1874. MNB 766 (Ma 687)

The *kouros* was the principal form
of Greek Archaic sculpture from
the end of the 7th century up to the
Persian wars. Many workshops,
scattered all over the Greek world,
produced these statues in varying
sizes and with diverse functions.
The fact that this one was discovered
in the sanctuary of Apollo in Actium
(Aktion) lends weight to the idea
that it represents Apollo.
The Louvre *kouros* should
be distinguished from earlier
examples by the satisfying solutions
it finds to certain problems
of reproducing the anatomy. The
effort of Greek sculptors, whatever
their origins, was centered on how
to render the athletic body of the
kouros more realistically. But certain
inaccuracies, such as the clumsy
junction between arm and forearm,
date the work to 550 B.C. at the latest.
Aside from growing anatomical
accuracy, stylistic differences can
be detected among *kouroi*.
The decorative harmony governing
the treatment of this particular
statue confirms it as being from the
Naxos workshops.

153. Head of a Horseman
Athens
c. 550 B.C.

H (head) 27 cm (10.6 in.)
Georges Rampin bequest, 1896. Ma 3104

When this marble head entered the Louvre collections it was deemed unclassifiable, since the head was evidently Archaic in style, but had asymmetric neck muscles. Furthermore, the hair of this piece, which has a few traces of color, is atypical, a veritable network under a delicately-worked laurel crown. Things seemed clearer when it became apparent that the head belonged to the body of a horseman, a fragment of which is conserved in the museum of the Acropolis (a cast is in the Louvre).
The victorious rider was no doubt shown turning and bowing his head in response to applause. There

is a longstanding hypothesis that there might be a second horseman, a pendent to the first. This arose from the presence of fragments of a horse's body much akin in style but which did not fit in the reconstitution of the first horseman. The Dioscuri have been suggested— Castor and Pollux—or, given the originality of the representation, the two sons of the tyrant Pisistratus, called Hippias and Hipparchus. Recent studies have shown that the fragments at the museum of the Acropolis belonged to very different horses. So we have to give up the idea of a companion for the "Rampin Rider." At all events, the face is Attic in the way its features are formed, and a tinge of Ionian grace brightens it with a smile.

154. Black-Figure Amphora
Signed by Exekias, potter
Attica
c. 540 B.C.

Terracotta. H 50 cm (19.7 in.) with lid
Acq. 1883. F 53

The signature of Exekias, the potter is to be found on a dozen vases including the Louvre amphora. On two vases he also claims authorship of the painting. The quality of the two scenes depicted here has prompted more than one suggestion that he painted this vase too. On one side Heracles is seen fighting Geryon, a monster with three hoplite bodies who is struggling to resist the hero's assault. The herdsman Eurytion has already succumbed. Shields are the central compositional pivot of the combat, and the artist gives proof of great narrative powers and an assured sense of balance. The lid decoration—an animal procession with alternating deer and sirens—recalls in its miniaturist detail the tall stemmed goblets contemporary with this vase. This was the period when the black-figure technique reached its peak, just before red-figure painting emerged and revolutionized the art of vase painting.

155. Red-Figure Amphora
Attica
c. 530–520 B.C.
Terracotta. H 58 cm (22.8 in.)
Acq. 1843. G1

Turned by the Athenian potter
Andocides who signed the base, this
amphora has a continuous design
containing two pictures of exceptional
interest and quality. On one side,
there is a fight attended by Athena
and Hermes, and on the other
a female zither player performs
before an audience and judges:
both images stand out against the
black background. The painter has
reversed the relationship of black

figures on a light ground, and is thus
able to indicate details within each
figure with much greater subtlety.
This new technique signaled
a revolution in the art of the painted
vase. The subtler paintbrush replaced
the stylet providing a wider range
of possibilities. The painter who
worked regularly with the potter
Andocides seems to have invented
this new style which first appeared
around 530 B.C. The red-figure
style established the superiority
of Athenian workshops, which
henceforth dominated the painted-
vase industry.

156. Head of a Sphinx
Thebes
Corinthian style c. 530 B.C.
Terracotta. H 18 cm (7.1 in.)
Acq. 1895. CA 637

Sphinxes were often part of funerary
or votive monuments. In particular,
as acroteria, they decorated buildings
ranging from aedicules (private
shrines) to full-scale temples. This
head belonged to a small sphinx
decorating a corner of a modest-sized
edifice. Shown seated, in profile with
erect forequarters, the sphinx's head
would have been turned to the side.
The feminine features which
are enlivened by a subtle smile are
framed by waves of hair spreading
from a central parting across the
temples down over her shoulders
in rolls. A diadem painted with lotus
flowers and buds crowns the
composition. It is a terracotta version
of a Greek sculpture of the period
dominated by *korai*. Similar works
are known, which link it to the
production of coroplaths at Corinth.
Athenian influence can, however,
be seen in the careful modeling and
attentive gaze.

157. Red-Figure Footed Crater
Signed by Euphronius the painter
Attica, c. 510 B.C.
Terracotta. H 44.8 cm (17.6 in.)
Campana coll. Acq. 1863. G 103

This red-figure vase, the form of which seems to have been introduced around 530 B.C. by the painter-potter Exekias, belongs to the greatest period of Greek pottery. It is signed by Euphronius who was active as a painter in Athens around the end of the 6th century B.C., the golden age for such pottery. The decoration around the bowl embodies an unswerving sense of proportion and balance. The principal scene here describes the battle between Heracles and the giant Antaeus before the terrified gaze of three young women. With his armor and the Nemean lionskin laid aside, the naked hero, who is certain of his strength, has a mortal grip on his enemy whose defeat is clear from the expression of anguish on his face. The elaborate detail on the two bodies demonstrates the artist's virtuosity in capturing anatomical essentials. A scene from everyday life on the other side counterbalances the myth. A musical contest is being held. The presence of engraved elements and the quantity of reddish-purple highlights indicate how close it is to the black-figure technique, which was still actively employed at that time.

158. Red-Figure Cup
Signed by Euphronius the potter,
decoration attributed to Onesimos
Attica
c. 500–490 B.C.

Terracotta, H 16.5 cm (6.5 in.); Ø 40 cm (15.7 in.)
Acq. 1871. G 104

Made by Euphronius at the
beginning of the 5th century B.C.,
this cup is distinctive not only for its
unusual scale but also for its lavish
ornamentation. The subject
is Theseus, a hero much loved by the
people of Athens where this was
made. The inside of the cup shows
an episode from Theseus' life on his
voyage to Crete with Minos. Minos
threw a ring into the sea, challenging
Theseus to recover it and prove that
he was the son of Poseidon. Theseus
dived in, escorted by a Triton shown

here holding his feet. In the sea
kingdom he is received
by Amphitrite. Between them rises
the great figure of Athena, protectress
of heroes. The flowing composition
with its complex interweaving
of lines is a subtle evocation of the
aquatic world. The outside of the cup
celebrates Theseus' victories over the
brigands plaguing Attica called
Sciron, Procrustes and Kerkyon; the
capture of the Marathonian bull was
his last exploit. In this masterpiece
of the late Archaic style, there
is a deliberate contrast between the
divine serenity of the scene within,
and the violent images without.

159. Statuette of a Butcher
Thebes (Boeotia)
c. 525–475 B.C.
Terracotta H 12 cm (4.7 in.)
Acq. 1902. CA 1455

The people of Boeotia, who are
to this day unfairly considered
by Athenians to be clumsy, have
often given proof of their artistic
skill, particularly in the making
of clay figurines. This one belongs
to a group which illustrates various
aspects of daily life; figures of cooks,
bakers and hairdressers are known.
Here a butcher is knocking out
a small pig on a tripod block.
Capturing the immediacy of the
action very effectively, this small
object was modeled by hand except
for the face which was cast from
a mould. Such figurines, which were
buried in tombs along with other
belongings of the deceased, may
have served as children's toys.

160. Mirror Stand
First quarter of the 5th century B.C.
Bronze. H 41 cm (16.1 in.)
Acq. 1888. Br 1688

Adapting a successful formula from
Egyptian art, Hellenic bronze
founders often shaped the handle
of the mirror into a female figure.
Here we have a caryatid bearing
a metal disk on her head, and she
would probably have held a flower
in her right hand. She is standing
on a stool with equine feet. This
particular artistic genre, of which
there are many examples during the
transition from Archaism to classicism, had a part to play in the stylistic
developments of this period. But
it also betrays a distinctive regional
flavor; it is attributed to the style
of Aegina. The rigid pose and the
fine folds down the tunic refer back
to earlier influences while the gravity
of the face and the suggestion of free
movement in the arms look forward
to the "Severe style."

161. Cup

Signed by the potter Brygus,
decoration attributed to the "Painter
of Brygus"
Athens
c. 490 B.C.

Terracotta. H 13.4 cm (5.3 in.); Ø 33.2 cm (13 in.)
Acq. 1881. G 152

The influence of Homeric legend
on Greek civilization is proverbial.
It comes as no surprise therefore that
so many vases should be illustrated
with scenes of the heroes of the *Iliad*
and the *Odyssey*. But this cup has
a unique quality. Made by the potter
Brygus—who signed one of the
handles—it was painted by an artist
who knew how to adapt to the
constraints of the decoration. Within
the circular field of the inner
medallion, Briseis, Achilles' captive,
is pouring a libation for Achilles' old
tutor, Phoenix; the relationship
between the figures reveals a great
skill in balancing the composition.
But over the outer bowl the "Painter

of Brygus" excels himself; he brings
to life the story of the sack of Troy
illustrating two episodes marked
by violence and passion. On one side
Andromache, armed with a pestle
—a woman's working tool—tries
to protect Astyanax, her son, from
attack by the Achaeans; on the other,
Neoptolemus, son of Achilles, bran-
dishes the child's body in an effort
to subdue King Priam who has
taken refuge at the altar of Zeus.

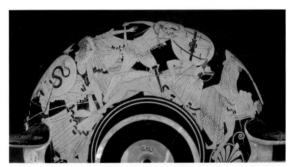

The Classical Greek World

The tribulations of the Persian wars, when the fate of Hellenism hung in the balance, brought about a decisive change in Greek art. Athens, whose hoplites and triremes blocked the advances of the Persian armies, emerged stronger from the conflict. Back in their devastated city, the Athenians piously buried the statues which the invaders had dethroned, in order to make way for new works of art.

Here, and throughout the Greek world, forms broke loose from conventions and became more realistic. True equilibrium shifted the movement across the hips, costumes fell more plausibly in simpler folds. The mobile athlete took over from the rigid *kouros* and the increasingly widespread use of bronze facilitated the change. But while bodies moved, gestures no longer sufficed; figures were given a sense of purpose, a feeling of imminent change.

Greek art became committed to realism. But this progression came to a standstill. The rhythm of athletic composition reached a caesura in the masterly equilibrium of the statues by Polyclitus, a symbol of classical perfection. The Ergastines of the Parthenon move at a unified ideal pace, remote from our world. Everything became subject to reason, harmony and transparency. However, the period which, in Athens, coincided with Pericles' government and the career of Phidias was short-lived. The atrocities of the Peloponnesian War upset the balance; new values founded on the individual emerged and art reflected the change. The female body, images of which multiplied, is seen under a web of drapery; faces are tinged with melancholy, and time and space are again linked in the image of the athlete. These tendencies increased during the 4th century B.C. In a world where classicism was under varying degrees of threat, foreign elements made themselves felt. The lissom grace of the figures by the sculptor Praxiteles, the passion burning in the faces by the sculptor Scopas defy their origins. At Xanthus and Halicarnassus, Greek genius encountered the ideology of the Barbarians; new disciplines like portraiture were mastered and three-dimensional work became more common. In this troubled world the exploits of Alexander the Great brought such changes in artistic conditions to an end.

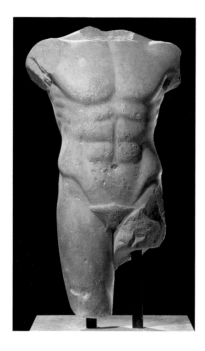

163. Male Torso
Found at Miletos
c. 480 B.C.

Marble. H 1.32 m (52 in.)
Rothschild donation, 1873. MNB 691 (MA 2792)

The imposing size of the Miletos torso distinguishes it from other athletic sculpture of the transitional period between the Archaic and Classic styles. It is dated to this period because of its somewhat rigid bearing despite the mobility of certain elements such as the shoulder blades. The arrangement of the shoulder muscles indicates that the right arm must have been drawn back while the left arm moved in front of the body. The anatomical mastery of the body itself combines all the lessons of the Archaic style with a hint of the *contrapposto* pose developed by sculptors after the Persian wars. The origins of the sculpture are unclear. Although it was found in Ionia, its forcefulness makes it closer to Peloponnesian styles. However, athletic sculpture was not unknown in Eastern Greece. Pythagoras of Rhegium, a forerunner and rival of the sculptor Myron, came from Samos. The Miletos torso could well be attributed to his influence.

162. Apollo and the Nymphs
Thasos, Passageway of the Theoroi
c. 480 B.C.

Relief, marble. H 92 cm (36.2 in.); W 2.09 m (82.3 in.)
Acq. 1864. Ma 696

The *Passageway of the Theoroi*, a group of reliefs placed at eye-level on the walls of a passage in Thasos, an island city in the northeast Aegean, offers us a rare opportunity to compare figures sculpted in the Archaic tradition with others whose modeling breaks away from the canon of the time. While the three Nymphs resemble a group of *korai* in their conventional presentational poses, Apollo with his lyre has a freedom of gesture and a suggestion of depth. These are signs of the arrival in Thasos of early experiments in the "Severe style." The influence of Athens around 480 B.C. possibly prompted these; but the relief was executed in Thasos, with an eclecticism characteristic of this island.

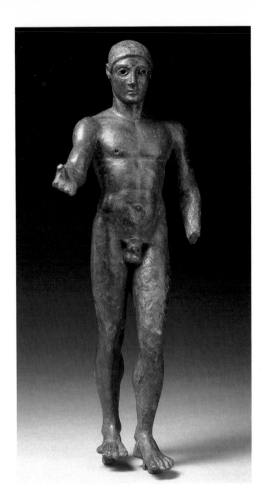

164. Athlete Making a Libation
Parian style?
c. 470 B.C.
Statuette, bronze. H 26.4 cm (10.4 in.)
David-Weill donation, 1937. Br 4238

The standing male nude is one
of the most eloquent of all statues
illustrating the transition from the
Archaic to the Classic styles. For
almost a century and a half, its
original rigid schema, with left leg
forward, remained unchanged.
At the dawn of the "Severe style,"
this statuette, which was found
in Phocis shows how the stiff pose
is moderated and the arms stretch
out in a more fluid and comprehensive gesture. His position is still
that of a *kouros*, particularly the
pronounced curve of the lower back.
But an unprecedented vitality now
runs through the musculature.
The *kouros* has become an athlete
whose body has begun to find its
natural poise.

165. Funerary Stele
Pharsalus, c. 460 B.C.

Marble. H 60 cm (23.6 in.)
Acq. 1863. Ma 701

The funerary stele, a stone erected over a tomb and sculpted with relief decoration, was a much exploited genre in Greek art. Athens shone most brilliantly at such work from the Archaic period onward. But the history of the stele in Attica was interrupted for half a century between 500 and 450 B.C. Elsewhere in the Greek world, such as in Thessaly where this stele originated, production continued. Two women, who would probably have been standing, are shown facing each other in a solemn, serene mood. At the center of the composition their hands are gathered in an apparent exchange of flowers and bags of grain. Perhaps they are mother and daughter, as is suggested by the more stately bearing of the right-hand figure. Alongside the continuing Archaic style of the left-hand arm, the locks of hair and line of drapery, we find new features such as more developed eyes, heavier jawlines and more pronounced expressions.

166. Female Helmeted Head
Aeginetan style, c. 460 B.C.

Marble. H 28 cm (11 in.)
Vogüé donation, 1917. Ma 3109

The island of Aegina, near the Attic coast, was the home during the late Archaic period of thriving workshops of sculptors working in marble as well as bronze. The style of this original head which was part of an idol of the goddess Athena, is the same as that of the pediment of the temple of Athena Aphaea. The resemblance is striking particularly with the central scene of the west pediment which shows the same goddess. The holes visible on the temples and ears were points where additional elements were fixed, most probably locks of hair and ornaments attached to the ear lobes. The firm, solemn expression, the round chin and thick eyelids (once lined with metal eyelashes) are signs of the beginnings of the Classic style, the so-called "Severe style."

167. Red-Figure Footed Crater
Attributed to the "Painter of the Niobides"
Attic style
c. 460–450 B.C.

Terracotta. H 54 cm (21.3 in.)
Acq. 1883. G 341

The decoration of this bowl is unusual and significant in that it distributes across several planes the protagonists of the two scenes illustrated. The composition, which by indicating the modeling with pale-hued lines, sometimes defines the figures and at others partly conceals their shape, can only be borrowed from some well-known picture. While the subject of one of the two scenes is easy to recognize, the punishment of Niobe and her children for their offense against Apollo and Artemis, the second scene remains obscure. It is customary to see the influence here of one of the most famous painters of the 5th century B.C., Polygnotus of Thasos, who painted great frescoes as well as easel paintings in Athens and in Delphi during the early classic period.

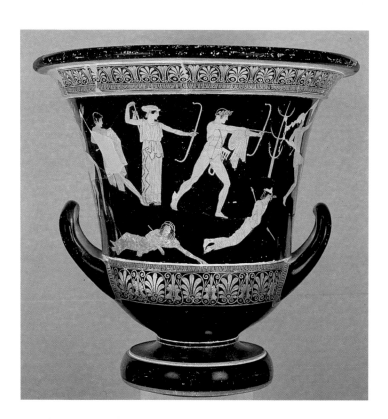

168. Metope Fragment:
Heracles with the Cretan Bull
Temple of Zeus at Olympia
c. 460 B.C.

Marble. H. 1.14 m (44.9 in.); 1.52 m (59.8 in.)
Acq. 1830, gift of the Hellenic Senate. Ma 716

In 468 B.C. the city of Elis commissioned the architect Libon to build a monumental temple to Zeus for the sanctuary of Olympia recently seized from Pisa. This great Doric temple was outstandingly decorated not merely on the pediments but also on the twelve metopes under the peristyle, on the east and west fronts. This frieze depicting the exploits of Heracles, the mythical founder of the Olympic Games, initiates or establishes the canon of the twelve Labors. The fight shown here between the hero and the Cretan bull formed the fourth metope on the west side. While the theme of one-to-one combat lends itself to the confines of the metope frame, the sculptor has skillfully filled all the available space in a composition where two diagonals intersect and where the two adversaries' heads turn towards each other in confrontation. This relief thus marks the high point in the development of the Severe style. Besides laying emphasis on diagonal compositions with frontal and profile elements juxtaposed, this style also plays on depths, defining form through the whole range of projection from bas-relief to sculpture in the round.

169. Metope from the Parthenon

Athens (Acropolis)

447–440 B.C.

High-relief, marble. H 1.35 m (53.1 in.);
W 1.41 m (55.5 in.)
Acq. 1818. Ma 736

This sculpted relief was part of the
Doric frieze of the Parthenon,
the temple on the Acropolis at Athens
dedicated to the city's goddess Athena.
In it stood the statue of Athena
by Phidias, who was the artist who
evolved the whole decorative
conception. The temple and its
decoration were finished within the
fifteen years which corresponded
to Pericles' governorship of Athens.
This is the tenth metope of the
southern facade, in which the theme
of centauromachy is treated.

The man-horse or centaur assails the
woman in a wild fury; the scene
is cleverly balanced within a confined
space. The artist has married the
flowing lines of the horse's body
to the firm lines of the drapery.
Although the shapes develop within
an idealized atmosphere there
is a close observation of reality in the
way the muscles and veins stand out
under the animal's skin. The two
figures seem to be moving in front
of a screen, in an interplay of lines
and volumes perfectly ordered
in a heightened feeling of harmony.

**170. Plaque from
the Parthenon Frieze**
Athens (Acropolis)
c. 440 B.C.

Bas-relief, marble. H 96 cm (37.8 in.);
W 2.07 m (81.5 in.)
Choiseul-Gouffier coll. Seized during the
Revolution. MA 738

The sculpted band which ran around
the whole length of the Parthenon
high up under the peristyle gallery
is one of the most accomplished
monuments of Greek sculpture.
Along over 160 meters (525 feet)
of frieze, around 360 figures join
in the procession at the great festival
of the Panathenaea when the entire
civic body of Athens assembled and
walked up to the Acropolis to offer
Athena a tunic embroidered by the
daughters of the most prominent
families. Here they are on the Louvre
marble proceeding along with two
leaders of the ceremony. Their
restrained gait expresses the
solemnity of the occasion, which
is orderly without being monotonous.
A slow rhythm runs through the
figures in which gravity and grace
are naturally allied. The figures,
it should be remembered, were close
to the central scene which showed
the gods gathering to attend the
homage paid to Athena. Doubtless
inspired by Phidias, the Parthenon
frieze marks the high point of classic
sculpture.

171. Aphrodite,
known as the **Venus of Arles**
Roman copy of an original attributed
to Praxiteles, c. 360 B.C.

Statue, marble (arms restored by Girardon who
reworked the areas around the breasts and the
folds of drapery). H 1.94 m (76.4 in.)
Found in Arles in 1651. Given by the town of Arles
to Louis XIV, 1683. Ma 439

While its identity cannot be confirmed, Louis XIV was no doubt justified
in seeing this statue from Arles
as a Roman copy of a classical
4th century B.C. Greek statue
of Aphrodite, the goddess of love.
Sadly this provided grounds for the
sculptor Girardon to restore her
arms and add an apple to her right
hand and a mirror to her left. These
two emblems were most certainly
not part of the original intention.
This can be inferred from other
versions of statues traditionally
attributed to the hand of the great
Athenian sculptor Praxiteles.
It is quite likely that the Arles
Aphrodite is a reproduction of the
famous Aphrodite of Thespiae
which Praxiteles sculpted around
360 B.C., using his mistress, the
courtesan Phryne, renowned for her
figure, as his model. The artist's bold
representation of nudity was
unprecedented, and he took these
revelations to an extreme in the
Aphrodite of Cnidos. The expression
of gentle melancholy and the sensual
forms fit in with the ancients' image
of Praxiteles as a sculptor of feminine
grace.

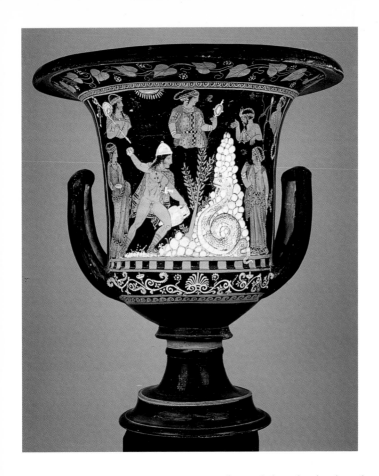

172. Footed Crater
Southern Italy
c. 330 B.C.

H 57 cm (22.4 in.); Ø 81 cm (31.9 in.)
Acq. 1825. N 3157

A large-scale scene on this high-stemmed crater depicts several figures. By using polychrome effects and arranging some of the figures on different levels, some of the latter seem to be half-hidden by folds of the land. The crater was produced in a workshop in southern Italy during the 4th century B.C., when Greek artists who had settled in the western Mediterranean were producing great quantities of vases which are outside the Athenian tradition and follow various regional variations. This is in the style of a workshop that has been located to Paestum, south of Naples, and to one painter in particular who signed just one work with his name, Python. The picture shows the battle between Cadmus and the dragon. Cadmus, son of King Agenor of Tyre, went in search of his sister Europa who had been carried off by Zeus, and was told by the Delphic oracle to found a city. Here he is fighting a dragon by a spring where the city of Thebes would later rise. This scene, which must have been painted around 330 B.C., probably takes its theme from contemporary theater, often a source of inspiration for the painters of Paestum.

173. Bell crater
Attributed to the Painter of Ixion
Campanian style, c. 320 B.C.

Terracotta H 45 cm (17.7 in.)
Acq. 1985. CA 7124

The well-known scene from the *Odyssey* in which Ulysses takes his revenge on rival suitors when he returns to Ithaca, massacring them in the midst of their banquet, is very seldom illustrated. However, this was the subject chosen by an Italiot painter practising in the latter half of the 4th century in a workshop in Campania. The "painter of Ixion" (thus named after another vase featuring this character) succeeded in adapting a composition from a great painting to the curve of a bowl. The dramatic aspects of the scene, which confronts the small group formed by Ulysses, his son Telemachus and a faithful servant (doubtless the swineherd Eumaeus), with the young suitors who are either in the grip of death or are trying to escape their fate, bring to mind descriptions in antique sources of paintings of great artists such as Zeuxis, who came from southern Italy. Ignoring the reverse side of the vase, the artist has concentrated his energies most profitably into recreating something of the heroic spirit which must have pervaded the large picture.

The liveliness and the effects of foreshortening, the psychological detail on the faces and the polychrome touches (mostly rubbed off) indicate a 4th century B.C. origin.

The Hellenistic World

The conquest of Alexandria (334–323 B.C.), which spread Hellenism over a huge area, shook the foundations of artistic activity. In Greek art beauty began to be sought for its own sake, and it was Greek art that was produced in Macedonia, Egypt and the Orient as far as the Indus. Of course over such a wide territory the many workshops merged local influences with Hellenistic tendencies to varying degrees. While Athens still set the example for others to follow and was a paragon of splendor—laden with the gifts of princes—other cities such as Alexandria, Pergamum and Antioch occupied important positions. Rhodes was the home of an influential school of sculpture.

The wealth of some of the courts led to increasing numbers of commissions and more ambitious undertakings. In that many-sided world, in those three centuries of Hellenism during which kingdoms and empires rose and fell unabatedly, it would be hard to discern one single line of evolution in artistic forms. Artistic development was often as unexpected as the historical events of the time. Besides which there are dauntingly few works that have survived. That is particularly the case of paintings where our only records are Roman copies in Campanian villas.

Lysippus, who lived at the turning point between the classic and Hellenistic period, introduced tridimensionalism into sculpture and gave his seal of approval to portraiture. His followers assimilated his lessons, carrying the evolution of forms in space and the study of human physiognomy still further. Realism, bordering at times on the austere, progressed alongside the already established motifs. New subjects enriched the repertoire; artists were at last drawn to represent children and the elderly, ugliness and suffering. The sense of movement increased to the point of violence. Such exuberance and tragic expression, found particularly in Pergamum, have often been described, perhaps justifiably, as "baroque" in style. But even at its peak, at the opening of the second century B.C., this was not the only form of expression. Concurrently we find the most sober realism, the most refined idealized forms, in places like Alexandria.

Moreover, within this profusion of images one can see time and again that the classic style had not been forgotten. And the gradual, inexorable advance of the Romans onto Greek soil, uncouth soldiers fascinated by Hellenistic culture, only hastened artists' return to the past. The last years of the second and first centuries B.C. saw the appearance of retrospective styles, in which neoclassical forms and archaizing motifs run alongside and sometimes merge with each other.

174. Statuette of Victory
Myrina
Beginning of 1st century B.C.
Terracotta. H 27.8 cm (10.9 in.)
Loan from the Musée de l'Université de Lyon,
1959. LY 1651

Intended to be hung on the wall
of a sepulcher, this figurine is one
of a great number of statuettes made
during the Hellenistic period
by workshops which were probably
located in Myrina, a Greek city
in Asia Minor, close to Pergamum.
These workshops started production
from the 6th century B.C. and
continued all through the following
centuries with little sign of originality.

But from the end of the 3rd century
new subjects appeared, Victory
among them. Many models can
be attributed to several hands,
as is indicated by signatures which
are more like trade marks.
However, the recurrence of certain
features might indicate a particular
hand. The Louvre Victory with its
graceful outline and close-fitting
garment is one of a similar group
produced at the beginning of the
2nd century B.C. and ascribed
to a single author known as
"Coroplathus of the Victories."

175. Winged Victory of Samothrace
Samothrace, c. 190 B.C.

Marble (statue) and limestone (the right wing
is a plaster reconstruction). H 3.28 m (129.1 in.)
Champoiseau expeditions, 1863, 1879, 1891.
Ma 2369

This is one of the most famous statues
to have come down to us from Greek
antiquity, and it is also one of the
few sculptures whose original setting
we know. It was found in a large
number of fragments on a terrace
overlooking the shrine of the Cabiri
on the island of Samothrace, in the
northeast Aegean. Symbolizing a sea
victory, this awe-inspiring winged
woman standing on a ship's prow
would have been seen to full effect
on top of the hill, thrusting out her
wings and surging upward. Her
right hand, which was found in 1950
and given to the Louvre, is open.
With her face turned toward the
beholder and her right hand raised,
Winged Victory would thus have
been announcing a victorious event.
But what event? The scale and style
of the statue are reminiscent of the
Pergamum altar, which was decorated
between 180 and 160 B.C. If the marble
of the prow does indeed come from
Rhodes, the *Victory of Samothrace*
might have commemorated a naval
victory by the men of Rhodes, which
occurred sometime in the early part
of the second century B.C.

176. Aphrodite,
known as the **"Kaufmann Head"**
2nd century B.C.

Marble. H 35 cm (13.8 in.)
Acq. 1951. Ma 3518

This delicately modeled female head is a fragment of a statue reproducing the nude Aphrodite which Praxiteles sculpted in the middle of the 4th century B.C., and which was placed by the Greeks of Cnidos at the heart of the goddess's sanctuary. This Athenian artist had a great impact as much because of the quality of his execution as for being the first to portray a female nude. The marble body of the goddess was colored by Nicias, the only painter with whom the sculptor was willing to collaborate. Aphrodite was shown having her ritual bath; it was a religious rather than a love scene. Her face is appropriately regal, with a certain grace softening her majestic aura. Her hair is pulled back in a chignon to expose the triangle of her forehead and locks of hair are kept in place with bands.

Most copies show these hairbands diverging. On the Kaufmann head they are parallel; a liberty which suggests that the Louvre head is a free Hellenistic recreation and not simply a Roman copy. The remarkable quality of the modeling which is flowing and sensual would lend weight to such a theory.

177. Homer
Rome
2nd century A.D.
Bust, marble. H 55 cm (21.6 in.)
Entered the Louvre in 1797. Ma 440

This imaginary portrait, of which
the original has disappeared,
is of Homer, the "father of Greek
poetry" and presumed author of
the *Iliad* and the *Odyssey*. Antiquity
placed him in the 8th century B.C.
and tradition had it that he was
poor and blind. Several ways
of representing him have been
suggested at different times. This
portrait, of which there are some
20 Roman copies, is the most striking
there is. The Hellenistic sculptor has
brought together within the same
figure, the decay of a face withered
by age and the exaltation
of a character defying misfortune
and the passage of time. His
expression now seems indifferent
to all things mortal and instead
seems to be in communion with the
spiritual universe. The artist, who
could create this sublime head,
adapted here in the shape of a herm,
would certainly have known the
altar reliefs at Pergamum.
It is therefore toward the middle
of the 2nd century B.C. that the
complete statue, with the poet shown
seated, must have been erected in
some great city of the Greek world.

178. Bearded Fighter
Asia Minor
Second half of 2nd century B.C.
Statuette, bronze inlaid with silver for eyes and
copper for nipples). H 25 cm (9.8 in.)
Jameson coll. Acq. 1950. Br 4307

The growth in the number of artistic
centers across the immense territory
conquered by Alexander ensured
a high yield of works of art.
Sometimes there is evidence
of an alliance between the Greek
and local styles; sometimes, as here,
the work is in the mainstream
of a great aesthetic tradition. With
the baroque expressiveness of the
fierce face and tangled hair, and
with the exaggerated musculature

in the modeling, this statuette
of a naked man in combat can
be placed within the 2nd century B.C.
Pergamum tradition of large ex-voto
objects. References to classical
depictions of Zeus with his
thunderbolt or Poseidon with his
trident support this attribution.
In any case the technique is extremely
refined; the reworkings, inlay and
correction of faults in the casting are
evidence of a consummate skill.

179. Aphrodite, known as the **"Venus de Milo"**
Melos
c. 100 B.C.

Statue, marble. H 2.02 m (79.5 in.)
Acq. 1821. Ma 399

The *Venus de Milo* was uncovered by pure chance on the Cycladic island of Melos in 1820. The Marquis de Rivière, French ambassador at Constantinople, subsequently acquired it and offered it to Louis XVIII who donated it to the Louvre in 1821. The statue was made in two sections which meet in the thick folds of drapery below the hips. The left arm was detachable and the right possibly restored in Antiquity. At the base, the left foot was worked on separately and the plinth would no doubt have been inserted into the top of a pedestal. Her position has been the object of much speculation. The most likely possibility seems that her right arm crossed her body, the hand lightly touching her hip, while her left arm was unquestionably raised. The statue is classical in theme but its lively treatment, the mobility of the silhouette, and realism of certain details make it a Hellenistic work, belonging to the period when the return to the Classic style was taking hold, in other words between the 2nd and 1st centuries B.C. Although there is no actual proof, by far the most plausible subject of this work would be Aphrodite. This would explain the beauty of the nude body emerging from the folds of drapery.

180. Battling Warrior,
known as **"The Borghese Gladiator"**
Antium
Early 1ˢᵗ century B.C.

Statue, marble. H 1.99 m (78.3 in.)
Borghese coll. in Rome. Acq. 1808. Ma 527

This figure has been famous since the early 17th century. Sometimes misinterpreted, the position of the warrior becomes clear if a shield is replaced on his left arm where there is still a buckle. The warrior is shielding himself—possibly from a horseman if we are to judge from the direction of his gaze—and preparing to parry a blow.
The restoration of the right arm, which is not antique, does not seem awkward. The work is signed on the tree trunk at the back of the composition: "Agasias, son of Dositheus, citizen of Ephesus, made [this statue]." Whether the tree-trunk prop indicates the signature of the artist who created the subject or that of the copyist who might have copied it from a bronze is open to question. The elongated figure follows the canon of proportions laid down by Lysippus in the 4th century, while the display of anatomical detail reminds us of the zeal of certain artists of the early classic period. This combination of tendencies raises the possibility of this being an original work combining the style of Lysippus with certain aspects of classicism. This would fit in well with the early 1st century B.C. date indicated by the style of the letters of the inscription.

The Etruscans

Of the many but often isolated peoples who inhabited Italy before Roman times, the Etruscans enjoyed a most remarkable expansion and developed a most coherent and outstanding culture. Their success was only matched by the Greek colonies of southern Italy, or "Magna Graecia" (to which a special room is devoted).

From the middle of the 8th century B.C., the cities of Etruria, which never unified, experienced rapid political, economic and cultural growth.

The Villanovan culture dominating Italy found its greatest expression in the applied arts—hammered bronze above all—marked by geometric influences then prevailing around the Mediterranean. A highly elaborate art developed, characterized by great technical skill (filigree, granulation) and close contacts with the East, and found its greatest expression in goldsmiths' work.

Etruscan civilization reached its climax between 675 and 475 B.C. Artistic exchanges with Greece were plentiful. Greek artists moved to Etruria and produced works of high quality, notably in the field of funerary paintings. There were huge imports of Greek vases (many Greek vases in the Louvre come from Etrurian necropolises), despite the development during the Archaic period of a truly Etruscan pottery known as bucchero. Etruscan art, however, remained profoundly and radically different from Greek art; less interested in the exploration of forms for their own sake, the Etruscans were more drawn to the expression of movement and immediacy. They were particularly fond of techniques requiring rapidity of execution, such as modeling in terracotta and bronze, and excelled at both. The Hellenistic period was marked by the Roman domination of Italy, but the influence of Greek world remained considerable. Art became more Hellenized, while the peoples of Italy as a whole became more uniform in outlook. Losing its political independence, Etruria gradually became absorbed into the Roman world.

181. Terracotta Plaque
Caere
Last quarter of the 6th century B.C.
Painted terracotta. H 1.23 m (48.4 in.);
W 58 cm (22.8 in.)
Campana coll. Acq. 1863. Cp 6627

Terracotta was particularly important in the decoration of Etruscan buildings, on acroteria, antefixes and larger elements, as well as in reliefs and statues. This plaque was discovered in a tomb at Cerveteri. Its funerary significance may be related to the illustration of spirits bearing away the soul of a dead woman or alternatively to the sacrifice of Iphigenia. The series of panels it belongs to appears to have been altered and might initially have been part of a public building. The style of painting is clearly marked by the influence of the Greek art of Ionia.

182. Sarcophagus of a Married Couple
Caere
Late 6th century B.C.

Terracotta. H 1.14 m (44.9 in.); W 1.90 m (74.8 in.)
Campana coll. Acq. 1863. Cp 5194

This unusual sarcophagus is a proud display of a couple from a great Etruscan family reclining together as was customary at a banquet. Influenced by Ionian art, the artist has expressed the couple's unity with particular sensitivity, relating their upper bodies and hands to each other in a lively harmony. The relationship between upper and lower halves of the body did not however concern him; this lack of interest in physical coherence is typical of Etruscan art. Technical features of this highly-finished work, and the quality of modeling link it to the great statues made in Veii at that time.

The river-god Achelous was able to change his form at will in order to confound his enemies. He has often been depicted as a bull-man. On this *repoussé* pendant, some of the locks of hair are in filigree-work. The rest of the hair, along with the beard, is granulated (tiny balls of gold are applied to a ground to create a decoration). The Etruscan goldsmiths perfected both these techniques and from the Orientalizing period onward the quality of the work for the ruling aristocracy of Etrurian cities was superlative.

183. Achelous
Early 5th century B.C.
Gold. H 4 cm (1.6 in.)
Campana coll. Acq. 1863. Bj 498

185. Portrait of a Man
Near Fiesole (Italy)
3rd century B.C.
Head, bronze. H 21 cm (8.3 in.)
Acq. 1864. Br 19

184. Cinerary Urn: Chariot Journey
Volterra
Late 2nd–early 1st century B.C.
Alabaster. H 84 cm (33.1 in.); W 60 cm (23.6 in.)
Ma 2357

On the cover, the bejewelled deceased
lady holds a fan in one hand and
a pomegranate, a symbol of immortality, in the other. On the side of the
urn, two mules are pulling the same
woman along in a covered chariot;
a horseman and several servants
accompany her. During the
Hellenistic period workshops in the
Etruscan city of Volterra specialized
in elaborately carved alabaster urns
to hold the ashes of the dead.
On some, the influence of contemporary Greek art is very apparent,
particularly of styles from Pergamum
and Rhodes. This is not the case here.
The subject, the journey to the land
of the dead, is treated as if it were
an everyday occurrence and given
a clumsy piquancy which anticipates
the vernacular art of the Romans.

The head of this somewhat soft
full-featured Etruscan is crowned
by a thick cap of clearly drawn locks
of hair. It is a very attentive portrait
of a man and the artist has done his
best to render his physical appearance
through an analysis of surfaces
which avoids psychological insight.
In this, it belongs to a group of Italic
portraits which are, nevertheless,
a long way behind the almost
excessive observation of detail seen
in certain Roman portraits at the
end of the Republic.

The Roman World

For a long time artistic activities were deemed by the Romans to be of secondary importance. However, wars in southern Italy and in the East during the 3rd and 2nd century B.C. brought the Romans into direct contact with Greece and the Hellenistic world on a massive scale. Attitudes changed profoundly. Art was no longer an indulgence for the privileged few. Rather it became an indispensable display of political power, in a way the Greeks had already mastered. Art from earlier periods was brought to Rome; and contemporary artists and works came too.

Nevertheless art initially remained subordinated to the gods, the state and aspiring leaders. Public projects were, therefore, important and an official art developed. This found its supreme expression in architecture or sculpture (the reliefs). Subjects, forms, and images copied from, or executed in imitation of the Greeks, were adapted sometimes with great subtlety to the new ends that the Romans found for them. But art was also a social tool, enabling an individual to assert himself, and display his real or assumed position in society; hence the importance of portraits mostly, in truth, of Hellenistic inspiration. The deepening crisis at the end of the 2nd century, which became more pronounced during the 3rd, marked a decisive artistic turning point. More and more clearly, works of art expressed the spiritual preoccupations of the individual. It can be seen most tellingly in funerary sculpture and is also noticeable in the development of portraiture. But art also existed to please the eye, as the development of mosaic floor decoration in Rome illustrates. Different "schools" emerged lending within each region a distinctive flavor to an art which stretched beyond the Mediterranean basin.

While sharing a similar overall direction, this art was in no way uniform from one province to another. The production of smaller works in silver, gold and bronze show that there was at once a common language and regional sources of inspiration occasionally linked, as in the East, to long-established local traditions.

186. Portrait of a Man
Rome, c. 100 B.C.

Head, marble. H 37.5 cm (14.8 in.)
Acq. 1888. Ma 919

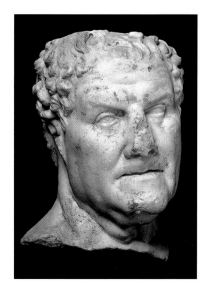

Executed in several sections (the top
and back of the head are missing),
this portrait of an old man has been
depicted with heightened realism (the
marks of age, the toothless mouth
and folds in the neck are pitilessly
reproduced), and there is nothing
schematic about it. An intense
vivacity quickens the mobile features;
the tilt of the head toward the right
gives it a certain pathos in keeping
with the tradition of Hellenistic
portraiture. After comparison with
coin effigies, the sitter has sometimes
been identified as Aulus Postumius
Albinus, a consul in 99 B.C. In any
event it is a portrait of one of the
very first citizens of Rome from the
end of the 2nd century B.C.

187. Scenes from a Census
Rome, c. 100 B.C.

Relief, marble. W 2.05 m (80.7 in.)
Acq. 1824. Ma 975

In the Rome of the Republic, the
census, which had long been
the basis for army recruitment, was
taken every four years. Citizens
were listed in official registers
according to their wealth. The scene
here shows this alongside a depiction
of a sacrifice to the god Mars
of a bull, a ram and a pig, which was
held at the close of procedures.
Part of a larger ensemble divided
between the Louvre and the Munich
Glyptothek, this bas-relief is one
of the oldest historical reliefs
so beloved of the Romans. As yet
unused to rendering contemporary
scenes faithfully, sculptors borrowed
certain forms from Greek art,
adapting them sometimes awkwardly
to their new function.

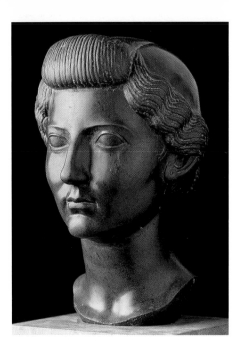

188. Livia
c. 30 B.C.

Head, basalt. H 34 cm (13.4 in.)
Acq. 1860. Ma 1233

Livia, wife of Emperor Augustus, is portrayed at around thirty years of age, with one of the most fashionable hairstyles of the early Roman empire: a knot of hair above her forehead, a small bun at the nape of her neck and a short plait over the back of her head, hidden here by a close-fitting veil. The hard sheen of the basalt gives the head a metallic look, accentuated by the hieratic effect of the strictly frontal pose and fixed features. It recalls contemporary cameo work cut in hard stone (*pietra dura*), which, under the influence of some exceptional craftsmen, flourished during the Augustan period.

189. Marcellus
Rome, 23 B.C.

Statue, marble. H 1.80 m (70.9 in.)
Louis XIV coll. Ma 1207

This is a portrait of Marcellus, nephew of Augustus who died prematurely in 23 B.C., by the Athenian sculptor Cleomenes. The sculptor's signature can be seen on the tortoise's shell. Cleomenes chose to depict Marcellus as the funereal Hermes erected on the tomb of the Greeks who died at the battle of Chaeronea in 447 B.C. This revival of classical art perpetrated by families of Greek sculptors in Rome, complied with the express wishes of Emperor Augustus. Along with the posthumous nature of the commission, it also explains its somewhat cold perfection and idealized features. The young man is somewhat transformed into a hero.

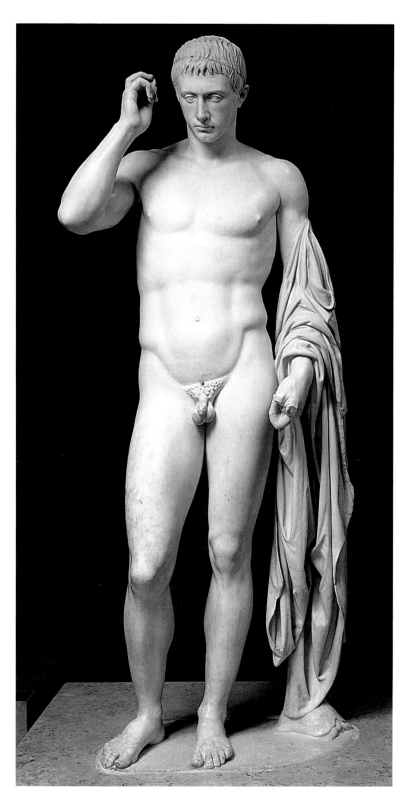

191. Imperial Procession
Rome, 13–9 B.C.

Relief, marble. H 1.20 m (47.2 in.);
W 1.47 m (57.9 in.)
Campana coll. Acq. 1863. MA 1088

To commemorate the Emperor Augustus's victorious return from Spain, the Roman Senate erected a monument in his honor between 13 and 9 B.C., known as the Altar of Peace (Ara Pacis) of Augustus. The carving is unusually elaborate. Processing in a double column behind the Emperor, we see members of his family, priests, magistrates and senators; it is a conscious transposition of the procession of the Panathenaea (no. 170) on the frieze of the Parthenon. Athens and its classic style were chosen by Augustus as the models for an official art characterized by measure, balance and refinement.

190. Juba I
Cherchell
Late 1st century B.C.

Head, marble. H 45 cm (17.7 in.)
Acq. 1895. Ma 1885

A king of Numidia, Juba joined Pompey's supporters against Julius Caesar, and killed himself on the latter's victory in 46 B.C.
The sculptor has emphasized his characteristic head of hair; long corkscrew curls pulled back by a royal band. But the idealized features, framed by the hair and beard, are treated in a deliberately impersonal, classicizing style; this is more the head of a god than of a man. The portrait was probably executed during the reign of his son Juba II, restored by Augustus to the throne of a small kingdom, and the capital (which is now Cherchell in Algeria) became a very active center of Greek culture.

192. Sarcophagus: Legend of Actaeon
Near Rome
c. 125–130

Marble. H 99 cm (39 in.); W 2.35 m (92.5 in.);
D 75 cm (29.5 in.)
Borghese coll. Acq. 1808. Ma 459

Three young women, the Hours
or Graces, are carrying heavy
garlands of fruit and above them are
scenes from the tragic story
of Actaeon: he came upon Artemis
bathing naked, was turned into
a stag and torn to pieces by his own
hounds. On the lid is a marine
procession. The elaborate borders
are influenced by the art of Asia
Minor, but the inclusion of small
scenes within the garlands was
a practise developed by Roman
workshops, and in vogue in Hadrian's
time. Of great quality and refinement,
the execution is notable for its
classicism, which occasionally spills
over into a rococo extravagance
in the tortuous convolutions of rocks
and trees.

short beard soften this impression. Looking more closely at the hairstyle (the uniformity of which often characterizes a series of imperial portraits) there is an attention to detail which distinguishes it from most other heads of this emperor. It is a powerful and original work.

194. Sarcophagus: Marine Procession

Rome
c. 140–150

Marble. H 95 cm (37.4 in.); W 2.37 m (93.3 in.); D 60 cm (23.6 in.)
Church of San Francisco a Ripa, Rome. Entered the Louvre in 1798. Ma 342

193. Hadrian
Second quarter of 2nd century

Head, bronze. H 43 cm (16.9 in.)
Acq. 1984. Br 4547

The frontal head with its direct gaze and slight frown gives Hadrian a severity and majesty bordering on the hieratic. This is further emphasized by the bronze with its unusual red patina. However, the swirling irregular locks of hair and

Marine processions were one of the most popular themes on sarcophagi from Roman workshops. They may have served to evoke the deceased's journey to a haven of happiness in the afterlife. The models are borrowed from Greek art but are reinterpreted by Roman sculptors more or less freely according to their talent. Here subtle variations in the detail enliven the symmetrical arrangement.

The harmonious classically-inspired composition is also given a restrained movement. There is a strong sense of volume with carving deep into the marble. The unfinished left side of the basin shows how sculptors worked stage by stage on the relief details.

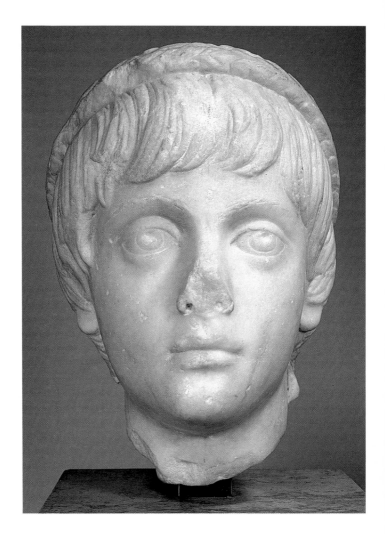

195. Portrait of a Young Prince
Annaba (Algeria)?
c. 170

Head, marble. H 21 cm (8.3 in.)
Acq. 1955. Ma 3539

Some of the greatest achievements
in Roman sculpture are children's
portraits. This sensitive portrait
by a sculptor of Greek origin
is probably of one of nine children
born to the Emperor Marcus
Aurelius, most of whom died young.
The delicacy of the modeling and
the fine treatment of the marble
surface, over which the light softly
plays, lend a particular charm to the
depiction of this child, whose
slightly melancholic expression
is a childlike imitation of the gravity
that can be seen on the faces
of adults in portraits of that time.

196. Sarcophagus:
Dionysus Discovering Ariadne
Rome
c. 235

Marble. H 98 cm (38.6 in.); W 2.08 m (81.9 in.);
D 62 cm (24.4 in.)
Found at St.-Médard-d'Eyrans (Gironde).
Acq. 1817. Ma 1346

Abandoned on the island of Naxos
by Theseus, Ariadne fell into
a slumber. Borne along in a tumultuous procession of satyrs and
maenads, Dionysus came upon her,
fell in love and swept her along
in his life of joy. For the Romans
who, at that period, were in the
midst of a spiritual crisis, this image
suggested the joys in the afterlife
in store for those who were faithful
to their god. The head of Ariadne,
which is unfinished, was intended
to portray the deceased woman.
This carefully-polished Greek
marble sarcophagus was sculpted
in Rome by artists at the peak
of their skill. Mastered to the point
of giving the marble a translucent
quality, their craft centers on the
creation of a play of light and shadow
which suggests the Dionysiac frenzy.
The effect is almost baroque in feel;
transposing the feeling of religious
ecstasy into a perfect form.

197. Sarcophagus: Lion Hunt
Rome
c. 235–240

Marble. H 88 cm (34.6 in.); W 2.20 m (86.6 in.)
Borghese coll. Acq. 1808. Ma 346

Two episodes from a lion hunt
are shown here. On the left they are
setting out; on the right the hunter
confronts the leaping animal.
The hunter is a likeness of the
deceased for whom the sarcophagus
was made, with the short hair and
beard that were fashionable in the
3rd century. He may never have
hunted lions, but this combat
symbolizes the victory that his moral
attributes will give him over the grip
of death. The clarity of the
composition and the direct treatment
betray a concern to give the work
movement without violence.

198. The Emperor Julian
c. 360

Statue, marble. H 1.75 m (68.9 in.)
Ma 1121

The sculptor represents Julian
(361–363) as a pagan priest, wearing
the intricate crown of office. This
emperor, who was a talented writer,
became the ardent defender
of ancient civilization and paganism
in the face of increasingly dominant
Christianity. Here he is dressed not
in a toga but in a *pallium*, a Greek
costume worn by philosophers,
which is draped tightly around
the right arm. The treatment of the
costume and above all that
of the face is a conscious evocation
of sculpture of the latter half of the
2nd century; but the somewhat
mechanical treatment of the fringe
with a boring tool, indicate the later
origin of this work.

199. Venus
4th century

Group, marble. H 76 cm (29.9 in.)
Found at Saint-Georges-de-Montagne (Gironde).
Acq. 1953. Ma 3537

A nude Venus is arranging her long hair. A small Cupid helps her hold the heavy mirror into which she gazes. A Triton to the right and a Cupid astride a dolphin to the left remind us that Venus was born of the sea. Somewhat ponderous and clumsy in execution, this small free-standing group was found with other statues of divinities in a large villa near Libourne. There was a ready market in the 4th century for such groups which are often devoid of religious significance and have only a decorative value.

200. Wrestler
1st century?

Statuette, bronze. H 27 cm (10.6 in.)
Autun. Acq. 1870. Br 1067

201. Old Woman Crouching
2nd century

Statuette, bronze. H 9.2 cm (3.6 in.)
Vichy. Acq. 1895. Br 2936

A popular spectacle during Roman times was the "pancratium", a fight between two bare-fisted wrestlers. With remarkable verve the artist has seized the instant when a wrestler has just kicked out and is tilting his torso to keep his balance. It is rare that a bronze statuette fills a space so satisfyingly; so much so that it is hard to choose the best angle to view it from. The deliberately exaggerated modeling helps to give this work its particular charm, although it remains firmly within the tradition of Hellenistic-period bronze wrestling groups.

The craftsman in bronze has successfully captured the figure of an old woman. She is huddled in a long robe, one foot bare, the other shod. With the skin of her cheeks and neck falling in folds and her eyes half-closed, she looks bewildered as she tilts a cup in her hand. The artisan has skillfully assimilated her headdress, a veil tied with a ribbon, into the upper half of the vessel which this statuette forms.
In keeping with the artistic tradition of Alexandria, bronze craftsmen were fond of depicting invalids and grotesque people. But seldom have they evoked so powerfully the exhaustion and wretchedness of one human being. Nevertheless the pitiless observation is tempered with a glimmer of humor.

202. Bacchus and Pan
Second half of the 2nd century

Group, bronze inlaid with silver. H 18.7 cm (7.4 in.)
Augst (Switzerland). Acq. 1865. Br 1061

203. Aphrodite as Universal Divinity
Roman period

Statuette, bronze. H 20 cm (7.9 in.)
From Amrith (Syria). Acq. 1868. Br 4425

From the end of the classical Greek period, antique artists often depicted Bacchus leaning on one of his companions, a satyr or Pan himself. But in this small group the two figures are less closely linked. Despite the gesture of his left hand, the god gazes ahead in apparent indifference to Pan who is kindly offering him a bunch of grapes. The somewhat heavy quality of the modeling and the emphasis given to the big eyes (which are inlaid with silver) date the work to the latter half of the 2nd century.

During Hellenistic and Roman times, Aphrodite was one of the most frequently reproduced figures in the bronze workshops of the Near East. She is often shown as a fulsome fertility goddess. But she also has the character of a universal divinity with some of the powers and accessories of other gods. Here a naked Aphrodite is laden with attributes; winged like a Victory, she is wearing a towered crown, and carries a horn of plenty and the rudder of Fortune. Also on her head she bears the emblem of Isis; slung across her back is a quiver, and a serpent twists around her arm. These small statuettes, produced in great quantities and widely distributed, bear witness to the religious fervor of the eastern Roman Empire.

204. Calliope
Pompeii, villa of Julia Felix
Between 62 and 79 A.D.

Fresco wall painting. H 45 cm (17.7 in.);
W 36 cm (14.2 in.)
Gift of Ferdinand IV, king of Naples, 1802. P 4

The Muse of epic poetry, Calliope,
stands on a console bearing
her name, with a roll of script in her
hand. Along with her eight sisters
and Apollo, she once occupied the
center of a large yellow panel,
in a configuration typical of the
last phase of wall painting
in Pompeii, before the eruption
(the "Fourth style"). Her reserved
attitude and the attention paid
to her costume distinguishes her
from her companions, however.
This is the first time the Nine
Muses can be referred to with any
certainty, thanks to inscriptions
bearing their names and functions.

205. Funereal Procession
Rome, tomb of Patron
Late 1ˢᵗ century B.C.
Fresco wall painting. H 1.68 m (66.1 in.);
W 39 cm (15.3 in.)
Campana Coll. Acq. 1863. P 37

This enigmatic scene once decorated the wall of the tomb of a Greek-born doctor, Patron. Thanks to the inscriptions we know who the main figures are; the wife of the deceased and her two daughters in the center, accompanied possibly by her grandchildren. Doubtless this slow and solemn procession had a religious meaning, perhaps a visit to the tomb. Aligning the figures at regular intervals across a simplified landscape, and using a sober and muted palette, the painter has created an exceptional atmosphere of sadness and quietude.

206.The Judgement of Paris
Antioch (Turkey),
"House of the Atrium"
Not long after 115

Mosaic, marble, limestone and glass paste.
1.86 m (73.2 in.) x 1.86 m (73.2 in.)
Acq. 1936. Ma 3443

The mosaic once decorated the
dining-room floor of a wealthy
home. It features Paris, the Trojan
shepherd-prince to whom the
messenger Hermes, appears, asking
him to judge which is the most
beautiful of the three goddesses,
Athena, Hera and Aphrodite.
Certain of her success, the latter
is leaning casually against a rock
on the right. Using very small cubes
with a wealth of color, the artist has
sought to rival the delicacy of brush
strokes: his model was without
doubt a painting and it came
as no surprise to find a fresco very
similar to this in Pompeii. For many
years the mosaics of the Roman
Orient, steeped in the tradition
of Greek art, retained this concern
to imitate painting in stone.
The border of elegant twists of vines
and ivy, trailing from two human
heads, and inhabited by insects,
lizards and birds, was inspired
by a 2nd century b.c. mosaic from
Pergamum.

207. Preparations for a Banquet
Carthage (Tunisia)
c. 180

Mosaic, marble and glass paste
2.25 m (88.6 in.) x 2.40 m (94.5 in.)
Acq. 1891. Ma 1796

In what is left of this large mosaic,
five servants are proceeding to the
right with food, plates and utensils
in preparation for a large feast. The
figures stand out against a uniformly
white background, and instead
of subtle tonal gradations the artist
makes use of highly contrasted
juxtapositions of light and dark
colors to suggest modeling. Stark
effects like these were sought after
in the expressionist style of Roman
art at the end of 2nd century.

208. Hunting Scenes
Daphne (Turkey), "Constantinian villa"
c. 325

Mosaic, marble, limestone and glass paste.
8.07 m (317 in.) x 8.04 m (316.5 in.)
Acq. 1939. Ma 3444

This mosaic, at the center of which
was a fountain, once lay in the
reception room of a large house
in Daphne. From its composition
it appears to be an adaptation
of a ceiling decoration, including the
gold mouldings (imitating stucco)
around each section. The outside
border comprises genre scenes taken
from Hellenistic art; at each corner
is a personification of an abstract
idea. Luscious plants surround the
flooring; at the corners four young
women, the Seasons, stand
on clumps of acanthus leaves.
In the central field are four hunting
scenes; one is mythological,
illustrating the exploits of Meleager
and Atalanta. The sheer variety
of images makes it a highly elaborate
work but the realistic, and
occasionally almost clumsy treatment
of the hunting scenes, contrasts

with the highly classical allure
of the large acanthus leaves and the
Seasons. Traditions inherited from
Greek art confront the new
tendencies of late Antiquity.

209. Phoenix on a Bed of Roses
Daphne (Turkey), late 5th century

Mosaic in marble and limestone.
6 m (236.2 in.) x 4.25 m (167.3 in.)
Acq. 1984. Ma 3442

The mosaics discovered at Antioch
(now Antakya in Turkey), the capital
of Roman Syria, and in the residential
environs of Daphne, are a superb
illustration of the high-quality
craftsmanship of one of the biggest
cities of the Roman empire. In late

Antiquity these floorings came to look like real carpets. On this mosaic, a rose pattern is reproduced *ad infinitum*. At the center stands a phoenix, a bird continually reborn from its ashes and a symbol of immortality. It was consciously used by artists to stress the eternal nature of the Roman empire. Around the border, one area of which was clumsily restored as long ago as Antiquity, ibexes stand on pairs of wings, with ribbons around their necks. The image comes from the art of the Sassanids, whose eastern empire (now Iran) rivaled Rome's; Antioch was at the crossroads of these two rival civilizations.

at banquets, they commonly served to remind guests to enjoy the fleeting moment. But never has the subject been treated so elaborately as on the two cups from the silver hoard of Boscoreale, near Pompeii. In almost strip-cartoon fashion, the skeletons are labeled and the scenes explained with inscriptions; they are celebrated Greek poets and philosophers, among them, Sophocles, Euripides and Epicurus and their words and gestures illustrate the frailty and vanity of the human condition with a caustic humor deriding the life of man.

210. Cup Decorated by Skeletons
Boscoreale, near Pompeii
1st century A.D.
Silver-gilt. H 10.4 cm (4.1 in.)
Boscoreale hoard. Rothschild donation, 1895. Bj 1923

This is not the only depiction of skeletons in Roman art. Shown

212. Gold Medallion
First quarter of 4th century

Gold. Ø 9.2 cm (3.6 in.)
Acq. 1973. Bj 2280

211. Marine Still-Life
3rd century

Dish, silver. Ø 45 cm (17.7 in.)
Found at Graincourt-lès-Havrincourt (Pas-de-Calais)
Acq. 1959. Bj 2214

This dish decorated with fishing
motifs, gives proof of the popularity
of silverware in Gaul. In an elaborate
manner, fish, shellfish, anchors, oars,
lobster pots, fishing nets and seabirds
adorn the center and rim of the dish.
The design, however, is not
innovative for many other contemporary objects have identical motifs.
These had been created much earlier
by craftsmen of the Hellenistic
period, and possibly in Alexandria.
They appeared first in fishing scenes,
but Roman silversmiths used them
purely for decorative purposes.

A gold coin of Constantine, issued
in 321 to commemorate the second
consulate of his two sons, is inserted
in a generous mount of perforated
gold leaf. This technique
(*opus interrasile*) was very popular
in goldsmiths' work from the
3rd century, coinciding with a fashion
for coin jewellery. This particularly
elaborate example was one of three
that formed a large necklace; most
probably it was commissioned by the
emperor as a gift. The busts around
the edges (originally there were six)
have not been identified.

213. Reliquary
Late 4th century

Silver-gilt. H 5.7 cm (2.2 in.); W 12 cm (4.7 in.)
From Castello di Brivio (Italy). Acq. 1912. Bj 1951

With the spread of Christianity, artists had to invent images to illustrate the new faith and biblical texts. This small box in precious metal, designed to keep relics, is richly decorated with reliefs in the *repoussé* technique, and the subjects are drawn from the Old and New Testaments. Three young Hebrews are thrown into the furnace on the orders of King Nebuchanezzar and are saved by an angel. We also see the Adoration of the Magi and the Raising of Lazarus.

214. Diptych
5th century

Ivory. H 29 cm (11.4 in.)
Acq. 1836. SMD 46

Over two ivory plates, six Muses bring inspiration to six poets and philosophers. Pagan in origin, the Muses have been given a wide significance. The refined execution is steeped in classicism as is most of the output of later Antiquity. The elegant design in strong relief once formed the cover of a diptych or two-fold panel. It would have been possible to write on the back of the panels which shut like a book. This was a much prized gift offered by men of note to their friends to commemorate special occasions such as their appointment to the magistrature.

215. Plate
Italy?
Late 1st century B.C.–early
1st century A.D.

Glass. Ø 13.3 cm (5.2 in.)
S 2476

The laying down of strips of vitreous
paste in various colors over a dark
ground gives this mosaic glass effect
which is to be found on a series
of small moulded receptacles, cups
and plates. A ropework border
in white reinforces the precious
nature of this plate and indicates the
quality of manufacture.
The workshops where items like
this were made were undoubtedly
in Italy.

216. Vase
Homs (Syria)
6th–7th century

Silver. H 44 cm (17.3 in.)
Durighello donation, 1892. Bj 1895

Metalwork made a great advance
during the early Byzantine period,
particularly in the field of liturgical
objects. This large amphora-shaped
vase, found on the site of ancient
Emesa, was doubtless designed
to hold the communion wine
of a church. Alternating with
foliated scrolls and horns of plenty,
the eight medallions on the decorative
band depict busts of Christ, the
Virgin Mary, angels and apostles.
Although it bears no stamp, the high
quality of the reliefs suggests
it originated from the capital of the
Byzantine empire, Constantinople.

Decorative Arts

Late Empire

Byzantine Art

Carolingian and Romanesque Art

Gothic Art

Renaissance, Italy

Renaissance, France

Renaissance, Flanders

First Half of the 17th Century

Louis XIV

Louis XV

Louis XVI

Empire

Restoration

Louis-Philippe

Napoleon III's Apartments

Introduction

The National Convention's decree of 27 July 1793 founding the Louvre museum provided for the inclusion of *objets d'art* in the collection from the outset. The decorative arts section took shape thereafter somewhat haphazardly, but mainly thanks to two major initial contributions. At the end of 1793 a part of the treasure of the Abbey of Saint-Denis entered the Louvre, including the coronation regalia of the kings of France and the precious vases which Abbé Suger had gathered together and mounted in the 12th century. In 1796, the greater part of the Renaissance bronzes and *pietra dura* vases from the royal collections were added.

This foundation collection, comprising objects as important historically as they were artistically, gave the future department of decorative arts a certain distinction and set standards of quality for subsequent acquisitions. Under the Restoration, two collections of *objets d'art* were purchased; that of Edme-Antoine Durand, wealthy connoisseur and traveler, in 1825, and that of Pierre Révoil, painter of historical scenes, in 1828. Under the Second Empire, Charles Sauvageot donated his collection in 1856, and in 1863 Napoleon III purchased the Marquis Campana's collection, which included a remarkable set of Italian maiolica. Thanks to these acquisitions, the Department of Decorative Arts, created under the Second Empire, became endowed by degrees with a coherent and homogeneous collection encompassing the Middle Ages and the Renaissance, with fine examples of ivory and metalwork, furniture, ceramics, glass and bronze.

The collection continues to grow to this day through gifts (Baron Adolphe de Rothschild, 1901; Baroness Salomon de Rothschild, 1922), and purchases. In the last years of the 19th century the chronological scope of the department was extended to "modern times." The transfer from the Mobilier National (the National Furniture Repository), in 1870 and again in 1901, of furniture, tapestries and decorative bronzes from former royal residences, constituted a prestigious nucleus from which the collection was to grow with gifts of furniture (Count Isaac de Camondo, 1911; Baron Basile de Schlichting, 1914; M. and Mme Grog-Carven, 1973), of silver and gold plate (M. and Mme David-Weill, 1946; M. Stavros S. Niarchos, 1955), of porcelain (Mme Adolphe Thiers, 1880) and with gifts in lieu of death duty and numerous acquisitions.

At last, with the creation of the Grand Louvre, the Decorative Arts Department has not merely been able to rearrange a part of its holdings (Middle Ages, Renaissance, early 19th century) on the first floor of the Richelieu Wing, but has likewise taken over the sumptuous apartments of the old Ministry of Finance, decorated under Napoleon III.

Late Empire

During the 3rd century A.D. the Roman Empire underwent a series of political, social and cultural crises from which it emerged profoundly transformed; this was the beginning of the Late Empire (3rd–4th century). Upon the death of Theodosius in 395, the Empire was permanently split into the Western Empire, of Latin civilization and the Eastern Empire, of Greek. Christianity, which had gradually been adopted throughout the whole Roman Empire and recognized by Constantine in 314, became the official religion under Theodosius in 385. Ultimately, relentless pressure from the barbarians led to the Great Invasions of the 5th century and the downfall of the Western Empire in 476. The art of the Late Empire broadly follows the traditional forms and techniques of Graeco-Roman art. This revival, especially evident in ivory carving in Rome around 400, was nevertheless permeated by original anticlassical currents. While Christian iconography gradually took shape, the continual attraction exerted by the arts of the Orient became increasingly palpable. The resulting primacy of idea over form represented an infringement of classical illusionism, especially where perspective was concerned. These tendencies became increasingly marked in the Eastern Empire during the 6th century.

217. Miracles of Christ
Rome, early 5th century

Plaque, ivory. H 19.7 cm (7.7 in.); W 78 cm (30.7 in.)
Acq. 1926. OA 7876–7878

This rectangular plaque formed the lateral side of a large leaf of an ivory diptych, which was divided into five sections. The three scenes depict some of Christ's miracles. Another lateral plaque from the same diptych, but almost certainly from the second leaf, is in Berlin. A third fragment showing the Adoration of the Magi was formerly kept at Nevers cathedral (now in the Musée de Nevers). These ivory reliefs are illustrative of the style used by Roman ivory carvers in the first years of the 5th century; the allusions to the classical art of antiquity are still very marked, despite the gradual disappearance of spatial perspective.

218. The Emperor Triumphant, known as *"The Barberini Ivory"*
Constantinople, first half of the 6th century

Ivory. H 34.2 cm (13.5 in.); L 26.8 cm (11 in.)
Acq. 1891. OA 9063

A gift to Cardinal Barberini from Claude Fabri de Peiresc, a scholar from Aix, in the early 17th century, the ivory must have been in Provence in the 7th century because on the back is a list of barbarian kings and officials from the region.
The "Barberini Ivory" is the only almost complete surviving leaf of an imperial diptych, with both leaves made up of five attached ivory units. The centerpiece shows the triumph of an emperor, Anastasius (491–518) or, more probably, Justinian (527–565) who is associated, in the upper section, with the glorification of Christ. The density of the composition and the very high relief—almost in the round—of the centerpiece, in addition to the fullness of the idealized faces of Christ and the emperor, are characteristic of a group of ivories worked in Constantinople in the first half of the 6th century.

Byzantine Art

Spared the Great Invasions of the 5th century, the Eastern Empire, now known as the Byzantine Empire, survived until 1453 when its capital, Constantinople, fell to the Turks. After a first flowering under the reigns of Justinian (527–565) and Heraclius (610–641), Byzantium was soon under threat from the rise of Islam which conquered the Southern Mediterranean coastline over the 7th century. Iconoclasm (726–843), the doctrine which forbade figurative religious art, ended this period in bloodshed. After the return to religious orthodoxy (843), the accession of the dynasty of Macedonian emperors (867–1056) opens the most brilliant period of Byzantine history, prolonged under the Comnenian dynasty (1081–1183). But the Crusades, coming in successive waves from the West, aggravated East-West clashes and the fourth Crusade turned against Constantinople itself. It was sacked in 1204, and the crusaders shared out the spoils of the empire between them. Little by little, however, the Greeks managed to regain their empire, which was restored in 1261. Then the Palaeologus dynasty began (1261–1453), the third and final period of Byzantine history, and the last gasp of an empire besieged by the Turks.

Byzantine art is a conscious successor to the art of the Christian Late Empire. Each great period of renewal in Byzantine history is matched by a series of deliberate backward turns, known as "renaissances" (the "Heraclian", "Macedonian", "Comnenian" and "Palaeologan" renaissances), which derive their central inspiration from the classical mainspring. It is this classicism that gives Byzantine art as a whole its profound unity and which finds expression, in every period, in its finest productions. It was not, for all that, impervious to other artistic currents, as can be seen in the Oriental luxury of Islamic art under the Macedonians, the research into decorative effects proper to the Comnenian period, or the note of pathos in the last period of Byzantine art under the House of Palaeologus.

219. Harbaville Triptych: Deisis and Saints
Constantinople, mid 10th century
Ivory with traces of gilding. H 24.2 cm (9.5 in.);
W 28.5 cm (11.2 in.)
Acq. 1891. OA 3247

The triptych is organized around
the depiction of the *deisis*; the Virgin
and St. John the Baptist intercede
with Christ enthroned, on behalf
of mankind. On the section beneath,
and on the two side panels, apostles,
martyrs, bishop—and soldier—saints
join in this prayer. This masterpiece
of Byzantine classicism is the most
elegant of the ivories from the
imperial workshop known
as "Romanos" (based on the plaque
in the Bibliothèque Nationale
in Paris in which Christ is crowning
Emperor Romanus II (945–949) and
his wife Eudoxia). It is an important
example of the rebirth of the
ornamental arts in Byzantium under
the Macedonian Emperors.

220. St. Demetrios
Constantinople, early 12th century

Medallion, gold and cloisonné enamel.
Ø 8.4 cm (3.3 in.)
Pierpont Morgan donation, 1911. OA 6457

This medallion and nine others in the same series (New York, Metropolitan Museum) were mounted round the frame of a large icon of the archangel Gabriel, formerly housed in the Djoumati monastery (Georgia). Three of the medallions depicted the *deisis* with which bust portraits of the saints were associated. This enamel is among the finest things created in Constantinople under the Comnenian dynasty. The striving for decorative effect and the perfect mastery of technique place it chronologically between the Crown Enamels of St. Stephen of Hungary (1071–1078) and the oldest enamels of the Venetian *pala d'Oro* around 1100.

Carolingian and Romanesque Art

As with Byzantine art, Medieval art is descended from the Late Empire. The connection is especially evident in the domain of Carolingian *objets d'art* because a particular ambition of Charlemagne and his successors—who were fascinated by imperialism—encouraged artists to draw inspiration, in the widest sense of the term, from ancient models and thereby bring about the so-called "Carolingian renaissance." While goldsmiths' work was perfected—and this had been the major art form of the preceding period—the end of the 8th and 9th century saw the revival of techniques that had been abandoned; glyptics, bronze casting (an example being the *Equestrian Statuette of Charlemagne*, no. 222), and above all ivory carving, prime examples of which are displayed in the Louvre.

In the 11th and 12th centuries, workshops multiplied and diversified. Now a cardinal role was played by different enameling techniques. While the *cloisonné* enamels of the *Maastricht Binding* (no. 225) are direct descendants of Carolingian and Ottonian *cloisonné* enamels, there is a marked development of *champlevé* enamels on copper, in the north and east as well as in the southern regions. The *Resurrection Armilla* (no. 229) and the *Reliquary of St. Henry* (no. 228) are evidence of the achievement of Saxon, Rhineland and Meuse workshops, on a par with the enamelers of Conques (*Griffon Medallion*, no. 230), and of Limoges (*Alpais Ciborium*, no. 231).

221. Leaves from the Binding of the Dagulf Psalter
Workshop of Charlemagne's palace, end of the 8th century

Ivory. H 16.8 cm (6.6 in.); W. of leaf 8.1 cm (3.2 in.)
From Bremen cathedral. MR 370–371

Charlemagne instructed Dagulf, the scribe, to illuminate a lavish psalter for Pope Hadrian I. Probably unfinished at the death of the pope in 795, the psalter remained in the royal treasury. These two ivory leaves of the binding illustrate the content of the manuscript, showing David overseeing the writing of the Psalms, and singing them, and St. Jerome receiving the order to correct the text of the Psalms and then working on them. These two ivories, which are the only ones that may be directly linked to a commission from Charlemagne, signal the beginning of the Carolingian renaissance. Their style refers directly to Late Empire models.

222. Equestrian Statuette of Charlemagne
9th century

Bronze with traces of gilding. H 23.5 cm (9.2 in.)
From the treasury of Metz cathedral. OA 8280

Inspired by classical equestrian statues, this statuette is made up of several bronze units that were cast separately and then assembled. The horse, which is not in proportion to its rider, may be a Late Empire work. The head and body of the rider are Carolingian bronzes. The sovereign, who is crowned, holds the orb of the world. His plump face with its thick drooping moustache, and his simple attire, correspond to Einhard's description of Charlemagne. The statuette may have been cast in Aix-la-Chapelle (Aachen) in the early 9th century. It is also possible, however, that the statue is a portrait of Charles the Bald, whose painted portrait in manuscripts shows a resemblance to his grandfather, Charlemagne.

223. Plaque, known as
"The Earthly Paradise"
France, c. 860–870?
Ivory. H 35.8 cm (14.1 in.); W 11.4 cm (4.5 in.)
Acq. 1863. OA 9064

The plaque is divided into several
sections showing, in descending
order, Adam and Eve, then fabulous
animals, wild animals and domestic
ones. It is not, in fact, a depiction
of the Earthly Paradise, but
an illustration to a text by St. Isidore
de Seville, outlining the different
orders of creation, the *Etymologiæ*.
The realism with which the animals
are treated and the soft delicacy
of the modeling reveal a deep
knowledge and a rare understanding
of models from antiquity or the Late
Empire. This ivory came from the
same workshop as the *flabellum*
(liturgical fan) from Tournus, in the
Museo Bargello, Florence.

224. Serpentine Paten

**1st century B.C. or A.D. (stone),
second half of 9th century (surround)**

Gold, pearls, precious stones, colored glass.
Ø 17 cm (6.7 in.)
From the treasury of the Abbey of Saint-Denis.
Entered the Louvre in 1793. MR 415

The paten is made up of two parts.
The serpentine saucer, inlaid with
golden fish, can be considered
as ancient, dating from the
1st century. The gold surround
is decorated with stones, between
which isolated motifs in *cloisonné*
goldwork evolve, a combination
found up to the early 11th century.
At Saint-Denis, this paten
accompanied an ancient agate
cantharus, the "Cup of the
Ptolemys," to which a goldwork
decoration was applied which
matches that on the paten (Paris,
Bibliothèque Nationale de France).
An inscription at the base of the

chalice states that it was given to the
abbey by Charles the Bald.

225. Maastricht Binding-Case
Second quarter of the 11th century

Gold, cloisonné enamel, precious stones, filigree
and niello on wood base. H 39.2 cm (15.4 in.);
W 32 cm (12.6 in.)
Acq. 1795. MR 349

This binding-case comes from the
treasury of St. Servais at Maastricht
(Netherlands); it contained
a manuscript of the Gospels
on which the dukes of Brabant took
solemn oath. An engraved inscription
inlaid with niello names the donor,
Beatrix, who was the wife either
of duke Adalberon of Carinthia,
or of Boniface of Tuscany (1036),
then of Godfrey the Bearded, duke
of Upper Lotharingia (and Brabant).
The *cloisonné* enamels are in the
style of pieces from the workshops
of Trier and Essen, and the style
of the gold embossed reliefs is close
to that of Ottonian works at the
beginning of the 11th century.

226. Coronation Sword of the Kings of France
10th–11th century (pommel),
12th century (cross-guards),
13th or 19th century (handle)

Gold, steel, glass or lapis-lazuli pearls.
H 1.005 m (39.6 in.); W 22.6 cm (8.9 in.)
From the treasury of the Abbey of Saint-Denis.
Entered the Louvre in 1793. MS 84

The coronation regalia of the kings
of France were kept in the treasury
at Saint-Denis. Since the 13th century
the coronation sword has been
thought to be the "Joyeuse" that
belonged to Charlemagne. The
pommel and the small metal plate
in the center of the hilt, with a foliate
motif, date from the early Middle
Ages; the handle, adorned until 1804,
with fleurs-de-lys within lozenges,
has a Gothic appearance; the cross-
guards, in the form of two little
winged dragons whose eyes are
inlaid with pearls, date from the
second half of the 12th century. This
swords and the spurs (also in the
Louvre) are part of the oldest
French regalia in existence today.

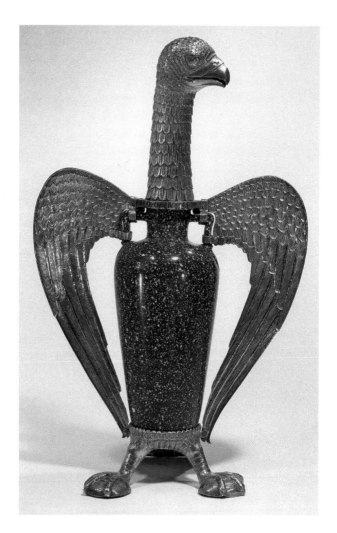

227. Eagle-Shaped Vase,
known as **"Suger's Eagle"**
Ancient vase; mount: France, before
1147

Porphyry, silver-gilt and niello inlay.
H 43.1 cm (17 in.); W 27 cm (10.6 in.)
From the treasury of the Abbey of Saint-Denis.
Entered the Louvre in 1793. MR 422

Suger, abbot of Saint-Denis and
adviser to Louis VI and Louis VII,
took a particular interest in adding
to the treasures of his abbey, and his
writings contain descriptions of the
precious vases he commissioned.
He writes that he found an antique
porphyry vase in a chest. He had
it converted into a liturgical vase

in an eagle-shaped mount. This
ewer joins other vessels in hard stone
(*pietra dura*) which Suger had
mounted and adorned: his chalice
(Washington, National Gallery), the
"Aliénor" vase, and the sardonyx
ewer which are both in the Louvre.
These were made by one of the
groups of goldsmiths who worked
for the Abbey of Saint-Denis; in this
instance, most probably goldsmiths
from the Ile-de-France.

228. Reliquary of St. Henry
Hildesheim, Lower Saxony, c. 1175

Engraved gilt brass, champlevé enamel and rock-crystal, silver on wood core. H 23.6 cm (9.3 in.);
W 16.1 cm (6.3 in.)
Acq. 1851. OA 49

This quadriform reliquary, enameled on both sides, rests on a hemispherical base, also enameled. On one side, Christ in Majesty is surrounded by three kings; on the other side we see St. Henry, last Ottonian Emperor of the Germanic Holy Roman Empire, canonized in 1152, with the Empress Cunegonde on one side and a clerk by the name of Welandus, probably the donor of the reliquary, on the other. The blue enamel ground flecked with gold, and the subdued coloring are characteristic of a group of works executed at Hildesheim at the time of the duke of Saxony, Henry the Lion (1142–1181).

229. "Armilla": the Resurrection
Meuse, c. 1170

Gilt brass, champlevé enamel. H 11.3 cm (4.4 in.);
W 14.7 cm (5.8 in.)
Gift of the Société des Amis du Louvre, 1934.
OA 3261

The *armilla* (a ceremonial bracelet)
and its pendant depicting the
Crucifixion (Nuremberg,
Germanisches Nationalmuseum)
might have been found in Russia
in the tomb of Prince André
Bogoloubski (d. 1174); the latter
supposedly received them from
Emperor Frederick Barbarossa
as a diplomatic gift. The style displays
the persistent classical traditions
of Meuse art around 1150–1160.
But the pure Byzantine grace of the
angels, their faces and that of Christ,
heralds the classicizing art
of Nicolas de Verdun after 1180.

230. Medallion Decorated with a Fabulous Animal
Conques(?), 1107–1119

Gilt brass, champlevé enamel. Ø 8 cm (3.1 in.)
Gift of friends of the Louvre, 1909.
OA 6280

A perfect expression of the
Romanesque *loi du cadre* (in which
the design fits the space perfectly),
this medallion is also a very early
example of the technique of *champlevé*
enamel on brass. With nine other
similar medallions (New York,
Metropolitan Museum, and Florence,
Museo Bargello), it was part of the
decoration on a casket. A second
casket still in Conques is decorated
with practically identical medallions,
two of which bear an inscription
which dates the construction of the
two caskets to the time of Abbé
Boniface (1107–1119).

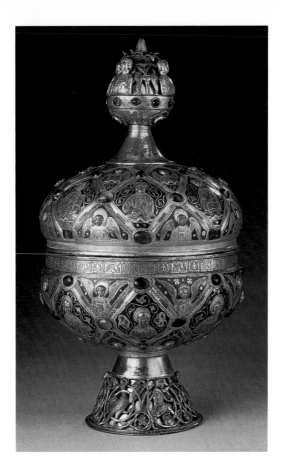

231. Alpais Ciborium
Limoges, c. 1200

Gilt brass, chased and engraved, champlevé enamel, cast and applied foot and finial, precious stones. H 30 cm (11.8 in.); Ø 16.8 cm (6.6 in.) Acq. 1828. MRR 98

This ciborium (a cup for reservation of the Eucharist) was found in the tomb of Bertrand de Malsang (d. 1316), abbot of Montmajour near Arles, where it may have been used as a funerary chalice. On the inside of the lid, around the engraved form of an angel, runs the inscription "MAGISTER G. ALPAIS ME FECIT LEMOVICARUM". It proves that the ciborium was made in Limoges itself, and is an essential document in the history of Limousin enamels of the Middle Ages. The ciborium is the masterpiece within a group of Limousin enamels executed around 1200.

Gothic Art

Throughout the first half of the 13th century, Limoges enamelers continued to produce outstanding works such as the *St. Mathieu* tablet from the Abbey of Grandmont (no. 232). But by the end of the century, Italian enamelers had perfected a new procedure which spread rapidly to the great centers of western Europe: the production of translucent *basse-taille* enamels, executed on silver (*Jeanne d'Évreux Virgin*, no. 236) or on gold (*Mirror Case* no. 234). The second half of the 14th century saw the triumph of enamels on *ronde-bosse* gold of which the fleur de lys on the *Scepter of Charles V*, no. 238) was originally an example. These pieces herald the technique of painted enamel which gradually supplanted other forms of enamelwork; the *Self-Portrait* by Jean Fouquet (no. 241) is one of the first examples of the technique. The growing wealth of the princely courts, especially of the French court, which was dominated by enthusiastic collectors of precious *objets d'art*, greatly fostered the craft of metalwork. There is perhaps no better expression of the perfection it attained than the *Jeanne d'Evreux Virgin* and the *Scepter of Charles V*. But the French Gothic style was even more influential in ivory carving. Statuettes, diptychs, triptychs, tabernacles and secular objects spread the style of the Parisian workshops throughout Europe.

232. Arched Plaque Decorated with a Figure of St. Matthew
Limoges, c. 1220–1230

Gilt copper, champlevé enamel. H 29 cm (11.4 in.); W 14 cm (5.5 in.)
Acq. 1825. MR 2650

The figure of St. Matthew is fixed on a base enameled with vigorous florid scrollwork. There are five other similar plaques with the apostles James (New York, Metropolitan Museum), Philip (St. Petersburg, Hermitage), Paul and Thomas (Paris, Petit Palais) and St. Martial (Florence, Museo Bargello), the "apostle" of the Limousin whom local worshippers associated with the apostolic college. They come from the altar of the former abbey of Grandmont near Limoges. Remarkable for their modeling, these apostles are the Limousin version of the classicizing style which appeared around 1200 in the Meuse and the north of France.

**233. Virgin and Child from
the Sainte-Chapelle**
Paris, c. 1250–1260
Ivory, traces of polychromy. H 41 cm (16.1 in.)
From the treasury of the Sainte-Chapelle in Paris.
Acq. 1861. OA 57

In the 13th and 14th centuries, the
growth of the cult of Mary led to the
production of numerous figurines
of the Virgin and Child, especially
in ivory. This statuette, described
in an inventory of the treasury
of the Sainte-Chapelle before 1279,
is considered to be the finest
achievement of Parisian ivory
workers, especially since it seems
to have inspired a whole series
of ivory statuettes in the second half
of the 13th century. The drapery and
her triangular face with its slit eyes
and slightly ironic smile place this
statuette in the full flowering
of Parisian monumental Gothic,
in the middle or third quarter
of the 13th century.

**234. Mirror Case: the Game
of Chess**
Paris, c. 1300
Ivory. Ø 12 cm (4.7 in.)
Gift of C. Sauvageot, 1856. OA 717

Gothic ivory workers produced not
only religious pieces but secular
articles as well, such as this mirror
case. The two flaps, held together
by a pin or hasp, and protecting
a small metal mirror, were sculpted
with courtly subjects or scenes
illustrating episodes from fashionable
romances. Perhaps the game of chess
shown here is inspired by a passage
in the story of Tristan and Iseut.
The delicate rounded modeling
of this relief and the smiling elegance
of the figures, clad in long floating
robes, are characteristic of art at the
court of Philip the Fair.

**235. Arm-Reliquary
of St. Louis of Toulouse**
Naples, before 1338

Rock crystal, silver-gilt, translucent enamels.
H 63 cm (24.8 in.); W 20 cm (7.9 in.)
Gift of Mme F. Spitzer, 1891. OA 3254

Brother of Robert d'Anjou, king
of Naples, St. Louis of Toulouse was
canonized in 1317.
This arm-reliquary, designed to keep
one of his relics, was made for Sancia
of Majorca, the wife of Robert
of Anjou. The translucent enamels
that cover part of the structure may
have been executed by a Sienese
metalworker (Lando di Pietro?).
With its pair (the arm-reliquary
of St. Luke, also made for Sancia
of Majorca), this is one of the rare
surviving works from the Angevin
court of Naples where French and
Italian metalworkers worked side
by side.

Given to the Abbey of Saint-Denis in 1339
by Queen Jeanne d'Evreux. Entered the Louvre
in 1793. MR 342 and 419

In the 13th and 14th centuries a new type of statuette came into vogue, in which the central figure holds the reliquary itself out towards the spectator. This Virgin in silver-gilt holds a lily, in gold plate and rock crystal, which once enclosed relics of the clothes, hair and milk of the Virgin. The rounded face of the Virgin, the layered hems and the folds of her robe that fall in long cones extending her form are characteristic of Parisian art in the first half of the 14th century. The enamels on the base (scenes from the childhood and the Passion of Christ) are an early dated example of translucent *basse-taille* enameling, perfected by Tuscan goldsmiths at the end of the 13th century.

236. The Jeanne d'Evreux Virgin and Child
Paris, between 1324 and 1339

Silver-gilt, basse-taille translucent enamels, gold,
rock crystal, precious stones and pearls.
H 69 cm (27.2 in.)

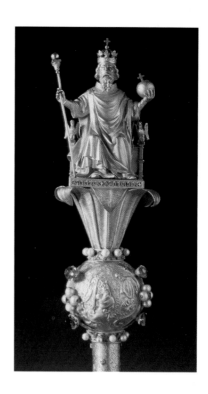

238. Scepter of Charles V
Paris, before 1380

Gold, pearls, precious stones, glass,
H 60 cm (23.6 in.)
From the treasury of the Abbey of Saint-Denis.
Entered the Louvre in 1793. MS 83

237. Tabernacle
Paris, second quarter
of the 14th century

Ivory. H 29 cm (11.4 in.); W 23.5 cm (9.2 in.)
Acq. 1882. OA 2587

Amidst the multifarious productions
of Gothic ivory workers,
"tabernacles" stand out because
of their elaborate design. These little
polyptychs are made up of folding
shutters that close around a central
section, shaped like a tiny chapel
in which stand one or more statuettes.
The center of the Louvre tabernacle
presents a Virgin and Child in high
relief. Her tall and sinuous silhouette,
the delicate cascading drapery and the
full face recall works of monumental
sculpture. The scenes on the shutters,
however, are closer to contemporary
diptychs and triptychs.

Charles V set aside a quantity
of vestments and royal insignia—
this scepter among them—for the
coronation of his son, the future
Charles VI. The detailed description
of the scepter in the inventory of the
Royal Treasury, dated 1379–1380,
shows that it has not undergone
much modification, save that the
fleur-de-lys was originally covered
with opaque white enamel. The
statuette of Charlemagne atop the
scepter, and scenes from his legend
on the knob are doubtless allusions
to Charles, the first name of the king
and his son, but also express the
desire of the first Valois monarchs
to link their power with the might
of the legendary Carolingian emperor.

239. Pair of Mirror Cases
Paris, before 1379

Gold, translucent basse-taille enamels.
Ø 6.8 cm (2.7 in.)
Acq. 1825. MR 2608–2609

John the Good and his sons, Charles V, Louis of Anjou, Philip of Burgundy and John of Berry were all avid collectors. There is almost nothing left of the vast treasure amassed by Louis of Anjou and described in an inventory of 1379 but these two mirror cases.

One depicts the Virgin and Child between St. Catherine and St. John, while the other shows God the Father between St. John the Baptist and St. Charlemagne. The bold style of these figures is influenced by the art of the Low Countries and the Rhineland. It is also typical of the milieu of the court of John the Good, and especially of Charles V, where many artists from these regions worked.

240. Support Figure: Kneeling Prophet
Paris, 1409

Gilt bronze. H 14 cm (5.5 in.)
Gift of J. Maciet, 1903. OA 5917

The kneeling prophet in the Louvre, and its pendant in the Cleveland Museum, were two of the bronze figures that supported the gold reliquary of St. Germain in the church of Saint-Germain-des-Prés. The reliquary, which was destroyed in the Revolution, is known to us from a 17th century engraving and from a contract drawn up in 1409 between the abbot and the three Parisian goldworkers who were to make it: Guillaume Boey, Gautier Dufour and Jean de Clichy.

241. Jean Fouquet
c. 1420–c. 1477–1481
Signed Self-Portrait
c. 1450

Painted enamel on copper. Ø 6.8 cm (2.7 in.)
Gift of H. de Janzé, 1861. OA 56

The fullness of the drapery and the vigor with which the heads are chased have been compared to the art of the best sculptors of the 1400s. It is a tangible expression of the "international" stylistic current in Gothic art around 1400.

This medallion, showing Fouquet's signature, was set into the frame, now lost, of his diptych in Notre-Dame de Melun, painted shortly after his journey to Italy, for Etienne Chevalier, counsellor to Charles VII, and treasurer of France in 1452. The diptych is now divided between museums in Berlin (*Etienne Chevalier Presented by St. Stephen*) and Antwerp (*The Virgin and Child Surrounded by Angels*). On the copper plaque, coated first with black, then gray-brown enamel, Fouquet laid his gold in thin hatched strokes, and then uncovered the black ground shining beneath it with the aid of a needlepoint. These techniques herald the art of painted enamel popular at the end of the century and during the Renaissance.

Renaissance, Italy

Italian Renaissance *objets d'art* are a testimony to a new lifestyle and new methods of working. The Louvre has a representative collection with greatest strengths in the fields of faience, glassware and bronze statuettes. These give us a good idea of decoration in homes as well as the special interest in the art of antiquity prevalent in 15th and 16th century Italy.

Faience (the name derives from the town of Faenza) is Italy's great contribution to ceramics. Faience is earthenware covered with an opaque tin-oxide glaze, usually white, onto which the painted decoration is then applied. The Louvre holds major examples from the principal centers of production, Faenza, Urbino, Casteldurante, Gubbio and Deruta.

Glassmaking made such rapid progress at the end of the 15th century in Venice that the two words remain inseparable. Thanks in part to the invention of a very white glass known as *"cristallo,"* the fame of Venetian glass brought in its wake a flood of imitations in the "Venetian style" throughout Europe, further encouraged by the emigration of many Italian artists. Despite its fragility, Venetian glassware has survived from the Renaissance and the Louvre's collection is one of the greatest in the world.

Bronze nevertheless remains the material most typical of Renaissance Italy; after the precious metals, it was the most highly favored for its diverse qualities and the illusion it gave of working "in the antique manner." Florence, Padua and Venice were the main centers of a flourishing industry in little statuettes and everyday objects, that were highly sought after.

242. Bowl Inscribed with the Arms of Florence

Florence, c. 1425–1450
Tin-glazed earthenware. H 8 cm (3.1 in.);
Ø 64 cm (25.2 in.)
Acq. 1897. OA 3946

The word *maiolica*, the name given
to Italian tin-glazed earthenware,
derives from Majorca. Throughout
the 14th century this island was
a transit point for luxurious glazed
artefacts from Spanish workshops
in Valencia and bound for Italy.
Although they were great admirers
of these pieces, a good many
of which carry the arms of families
from Pisa and Florence, the Italians
developed their own original style,
which reflected the general artistic
climate of the Florentine *quattrocento*.
The iconography on this bowl,
a heraldic banner borne by a lion
who stands on a field of lily stems
(denoting the city of Florence), bears
witness to the great quality of this
city's *maiolica* production in the first
quarter of the 15th century.

243. Cup Decorated with an Allegorical Procession

Venice, last quarter of the 15th century
Enameled glass. H 27.5 cm (10.8 in.);
Ø 14 cm (5.5 in.)
Baroness Salomon de Rothschild bequest, 1922.
OA 7564

During the 15th century, the glassmaking traditions of ancient Rome
were revived in Venice thanks
to numerous contacts with Byzantium
and Mamluk Syria where these
traditions had been maintained.
Enameling, one of the most spectacular aspects of Syrian glassware,
was a technique widely used by the
master glass-makers of Venice.
Prominent among them was Angelo
Barovier who died in 1460. Although
this cup appears stylistically to date
after the death of Angelo Barovier,
it gives us a good idea of the splendor
of Venetian glassware at the end of
the 15th century. While the meaning
of the allegorical procession around
the bowl eludes us, it is thought
perhaps to be an allegory of marriage.

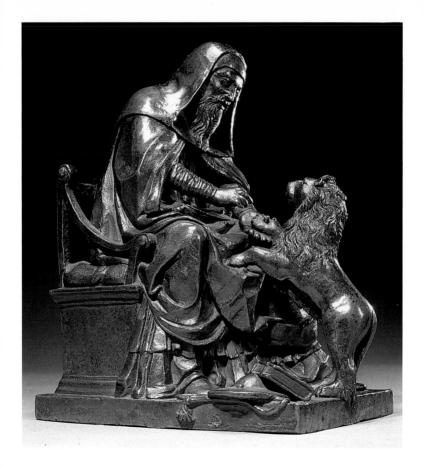

244. Bartolomeo Bellano
c. 1440–1496/7
Saint Jerome and the Lion
Padua, end of the 15th century

Bronze with crackled black patina.
H 25 cm (9.8 in.); W 20.5 cm (8.1 in.)
Gift of Mme Gustave Dreyfus and her children,
1919. OA 7250

A pupil of Donatello and a native
of Padua where the art of bronze
flourished, Bellano is renowned for
works with a strong narrative bias.
This bronze statuette illustrates the
famous episode in which the saint
pulls a thorn from a lion's paw.
As the only one of its kind, the
statuette seems to have been cast
directly from the wax model. It can
be dated to around 1490–1495
because of close similarities

to Bellano's sculptures on the
monument to Pietro Roccabonella
in San Francesco, Padua. He began
work on these in 1491; they exhibit
a similar simplified treatment
of volumes and an equally sensitive
rendering of the human face.

245. Andrea Briosco,
known as **Riccio**
1470–1532
Paradise
Padua, 1516–1521

Bas-relief, bronze with brown patina.
H 37 cm (14.6 in.); W 49 cm (19.3 in.)
Entered the Louvre in 1798. MR 1711 (OA 9099)

This bas-relief—one of a series of eight—comes from a tomb in the church of San Fermo Maggiore in Verona. The tomb was constructed by Riccio, the renowned Paduan sculptor, in honor of Girolamo della Torre, a physician and professor of medicine, and of his son Marcantonio, also a professor of medicine and a friend of Leonardo da Vinci. The reliefs derive from Book VI of Virgil's *Aeneid*, and depict in pagan mode the journey of the soul of the deceased into the underworld. *Paradise* depicts the soul of the dead (on the left) as a winged cupid carrying a book and being welcomed by dancers on the Elysian Fields of the pagan underworld. Top right, again as cupid, the soul is shown drinking the waters of Lethe, the river of oblivion, while at bottom right he is shown back in his earthly form as bearded old man asleep, awaiting his return to earth and crowned with Fame. Known for his many mythical and fabulous creatures, Riccio's achievement here is based on an alliance between a classicism derived from antique models, and the lyrical realism typical of artists in northern Italy.

246. Nicola da Urbino
known between 1520 and 1538
**Plate from the Service
of Isabella d'Este**
Urbino, c. 1525
Tin-glazed earthenware. H. 4 cm (1.6 in.);
Ø 27 cm (10.6 in.)
Gift of Baroness Salomon de Rothschild, 1922.
OA 7578

The most original contribution made
by the Italians to the history of faience
was with the *Istoriato*, a decorative
genre in which pieces were painted
with historical scenes. During the
first half of the 16th century, centers
like Casteldurante and Urbino
brought this art to an unsurpassed
degree of perfection. Nicola
di Gabriele Sbraga, who signed his
works Nicola da Urbino after the
name of his town, stands out among
the most brilliant painters of *Istoriati*.
One of Nicola's most prestigious
achievements was the service commissioned around 1525 by Isabella
d'Este, the famous patron and
connoisseur of the arts. The plate
in the Louvre was part of this service.
The marchioness of Mantua's
coat-of-arms is in the foreground
of the decoration, and her motto
is on a scroll on the ground. The
scene itself is an imitation of a work
by Raphael in the Vatican—an illustration from Genesis, *Abimelech
Observing Isaac and Rebecca*.

247. Gnome on a Snail
Florence, second half
of the 16th century
Bronze with black cracklework and brown patina.
H 37.5 cm (14.8 in.); W 19.5 cm (7.7 in.)
Acq. 1933. OA 8252

Sitting astride a snail, holding
a whip handle in his right hand, the
naked gnome seems in a ludicrous
way to want to speed the animal
along. The bold association
of a deformed human figure with
a monstrous snail, treated
naturalistically, is typically mannerist
in feel. This gnome is akin
to a marble of the same subject
in the Villa Careggi near Florence,
and attributed to the workshop
of Valerio Cioli (1529–1599). Despite
its diminutive size it is related
to sculptures designed for villa
gardens. The gnome's complex
position has been worked out
so as to stand scrutiny from different
angles.

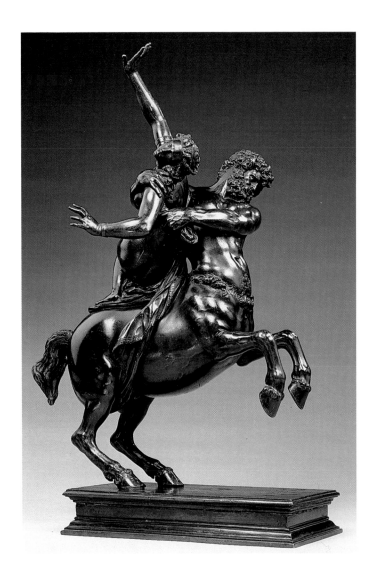

248. Giambologna (Jean Boulogne)
1529–1608
Nessus and Deianeira
Florence, c. 1575–1580

Bronze with red-brown patina. H 42.1 cm (16.6 in.);
W 30.5 cm (12 in.)
Coll. of the French Crown. Inv. Cour. 176

A native of Douai, Jean Boulogne
made his career in Florence
where his name was Italianized
as Giambologna. Besides large marble
sculptures, Jean Boulogne made
numerous models for small bronzes.
These were cast in his workshop and
disseminated by his pupils. They
were much sought after throughout
Europe, and served as diplomatic
gifts at the court of the Medici.
The Louvre group is of exceptional
quality and one of the very rare
examples which has the artist's
signature ("Ioa bolongie" on the
centaur's headband). It was most
probably the bronze given
to Louis XIV by Le Nôtre in 1693,
and shows Jean Boulogne's genius
for capturing two figures in action.

Renaissance, France

In France, during the Renaissance, *objets d'art*—along with the arts in general—came under Italian influence. The presence of Italian artists in France, working especially on royal palaces like Fontainebleau, was a stimulus to local artists. And there was another new phenomenon: the circulation of prints which familiarized the French with forms and decorations developed not only in Italy but in Germany and Flanders as well. In return, the brilliance of the "School of Fontainebleau," and the dissemination of models created by a new type of artist, the ornamentalist—such as Jacques Androuet du Cerceau or Etienne Delaunc—ensured that France had a place of honor in the domain of *objets d'art*.

Works in precious metal from the period are remarkably rare today, but they convey something of the luxury of the Court of France, in particular its taste for polychromy, enamel effects, decorations inspired by the grotesque or the moresque, and historical scene-painting.

Enamel painting on copper was a specialty of Limoges throughout the 16th century; originally designed for devotional paintings, it was later used on decorative tableware. Like Italian maiolica, its popularity was immense both in France and abroad.

French ceramics belonged to one of two camps; on the one hand there was Italianism, brought to Lyons and Nevers, and assimilated by an obscure Rouen artist, Masséot Abaquesne, who produced tin-glazed earthenware using the Italian technique; on the other, there was traditional production, which flourished in provincial centers such as Beauvaisis or Saintonge, and was dominated by the mythical figure of Bernard Palissy.

249. Léonard Limosin
c. 1505–c. 1575
St. Thomas with the Features of Francis I
Limoges, c. 1550
Enamel on copper, H 91 5 cm (36 in.);
W 43.5 cm (17.1 in.)
Entered the Louvre in 1816. MR 211

From the 15th to the 17th century Limoges was the center of production for enameled copper plaques. It was Léonard Limosin who brought the technique to perfection. In 1547 he finished twelve paintings in enamel depicting the apostles, now in the Musée de Chartres. The cartoons were painted by Michel Rochetel after drawings

250. Léonard Limosin
c. 1505–c. 1575
**Portrait of the Constable
of Montmorency
Limoges, 1556**

Enamel on copper, mount in gilt wood.
H 72 cm (28.3 in.); W 56 cm (22 in.)
Seized during French Revolution. Entered the
Louvre in 1794. N 1254

by Primaticcio. The series was a gift from Henry II to Diane de Poitiers for her Château d'Anet. Léonard Limosin may well have been commissioned to reproduce the series as the Louvre possesses two other apostles from the Feuillantines convent which were in Alexandre Lenoir's Museum of French Monuments during the Revolution. This portrait of St. Thomas differs from the one at Chartres in that the head is a portrait of Francis I, and the surrounding motifs are inverted.

In 1556, Léonard Limosin—who was an enameler at the court of Francis I and then of his successors—painted this portrait of Anne de Montmorency (1493–1567), High Constable of France, in 1538. Most probably painted from a pencil drawing, the portrait is a good example of Léonard Limosin's masterly skill. It is still in its original frame which is made up of eight panels of different shapes, depicting the high constable's heraldic device, children's and women's heads, and two satyrs, the model for which came from the Galerie François I at Fontainebleau.

Detail

251. Masséot Abaquesne
known from 1526 until his death
before 1564
Altar Step for La Bastie d'Urfé
Rouen, 1557

Tin-glazed earthenware. W 3.260 m (128.3 in.);
D 1.840 m (72.4 in.) and 54 cm (21.3 in.);
flags 11 cm (4.3 in.)
Gift of Beurdeley, father and son, 1880. OA 2518

In a contract drawn up at Rouen,
on the 22 September 1557, Claude
d'Urfé commissioned enameled
paving flags from Masséot Abaquesne.
These were almost certainly the tiles
used to pave the chapel at his home,
La Bastie d'Urfé in the Forez.
The Louvre possesses the altar step
from this chapel. It is not known
whether Masséot Abaquesne was
a businessman or artist, or if the
latter, where he trained. Both
the earthenware technique and the
"Raphaelesque" decoration,
commonly used in Urbino
workshops at the time, indicate
an Italian influence.

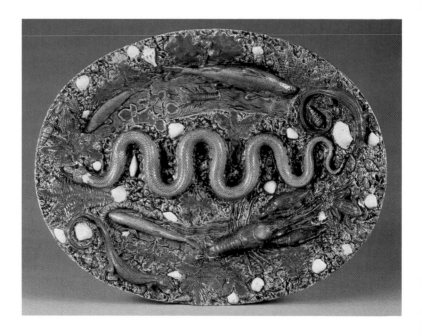

252. Bernard Palissy

1510?–1590
**Dish Decorated with
"Rustic Figulines"**
France, c. 1560
Glazed clay, H 7.4 cm (2.9 in.); L 52.6 cm (20.7 in.);
W 40.3 cm (15.9 in.)
Acq. 1825. MR 2293

Bernard Palissy is the most famous
figure in the history of French
ceramics. As a writer, architect,
chemist, and devoted artist he was
an archetypal Renaissance humanist.
One of the most characteristic aspects
of his work can been seen in the
large dishes adorned with reptiles,
shells and plants cast from life.
Known as "rustic figulines", they can
be linked in design to the two
grottoes, which have now disap-
pear-ed, designed for Catherine de'
Medici in the Tuileries, and for the
Constable of Montmorency
at Ecouen (see no. 250).

253. Pierre Reymond

c. 1513–after 1584
Oval Plate
Limoges, 1578
Enamel on copper. H 39 cm (15.3 in.);
W 51.5 cm (20.3 in.)
Acq. 1825. MR 2419

The 16th century saw the emergence
of decorative table services in enamel
often painted in gray monochrome
(grisaille) with highlights—as here—
in salmon pink and gold enamel.
These dishes are decorated either
with monthly tasks or with
illustrations from the Bible. Here,
Shaphan reads the "book of law"
to Josiah, King of Judah, who upon
hearing the book institutes major
religious reforme.
The rim is adorned with a frieze
of monsters and animals with
an escutcheon bearing the date 1578
at the top. The motifs often derive
from contemporary engravings:
in this case from a vignette
by Bernard Salomon published
in Lyons from 1554.

254. Charles IX Shield
Paris, c. 1572

Embossed iron and gold plating, enamel.
H 68 cm (26.8 in.); W 49 cm (19.3 in.)
Acq. 1793. MR 427

This shield is a rare example
of the luxury enjoyed by the last
Valois kings; it is accompanied
by a matching helmet. Charles IX
(1550–1574) first received the helmet
and a scimitar from Pierre Redon,
metalworker and page-in-waiting
to the king. The shield was made
later and settlement for it was made
to Redon's widow, Marie de Fourcroy,
in 1572. The central bas-relief depicts
the victory of Marius over Jugurtha,
king of Numidia, in 107 B.C.
This is surrounded by the favorite
motifs of the School of Fontainebleau:
cuirasses, masks, trophies, and
ornamental fruit. Round the rim,
the king's monogram K alternates
with medallions in *cloisonné* enamel.

255. Mace from the Order
of the Holy Ghost
Paris, 1584–1585

Silver-gilt and enamel. H 1.10 m (43.3 in.);
W 32 cm (12.6 in.); weight 4.24 kg (9 lb 5 oz)
Formerly in the treasury of the Order of the Holy
Ghost. MR 564

The Order of the Holy Ghost
(Ordre du Saint-Esprit) was founded
in 1578 by Henry III (1551–1589)
who ordered a set of ten silver-gilt
objects to be made in Paris for this
Order of Chivalry. The mace was
duly delivered in early 1586 by the
metalworker François Dujardin.
It is surmounted by the royal crown,
and the upper part of the mace has
four bas-reliefs depicting ceremonies
of the Order, after drawings
by Toussaint Dubreuil (kept in the
Cabinet des Dessins in the Louvre).
Below, in enamel, are the arms
of Henry III, king of France and
Poland. The rod is decorated with
fleurs-de-lys, flames, crosses of the
Order and crowned H ciphers.
The mace is evidence of the quality
of Parisian metalwork in the
16th century.

Renaissance, Flanders

256. Bernard van Orley (after)
The Month of September
seventh piece from the set
of **Maximilian's Hunts**
Brussels, c. 1528–1533

Tapestry, silk and wool, gold and silver thread.
7 warps per cm; H 4.48 m (176.4 in.);
W 5.58 m (219.7 in.)
Coll. of the French Crown. OA 7320

Woven in Brussels, the largest center of tapestry weaving in the 16th century, this piece belongs to a set of twelve tapestries depicting hunting scenes in the countryside around Brussels. The set is organized around the twelve months of the year; it has been attributed to Bernard van Orley, a Flemish painter who was prominent in tapestry design.
In all probability woven in the workshop of Jan Ghieteels, the set has been dated to sometime between 1528 (from the communal stamp which became obligatory that year) and 1533 (from the building progress on the old ducal palace in Brussels shown in the tapestry for the month of March). Called *Maximilian's Hunts* because of the supposed portrait of Maximilian I killing the wild boar in the tapestry for the month of December, the set belonged to Cardinal Mazarin and then to Louis XIV.

First Half of the 17th Century

French *objets d'art* from the first half of the 17th century are still not widely known. Yet the period was a productive one, perhaps thanks to Henry IV who encouraged artist-craftsmen by allotting them apartments in the Louvre itself. Contributions from abroad (Flemish weavers, and cabinetmakers from Flanders and Germany) favored the introduction and development of various techniques.

The Louvre collection takes account of all this activity. The various tapestry manufactories which were dotted around Paris, for example, are represented by hangings designed by Simon Vouet (no. 260), painter to Louis XIII. As for furniture, the traditional solid wood carving by Parisian and provincial furniture makers came up against a new, imported technique which was to revolutionize the history of furniture: that of veneered wood or cabinetmaking. Ceramics are represented by large items of tin-glazed earthenware from Nevers. While much fine French metalwork from the 17th century was melted down, we have an example in the golden coffer said to have belonged to Anne of Austria and in certain mounts in enameled gold, made for hard stone (*pietra dura*) vases. The new technique of painting on enamel was introduced in watchmaking, as examples from Blois clockmakers and enamelers show. Decoration in general, on tapestries, ebony cabinets, tin-glazed earthenware, and watches displays a similar contrast of modes; scenes of mythological, religious or literary derivation are framed by naturalistic images where flowers abound.

258. Ottavio Miseroni
d. 1624
Cup Belonging to Emperor Rudolph II
Prague, 1608

Bloodstone, silver-gilt. H 19 cm (7.5 in.);
W 57.5 cm (22.6 in.); D 33 cm (13 in.)
Coll. of the French Crown. Entered the Louvre in
1796. MR 143

The Louvre acquired, shortly after
the Revolution, the collection
of hard stone (*pietra dura*) vases
which Louis XIV had assembled
at Versailles. He began with the
purchase of almost the entire
collection of Cardinal Mazarin after
his death, which included this cup.
It had been made for Emperor
Rudolph II (1552–1612) and his
monogram is inscribed on it. In the
16th century, Milan was famous for
its *pietra dura* vases. It was from that
city in 1558 that Rudolph II invited
the engraver Ottavio Miseroni
to Prague to run a workshop.
This vase is typical of his style, both
in form and in the carved motifs.
It is one of the largest *pietra dura*
vases ever produced.

257. Barthélemy Prieur
1536–1611
Henry IV as Jupiter
Paris, c. 1608

Statuette, bronze, black lacquer and light brown
patina. H 67 cm (26.4 in.)
Acq. 1986. OA 11054

Barthélemy Prieur was one of the
greatest French sculptors at the end
of the 16th century and beginning
of the 17th. There are, sadly, very
few works remaining that can
be safely attributed to him (no. 315),
hence the importance of his signature
on the base of this statuette. The
portrayal of the king, which is typical
of the classicizing Renaissance,
is quite unique. Henry IV is shown
as a nude god. This bronze has
a pendant in the Louvre showing the
queen, Marie de Médicis, as Juno.

259. Cabinet in Two Stages
France, 1617
Walnut. H 2.54 m (100 in.); W 1.82 m (71.6 in.);
D 80 cm (31.5 in.)
Révoil coll. Acq. 1828. MRR 61

This cupboard is carved with
decorations of a striking exuberance
and virtuosity. Its form is typical
of French cabinets from the
Renaissance and the first half of the
17th century, divided into two
cupboards each with two doors.
As so often, the carved panels
of the doors derive from Flemish
engravings. Top left we see *Bellonius*
Leading His Troops and right, *The*
Victory of Wisdom over Ignorance,
after Barthélemy Spranger; below,
the reliefs are copies of two prints
from the series of Planets, after
Martin de Vos; to the left is *Mars*,
standing above *Virility Accompanied*
by Prudence. To the right is *Jupiter*,
placed above *Memory Leaning on his*
Still and Conversing with a Man Who
Symbolizes Old Age.

260. Simon Vouet (after)
Moses in the Bullrushes
Third piece from a set of tapestries
of **The Old Testament**
Paris, Louvre workshop, c. 1630

Tapestry, wool and silk, 7 to 8 warps per cm;
H 4.95 m (194.9 in.); W 5.88 m (231.5 in.)
Transferred from the Mobilier National, 1907.
OA 6086

In 1627 the painter Simon Vouet
was summoned home from Italy
by Louis XIII. The king immediately
commissioned him to design, among
other things, a set of eight tapestries
of scenes from the Old Testament
to adorn the walls of the Louvre

Palace. *Moses in the Bullrushes* was
one of two pieces woven in the
Louvre workshops, installed
by Henry IV under the Grande
Galerie, where the weavers Pierre
Dubout and Girard Laurent worked.
These workshops were the beginning
of the Gobelins manufactory, created
after 1662.

261. Cabinet
Paris, middle of the 17th century

Oak and poplar, ebony veneering, blackened fruit wood. H 1.85 m (72.8 in.); L 1.58 m (62.2 in.); D 56 cm (22 in.)
Transferred from the Mobilier National, 1900.
OA 6629

The Parisian cabinetmakers of the first half of the 17th century made predominantly one item of furniture, the cabinet, for which they elaborated a formula of their own. The upper stage contains a row of drawers under which two large doors open; the interior contains two rows of five drawers which surround two little doors that conceal a niche.

The separate base consists of a row of drawers with aprons beneath; these stand, at the front, on columns and caryatids; at the back they rest on columns, pilasters or paneling. The decoration of the ebony veneering is often framed by wavy mouldings. The Louvre cabinet, which is further enhanced by statuettes in ebony and, on the inside, by small ivory columns, belongs to one of the most elaborate styles of cabinet.

Louis XIV

Louis XIV used every aspect of the applied arts in his quest to make himself the most powerful monarch in Europe. His court at Versailles and the other royal palaces, with their furniture, paintings, silver and sculpture, was imitated by foreign monarchs all over Europe. The Royal Manufactory of the *Meubles de la Couronne* was founded in the Gobelins in 1667. It was here, under the guidance of Charles Le Brun, that the items of decoration required by the pomp of the royal residences were produced, including tapestries, furniture, metalwork (especially silver) and marble mosaics. The royal carpets were woven at the Savonnerie manufactory. In the Louvre, André-Charles Boulle dominated the cabinet-making of the period. Commissions from the sovereign were so abundant that, as under Napoleon, they determined the general style of the period: a combination of stylized foliate motifs and themes from the Graeco-Roman repertory. The Louvre houses some particularly spectacular examples of the activity of this period.

The Gobelins manufactory is represented by several tapestries woven after 16th century and contemporary cartoons as well as two tables in mosaic marbling bearing the royal arms. Louis XIV's silverware has disappeared, but a large silver mirror in the French style, made in Augsburg around 1700, gives us some idea of it. Huge carpets designed for the Louvre and the Tuileries display the art of the Savonnerie manufactory (no. 285). New types of furniture appeared and Boulle's technique is exhibited in numerous works of marquetry in brass and tortoiseshell, horn and pewter, that show the importance that bronze ornaments began to assume on furniture. Gilding was used to decorate furniture, one of the oldest gilt pieces being the pedestal table in the Louvre which passed from Fouquet to Louis XIV. The Louvre collections testify to the latter's qualities as a great collector; the larger part of his collection of Renaissance bronzes and hard stone (*pietra dura*) vases was assigned to the museum during the Revolution.

262. Vase
Italy, 16th century (stone); Paris, middle of the 17th century (mount)

Lapis-lazuli, silver-gilt, enameled gold. H 41.5 cm (16.3 in.); W 37.5 cm (14.8 in.); D 13.5 cm (5.3 in.) Coll. of the French Crown. Entered the Louvre in 1796. MR 262

The vase is made up of four sections in lapis: a particularly voluminous gadrooned body, a baluster in two sections and a base. The mounts of hard stone vases were often altered as fashions changed, as is true of this vase, which was not given its present mount until the mid-17th century in Paris. It is done in a style typical of the period, combining naturalism—in the sprays of flowers in enameled gold—and mythology, in the silver-gilt statuettes (Neptune and four Egyptian sphinxes), and in the enameled gold figures (head of a satyr, shark's mouth, and two grotesque masks). This vase was part of Louis XIV's collection before 1673, and later it adorned Marie-Antoinette's bedroom at Versailles.

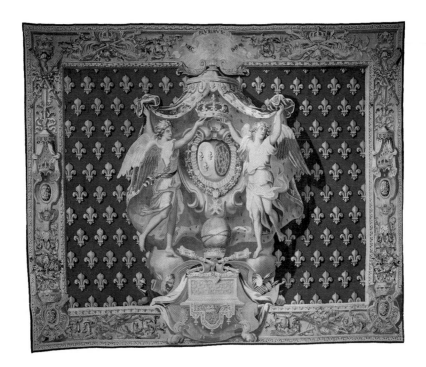

263. Chancellerie Tapestry with Louis Boucherat's Monogram
Beauvais, 1685

Tapestry, wool and silk. 8 to 9 warps per cm;
H 3.81 m (150 in.); W 4.40 m (173.2 in.)
Transferred from the Mobilier National, 1902.
OA 5703

The *Chancelleries* were tapestries
on blue backgrounds with fleurs-de-
lys, bearing the arms of the King
and the attributes of the Seal,
designed as a gift to the chancellor
of France. The Louvre *Chancellerie*
woven in Beauvais after a motif
by François Bonnemer for the middle
section, and by Jean Le Moyne
of Paris for the borders, was
purchased by the king in 1686 for

five thousand livres. It was given
to Louis Boucherat who was
chancellor of France from 1685 until
his death in 1699. His monogram
and the date of his appointment
can be seen in the middle of the lower
border. The Beauvais manufactory,
set up by Louis XIV's finance
minister Colbert in 1664, was
a private enterprise under the king's
protection.

264. Jules Romain (after)
The Arrival in Africa
First piece from a set of tapestries
depicting **The History of Scipio**
Paris, Gobelins manufactory,
1688–1689
Tapestry, wool and silk, 8 to 9 warps per cm;
H 4.50 m (177.2 in.); W 5.48 m (215.7 in.)
Transferred from the Mobilier National, 1901.
OA 5393

After 1683, the new superintendent
of buildings, Louvois, successor
to Colbert, kept the Gobelins low-
warp tapestry workshops active
by having them copy tapestries stored
in the Royal Furniture Repository
(Garde-Meuble Royal); this also
avoided commissioning new cartoons
which would have been too costly.
He selected masterpieces of 16th
century tapestry from Brussels. *The
History of Scipio*, after Jules Romain,
made for the Maréchal de Saint-
André in 1550, was copied in ten
pieces. *The Arrival in Africa* shows

the moment when Scipio first catches
sight of the coast where he will
disembark in pursuit of Hannibal,
whom he will vanquish at the battle
of Zama. The Gobelins copy perfectly
reproduces the delicate weaving
of the Renaissance original, and
shows the standard of excellence
achieved by the weavers of the royal
manufactory.

265. Carpet Bearing the Arms of France for the Grande Galerie at the Louvre

Paris, Savonnerie manufactory, c. 1670–1680

Wool 8.95 m (352.4 in.) x 5.10 m (200.8 in.)
Transferred from the Mobilier National, 1901.
OA 5432 bis A

Set up in a former soap factory in Chaillot during the reign of Louis XIII, the Savonnerie carpet manufactory flourished under Louis XIV. Following an order for 13 carpets for the Galerie d'Apollon in the Louvre, the manufactory received one for 93 further carpets to cover the floor of the Grande Galerie nearly 500 meters (1,640 feet) in length, as part of the king's refurbishment scheme. These carpets were woven in the workshops of the Lourdet and Dupont families between 1670 and 1689, following cartoons by François Francart, Baudoin Yvart and Jean Le Moyne, after Charles Le Brun.

They celebrate the themes of glory and royal virtues. The carpets were sadly never laid in place. Some went to royal residences and others served as diplomatic gifts.

266. André-Charles Boulle
1642–1732
Wardrobe
Paris, c. 1700

Made of oak and pine, with ebony, tortoiseshell, brass and pewter veneering, gilt bronze. H 2.65 m (104.3 in.); W 1.35 m (53.1 in.); D 54 cm (21.3 in.) Coll. of the French Crown. Transferred from the Mobilier National, 1870. OA 5441

Working in the Louvre from 1672 until his death, Boulle did not invent the marquetry technique which bears his name, but he was able make the best use of it. The technique comprised cutting a motif out of two superimposed, contrasting materials, one light and the other dark; the motif obtained from one is then inserted into the space left in the other. When the decoration is light on dark, it is called *en partie*; an example is the center of the wardrobe where brass arabesques are fitted in a tortoiseshell background. *En contrepartie* is the name for dark colors used on a light background, as round the edge of the doors here, where tortoiseshell scrolls wind over a brass background. Boulle applied this technique to magnificent furniture in original shapes of his own creation, richly ornamented in gilt bronze. The ebony veneering recalls furniture of the preceding period.

267. Table
Paris, beginning of the 18th century

Gilt walnut, portor marble. H 86 cm (33.9 in.); W 2.00 m (78.7 in.); D 87 cm (34.2 in.) Transferred from the Mobilier National, 1901. OA 5049

Gilt-wood furniture—especially tables and chairs—became more widespread during the second half of the 17th century. This table illustrates the ornamental style at the end of Louis XIV's reign. It bears the arms of the Malon de Bercy family (azure, three ducks, or, arranged two and one) under the crown of a marquis. The table comes from the Château de Bercy, east of Paris. In the early 18th century, when the table was made, the owner of the château, Charles-Henri de Malon de Bercy (1678–1742), superintendent of finances, son-in-law of the Contrôleur Général des Finances, Desmaretz, and great-nephew of Colbert, had major alterations made to the building under the direction of the architect Jacques de La Guêpière; the interior decoration was renovated in 1713–1714 by the team of wood carvers who worked for the Bâtiments du Roi (the royal administration of works).

Louis XV

With curved lines and asymmetry in decoration, and drawing inspiration
from nature (rocks, trelliswork, flowers), the Louis XV style, many elements
of which can be found in the last objects created for Louis XIV, enjoyed
universal and lasting success Ornamentalists (Meissonnier, Pineau, the Slodtz
family), artists (Boucher, Cressent), and *marchands merciers* (dealers in furniture
and works of art) like Hébert and Duvaux, encouraged by patrons such
as Madame de Pompadour, turned out an endless succession of new models
in every branch of the decorative arts.

After a brief eclipse at the start of Louis XV's reign, marquetry came back
into fashion when cabinetmakers worked not only in wood and bronze but
in lacquer and porcelain. Gilt bronze was used for a wide range of purposes
and Parisian goldsmiths were employed by every court in Europe. Jewelers
decorated their snuff-boxes and watches with polychrome materials from
enamel and tortoiseshell to porcelain and hard stone (*pietra dura*). Although
high-temperature kiln firing (*grand feu*) of faience reached a peak of perfection
at Rouen and Moustiers, it declined after the middle of the century when
a technique of muffled kiln firing (*petit feu*) was perfected at Strasbourg and
Marseilles enabling a wider range of colors to be used. Meanwhile, the
manufactory at Vincennes produced outstanding examples in the new
technique of porcelain before moving to Sèvres in 1756.

However, in time, certain connoisseurs (Caylus, Marigny) and architects
(Blondel, Soufflot) grew tired of the rococo style (style rocaille). This current
of opposition became increasingly active after 1760, and led to the Greek
or Transition style, which derived both from classical models and the art of the
Louis XIV period. Forms became rectilinear and architectural, while
decoration, drawing on archaeological finds, made use of pilasters, Greek
borders, vases, marks, scrolls and laurel wreaths. Furniture made by Leleu
(no. 281) for the prince of Condé is a perfect illustration of this reaction,
which gave rise to the Louis XVI style.

268 The Regent

Diamond, 140.64 metric carats.
Diamond collection of the French Crown. MV 1017

Although it is now surpassed
in weight by other famous diamonds,
the exceptional luster and perfect cut
of the Regent give it an uncontestable
reputation as the most beautiful
diamond in the world. Discovered
in India in 1698, it was acquired
by Thomas Pitt, Governor of Madras,
who sent it to England where it was
cut. In 1717 the Regent purchased
it from Pitt for the French Crown.
It first adorned the band
of Louis XV's silver-gilt crown (now
in the Louvre) at his coronation
in 1722, going then to Louis XVI's
crown in 1775. Later in 1801
it figured on the hilt of the First
Consul's sword (Fontainebleau,
Musée Napoléon Ier), and then
on the emperor's two-edged sword
in 1812. In 1825 it was worn on the
crown at the coronation of Charles X,
and during the Second Empire
it embellished the "Grecian diadem"
of the Empress Eugénie.

269. Daniel Govaers or Gouers
1717–before 1754
Snuff-Box
Paris, 1725–1726

Enameled gold, gold-inlaid tortoiseshell, miniatures,
diamonds. H 3 cm (1.2 in.); W 8.5 cm (3.3 in.);
D 6.5 cm (2.6 in.)
Anonymous gift, 1978. OA 10670

From the time of Louis XV, French
sovereigns would make gifts,
particularly to foreign diplomats,
in the form of boxes decorated
with their portraits and adorned with
precious stones. Daniel Govaers
supplier to Louis XV, made this
snuff-box, the oldest in the Louvre's
considerable collection.
On 3 February 1726 it was given
by the king to Baron Cornelis Hop,
the Dutch ambassador (1685–1762).
The top and bottom are in tortoiseshell inlaid with gold, the sides
in enameled gold. Inside the lid are
two miniatures attributed to Jean-
Baptiste Massé, after Jean-Baptiste
Van Loo, portraying the young
Louis XV and Queen Maria
Leczinska, married in 1725.

270. Henri-Nicolas Cousinet
died c. 1768
**Chocolate-Pot on Lamp Stand:
Set Made for Queen Maria Leczinska**
Paris, 1729–1730

Silver-gilt, ebony. Chocolate-pot: H 19.4 cm (7.6 in.);
stand: 12 cm (4.7 in.); lamp: H 4.5 cm (1.8 in.)
Gift of the Société des Amis du Louvre with the
support of Mr. Stavros S. Niarchos, 1955. AO 9598

The pot, which originally bore the
arms of Queen Maria Leczinska
(now effaced), was probably made
when the Dauphin (her son, and
heir to the throne) was born, after
three older sisters, in 1729. Marine
motifs alluding to the Dauphin
(literally dolphin) appear on the pot
and stand. They also bear witness

to the arrival of the rococo style
in royal commissions with reeds,
flowers, waves, shells, asymmetrical
cartouches and clasps. The chasing
on these motifs is eloquent testimony
to the quality of Parisian silversmiths,
and in particular to the skill
of Cousinet, who later earned the title
of Sculptor to the prince of Condé.

271. Winter
Rouen, c. 1740

Tin-glazed earthenware with "grand feu" decoration. H 2.09 m (82.3 in.); W 60 cm (23.6 in.) Acq. 1882. OA 2611

This bust is one of a set, illustrating the four seasons. A statue of Apollo, now in the Victoria and Albert Museum in London, originally completed the ensemble. Although there is no signature, this sculptural bust can be attributed to Nicolas Fouquay's manufactory at Rouen. The decoration is much akin to examples signed by the painter Pierre Chapelle.

272. Charles Cressent
1685–1768
Wall-Clock: Love Conquering Time
Paris, c. 1740

Gilt bronze, brass and tortoiseshell marquetry.
H 1.40 m (55.1 in.); W 50 cm (19.7 in.)
Coll. of the French Crown. Transferred from the
Cour de Cassation, 1953. OA 9586

Cressent, who was a cabinetmaker
by trade though he trained
as a sculptor, is celebrated for the
quality of the bronze mounts on his
furniture. He created the models
and supervised their execution.

Their quality is especially impressive
on this wall-clock, where the
cabinetwork is limited to side panels
finished in Boulle marquetry. The
dial and mechanism are by Nicolas
Gourdain, who was received
as a master clockmaker in Paris
in 1724 and died in 1753. A cupid
dominates the composition, the
asymmetry of which is typical
of the rococo style. Cressent was
obliged to sell up three times, and
included a wall-clock of this type
in his 1749 auction sale.

273. Wall-Clock
Strasbourg, Paul Hannong
manufactory, c. 1750

Tin-glazed earthenware with "petit feu" decoration.
H 1.12 m (44.1 in.); W 45 cm (17.7 in.)
Gift of Count Isaac de Camondo, 1911. OA 6568

Around the middle of the
18th century, growing competition
from porcelain manufacturers forced
potters to develop new techniques.
The use of decoration *au petit feu*,
in which successive layers of various
metal oxides were fired at a low
temperature onto fired enamel

greatly extended the range of available
colors. This clock comes from Paul
Hannong's factory at Strasbourg.
It is an example of the *petit feu*
process at its best, combined with
a form of great complexity, possibly
inspired from a model by the
Parisian cabinetmaker Charles
Cressent (no. 272).

274. Jacques Dubois
c. 1693–1763
Desk
Paris, mid-18th century

Oak, pine and fruit wood, oriental lacquer, black
French lacquer, gilt bronze, leather. H 81 cm
(31.9 in.); W 1.87 m (73.6 in.); D 1.02 m (40.2 in.)
Château du Raincy. Seized during French
Revolution. Transferred from the Ministry
of Justice, 1907. OA 6083

Before the Revolution this desk was
in the Château du Raincy which
belonged to the duke of Orleans.
It bears the stamp of Jacques Dubois,
a Parisian cabinet maker. Alongside
its standard production, this workshop turned out some of the most
luxurious examples of 18th century
furniture. This desk reflects the taste
for lacquered furniture at its best.
The great Parisian *marchands
merciers* were responsible for this,
having, during the 1730s, conceived
the idea of producing furniture
adorned with lacquered panels taken
from objects imported from the Far
East (chests, cabinets, screens).
The skirting around this desk
is decorated with lacquer paintings
of landscapes; the framing and feet
are in black lacquer.

276. François-Thomas Germain
1726–1791
Fire-Dog
Paris, 1757

Gilt bronze. H 59 cm (23.2 in.); W 60 cm (23.6 in.);
D 45 cm (17.7 in.)
Acq. 1935. OA 8278

275. Naiad
Vincennes, Royal Porcelain
Manufactory, 1756

Soft-paste porcelain, gilt bronze. H 26 cm (10.2 in.)
Mme Adolphe Thiers bequest, 1880. TH 693

This naiad, more familiarly known
by its 19th century name *La Source*
(*The Spring*), was undoubtedly the
most important figure produced
at the Royal Porcelain Manufactory
at Vincennes. It is dated 1756, the
same year the manufactory moved
to Sèvres. Its modeler is unknown,
but the fine painted decoration
is by C.-N. Dodin, one of the most
prolific artists in the manufactory.
The *marchand mercier* Lazare
Duvaux purchased it in 1757 and
sold it to his colleague Hébert.
The latter most probably added the
extraordinary bronze mounting.

This fire-dog is signed in full by the
goldsmith François-Thomas
Germain who, on the death of his
father in 1748, took over both
Thomas Germain's title as sculptor-
goldsmith to the king and his
Louvre lodgings. This freed him
from guild regulations, and allowed
him to extend the scope of his craft.
He produced several major
gilt-bronze ensembles, including the
fireplace in the Bernstorff Palace
in Copenhagen (1756), the wall-
lights now in the Getty Museum
(1756) and this fire-dog. The scrollwork is rococo, but the pan, tripod
and its drapery are early signs
of what came to be called at that
period the "Greek" style, the first
phase of neoclassicism.

277. François-Thomas Germain
1726–1791
**Dish Cover Belonging to Joseph I
of Portugal**
Paris, 1758

Silver, cast and chased. H 47.5 cm (18.7 in.);
W 57.3 cm (22.6 in.); D 53.6 cm (21.1 in.)
Acq. 1983. OA 10923

Germain made silverware
for Louis XV and for a number
of foreign monarchs, such as Joseph I
of Portugal (1714–1777) for whom
he made several dinner services, one
of which included this dish cover,
between 1756 and 1765.
With a brilliantly executed genre
scene resting on a fluted base,
adorned with naturalistically
modeled fauna it is as much a work
of sculpture as a piece of decorative
silver. In the 19th century, some
of the gold and silverware belonging
to the Portuguese court went
to Emperor Pedro I of Brazil, who
had his monogram engraved on this
article.

278. Edme-Pierre Balzac
1705–after 1781
Wine Cooler from a Service Belonging to the Duke of Penthièvre
Paris, 1759–1760

Silver, cast and chased. H 24.5 cm (9.6 in.);
Ø 23.5 cm (9.2 in.); W 28.5 cm (11.2 in.)
Acq. 1987. OA 11117

This wine cooler (one of a pair) was part of a famous table service, eight items of which are in the Louvre. It belonged to Louis-Jean-Marie de Bourbon, duke of Penthièvre (1725–1793), grandson of Louis XIV and marchioness of Montespan. In the 19th century it passed to his grandson, the duke of Orleans and future king, Louis-Philippe (1773–1850), who added his coat-of-arms to each piece. The service consists of two parts made at different times. The earlier part was made by Thomas Germain around 1730. The second part made in the rococo style to match, is the work of two other great silversmiths, Edme-Pierre Balzac and Antoine-Sébastien Durand.

279. Pot-Pourri Vase and Cover Belonging to Mme de Pompadour
Sèvres, Royal Porcelain Manufactory, 1760

Soft-paste porcelain. H 37 cm (14.6 in.);
W 35 cm (13.8 in.)
Acq. 1984. OA 10965

The form of this pot-pourri recalls the gold vases that decorated royal tables. The design is by J.-C. Duplessis, a goldsmith responsible for models at the Sèvres manufactory. The delicate pink ground surrounds a palm-fringed cartouche within which C.-N. Dodin painted a *chinoiserie* scene. Purchased by Mme de Pompadour in 1760, this *pot-pourri* was found on her bedroom mantelpiece in her Parisian hôtel (town house)—the present Elysée Palace—at her death in 1764.

280. François Boucher (after)
Eros and Psyche
Paris, Gobelins manufactory, c. 1770

Tapestry, wool and silk, 10 to 11 warps per cm;
H 4.25 m (167.3 in.); W 3.80 m (149.6 in.)
Palais Bourbon, fourth piece of an alcove set from
the bedroom of the duchess of Bourbon.
Coll. of the French Crown, 1825. Transferred from
the Mobilier National, 1901. OA 5118

This tapestry belongs to a set of four, celebrating the *Loves of the Gods*, woven in Jacques Neilson's workshop at the Gobelins. François Boucher was artistic director of the Gobelins manufactory, supervising work there from 1755 until his death in 1770. It was he who made the sketches for the central scenes which simulate paintings hanging on a wall. The crimson surround follows designs by Maurice Jacques. These two artists collaborated on numerous tapestries on the theme of the Loves of the Gods—considered the most successful and spectacular of productions from the Royal Manufactory.

281. Jean-François Leleu
1729–1807
Commode Belonging to the Prince of Condé
Paris, 1772

Oak, purplewood veneering, marquetry in various woods, gilt bronze, red brecciated marble.
H 88 cm (34.6 in.); W 1.17 m (46.1 in.);
D 56 cm (22 in.)
Acq. 1953. OA 9589

Louis-Joseph de Bourbon, prince of Condé (1736–1818), purchased the Palais Bourbon in 1764 and subsequently entrusted its decoration to innovative architects. From 1772 to 1776 many items of cabinetwork were ordered from Leleu (some now in the Wallace Collection, London and the Petit Trianon), this commode among them, which was delivered in 1772 and installed in the prince's bedroom. With its architectural appearance and Graeco-Roman bronze decoration, it is typical of the "Greek" style which came into vogue in the 1760s. The remarkable marquetry is a reminder that Leleu worked under the great master of marquetry Jean-François Oeben who had been apprenticed to the youngest son of André-Charles Boulle at the Louvre.

Louis XVI

Under Louis XVI, there was an ever-increasing interest in interior decoration, furniture and the decorative arts, especially from the middle classes. The quality of workmanship improved and new ideas were plentiful. Architects and ornamentalists (Gondoin, Belanger, Dugourc) supplied patrons with highly imaginative designs which were realized by luxury traders (*marchands merciers*) like Poirier, Daguerre or the Darnault brothers, by cabinetmakers like Riesener and Carlin, and metal-founders like Gouthière and Thomire. Forms were more graceful than during the Greek-style period, and decoration combined classical motifs, scrollwork and "arabesques" with more figurative themes, flowers and trophies. Some objects inspired by a Turkish or Chinese style were naively exotic in appearance. Fabrics and trimmings became so important that they provided inspiration for subjects in other forms. Materials increased in variety. While Boulle marquetry came back into fashion, it was not unusual to find furniture veneered in mother of pearl, marble mosaic or made almost entirely out of metal like the Weisweiler table (no. 284). Mahogany (from the Americas) became more widely used. New techniques took over in ceramics: hard-paste porcelain and creamware. The Louvre ensembles, such as the vases belonging to the duke of Aumont, Bellevue's lacquered furniture, the furniture by Riesener for Marie-Antoinette in the Tuileries, the Jacob and Sené chairs designed for the Château de Saint-Cloud are typical of developments in progress on the eve of the French Revolution.

282. Robert-Joseph Auguste
1723–1805
**Service Belonging to George III
of England**
Paris, 1776–1785

Silver, cast and chased.
Acq. 1976. OA 10602–10624

R.-J. Auguste made numerous items,
many since lost, for the French court
under Louis XVI. However, like
other Paris silversmiths, he undertook
commissions for many of the foreign
courts. This selection comprising
some 23 pieces is only a small portion
of a service engraved with the
monogram of George III of England
and Hanover (1738–1820) which was
commissioned for use at the
Hanover court. It was subsequently
augmented by German silversmiths
copying the same motifs. The service
offers a sampling of the different
types of table objects to be found
in the 18th century: tureens, cloches,
dishes, wine glass coolers (monteiths),
cruet stands, mustard pots and
candelabra.

283. Georges Jacob
1739–1814
Armchair
Paris, 1777

Gilt walnut. H 94 cm (37 in.); W 70 cm (27.6 in.);
D 76 cm (29.9 in.)
Baroness Gourgaud bequest, 1965. OA 9987

Under Louis XVI, the fashion for
"Turkish Rooms" which conjured
up an imaginary Orient owed much
to the Count of Artois, brother
of Louis XVI and future Charles X
(1757–1836). In his priory-house
of Le Temple in Paris, he had
a "Turkish Room" fitted out for him
by the architect Etienne-Louis
Boullée in 1776–1777. The imagina-
tively designed chairs, one of the
first sets made by Jacob for the royal
family, include two "ottomans," two
armchairs—one shown here—and
four chairs which were originally
painted white and covered with
a lampas (a flowered silk) in yellow,
white and gray. The daring line
of this furniture prefigures that
of chairs from the Empire period.

284. Adam Weisweiler
1744–1784
**Writing Table Belonging to Queen
Marie-Antoinette**
Paris, 1784

Oak, ebony veneering, lacquer, mother of pearl,
steel, gilt bronze. H 82 cm (32.3 in.);
W 47 cm (18.5 in.); D 44 cm (17.3 in.)
Coll. of the French Crown. Transferred from the
Mobilier National, 1901. OA 5509

The famous *marchand mercier*
(supplier of luxury goods) on the rue
Saint-Honoré, Dominique Daguerre,
delivered this writing table to the
Garde-Meuble (royal furniture
repository) in 1784. It bears the mark
of Weisweiler the cabinetmaker who
became master craftsman in 1778.

On the outside, cabinetwork plays
only a minor part in a table which
is very modern for its use of steel for
its skirting and bronze feet. The top
surface is made up of three lacquered
panels; the central panel can be raised
like a sloping desk top.
But Weisweiler's artistry is most
obvious in the style of the interlacing
stretcher and in the refined
decoration on the drawers, veneered
on the inside with a lozenge mosaic.
In 1789, the table was in Marie-
Antoinette's inner room in the
Château de Saint-Cloud.

285. Charles Ouizille
1744–1830
**Incense Burner Belonging to Queen
Marie-Antoinette**
Paris, 1784–1785

Gold, agate, bloodstone, miniatures. H 27.5 cm
(10.8 in.); W 12 cm (4.7 in.); D 9.2 cm (3.6 in.)
Acq. 1982. OA 10907

This agate incense-burner stands
on a square base made of bloodstone,
decorated with four cameo-like
miniatures by the painter Jacques-
Joseph De Gault. The gold mount
is from Ouizille the jeweller,
purveyor to Queen Marie-Antoinette.
This exceptionally refined piece
is evidence of the queen's love
of precious stones; it belonged to her
personal collection of *objets d'arts*
at Versailles. When she left the
château in October 1789, she
entrusted them to the *marchand
mercier* Dominique Daguerre who
kept them until her death.

286. Georges Jacob
1739–1814
**Armchair from the Games Room
at the Château de Saint-Cloud**
Paris, 1787–1788

Gilt walnut. H 1.01 m (39.8 in.); W 75 cm (29.5 in.);
D 64 cm (25.2 in.)
Acq. 1948. OA 9449

In 1785 the duke of Orleans sold
the Château de Saint-Cloud
to Louis XVI. Sumptuous furniture
was produced to decorate it during
the last years of the ancien régime,
and Jacob supplied the furniture for
the games room. Though now
dispersed, it comprised 2 sofas,
2 *bergères*, 22 armchairs, 16 of which
were *meublants, à la Reine* (i.e., with
straight backs, like the one shown,
of which the Louvre possesses 2) and
6 *courants, en cabriolet* (with curved
backs). There were in addition
24 chairs, 6 *voyeuses*, 4 stools, a fire-
screen and a folding screen. The set
was covered with a silk by Pernon,
the Lyons maker. It was decorated
with a rose-tree motif, the design for
which has survived; this has enabled
new covers to be woven for the
Louvre ensemble so they regain their
original appearance.

Empire

Under the Empire (1804–1815), the luxury industries benefited from the stability and prosperity of the regime, and in particular from the support which Napoleon lavished on them, with orders, purchases, and the organization of exhibitions displaying their products. A remarkably coherent style spread throughout the Empire.

The Louvre collection brings together furniture from various imperial residences. They are typical of the dominant style, which was imposing and rather severe; made in gilt wood or mahogany, along rigid lines, they are embellished with very high quality bronzes. Many were made by Georges Jacob's son, Jacob-Desmalter, an abundant supplier to the Mobilier Impérial (imperial furniture repository). Collaborating with him at times was the bronze-worker Pierre-Philippe Thomire, who was also one of the principal purveyors to Napoleon I.

Reviving the sumptuous tradition and court ceremony of the ancien régime, the emperor commissioned splendid services in porcelain and precious metals. The Louvre exhibits a representative cross-section of pieces by Martin-Guillaume Biennais (1764–1843), private goldsmith to the emperor. Aiming both for prestige and promotion of the national industry, the Sèvres manufactory produced items designed for use at court or as official presents.

287. François-Honoré-Georges Jacob-Desmalter
1770–1841
Jewel Cabinet Belonging to the Empress Josephine
Paris, 1809
Oak, exotic yew and purplewood veneering, mother-of-pearl, gilt bronze. H 2.75 m (108.3 in.); W 2.00 m (78.7 in.); D 60 cm (23.6 in.)
On loan from the Musée National du Château de Fontainebleau, 1964. OA 10246.

In 1809, Jacob-Desmalter, principal supplier to the Mobilier Impérial, delivered his most precious order, the jewel cabinet designed for the Empress Joséphine's great bedroom at the Tuileries (and soon to be used by Marie-Louise). This impressive piece of furniture which was designed by the architect Charles Percier is embellished with luxuriant bronze ornaments: the central panel depicts the *Birth of the Queen of the Earth to Whom Cupids and Goddesses Hasten with Their Offerings* by P.-P. Thomire, after a sculpture by Chaudet. Jacob-Desmalter must have completed the "great jewellery box" in 1812, accompanying it with two smaller items of furniture in the same style but using indigenous woods.

288. Martin-Guillaume Biennais
1764–1843
**Part of a Tea Service Made
for Napoleon I**
Paris, 1809–1810

Silver-gilt. Tea urn: H 80 cm (31.5 in.);
W 45 cm (17.7 in.); teapot: H 18 cm (7.1 in.);
W 32 cm (12.6 in.); tea-caddy: H 14.5 cm (5.7 in.);
W 15.5 cm (6.1 in.); milk jug: H 27 cm (10.6 in.);
Ø 11 cm (4.3 in.)
Gift of the Société des Amis du Louvre, 1952.
OA 9537 (2, 4, 5)

Shortly after his marriage to Marie-
Louise of Austria in 1810,
Napoleon I ordered an opulent
28-piece tea and coffee set from his
silversmith Biennais. Half the set
is now on show in the Louvre.
The forms and decoration (the latter
supplied by Percier the architect) are
classical in inspiration, with
an "Etruscan" form for the teapot,
palm fringes and water leaves,
winged figures and a reproduction
of an Augustan frieze, the
Aldobrandine Nuptials, on the

tea-caddy. The style is typical
of Biennais's prolific and remarkably
consistent production: the ovoid
form of the milk-jug, and wide rims
with motifs chased on a matted
ground.

289. Fuseau Vase Belonging to Madame Mère
Sèvres, Imperial Porcelain Manufactory, 1811
Hard-paste porcelain and gilt bronze. H 1.07 m (42.1 in.); W 36 cm (14.2 in.); Ø 33 cm (13 in.)
Gift of Mme Maria Teresa Castro de Polo, 1986. OA 11056

The baptism of the king of Rome on 10 June 1811 gave the emperor the opportunity of offering a large number of gifts in Sèvres porcelain. The spectacular vase in the Louvre was destined for Madame Mère, grandmother and godmother of the new-born. Standing out against the precious tortoiseshell ground is the portrait of the emperor crossing Mont-Saint-Bernard painted by J. Georget, after the famous painting by David.

Restoration

The accession of Louis XVIII (1815–1824) did not bring about any marked change in the development of the decorative arts. The king, who was economically minded, settled into Napoleon's quarters, content merely to do away with the symbols of empire. The court was quite austere, and only the duchess of Berry provided any real patronage. Charles X (1824–1830) proved more demanding; he commissioned a ceremonial bed in gilt and carved wood from Brion. In the Louvre collection the period is represented in the main by porcelain and bronzes. Biscuit-ware (unglazed porcelain), in the 18th century tradition, was used for numerous statues and busts of members of the royal family. Painted motifs, in the style of miniatures, had great success on Sèvres and Paris porcelain.

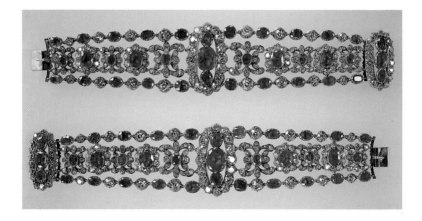

290. Paul-Nicolas Menière
1745–1826
Evrard Bapst
1771–1842
**Pair of Bracelets Belonging
to the Duchess of Angoulême**
Paris, 1816

Gold, rubies, diamonds. L 18 cm (7.1 in.);
17.6 cm (6.9 in.)
Claude Menier bequest, 1974. OA 10576

This pair of bracelets is part of a jewelry set which included a diadem, a necklace, a comb, earrings, a belt and three clasps. The rubies and diamonds came from an adornment made in 1811 by the firm of Nitot for the Empress Marie-Louise. On his accession, Louis XVIII had the imperial jewels dismantled and brought up to date. In 1816, following designs by his son-in-law Evrard Bapst Menière reset Marie-Louise's rubies and diamonds for the duchess of Angoulême. The duchess of Berry and the Empress Eugénie also wore this ensemble.

291. Casket for the King's Snuff-Box

Sèvres, Royal Porcelain Manufactory, 1819

Hard-paste porcelain, silver-gilt. H 20 cm (7.9 in.); W 35 cm (13.8 in.); D 25 cm (9.8 in.)
From the Musée des Souverains. MS 214

This casket was designed to contain Louis XVIII's snuff-box and a variety of small oval plaques in porcelain that could be fitted onto the inside of the snuff-box lid as disired. The painter Béranger is responsible for the spectacular imitation cameo painting which decorates the top. According to the catalogue entry for the 1820 exhibition of products from the royal manufactories where this casket was displayed, the painting depicts "Cybele (earth), Vulcan (fire) and Pluto (metals) offering to Painting the means and materials to practice its art on porcelain and to render the results permanent." This iconography reflects the theories of A. Brongniart, the director of the manufactory, who saw the transfer of easel paintings onto porcelain as a means of preserving their original colors.

Louis-Philippe

The reign of Louis-Philippe (1830–1848) was a period of diversification and renewal in the decorative arts. A return to previous styles led to a wide range of new sources of inspiration: neo-Gothic, neo-Renaissance, neo-Louis XV. Such eclecticism affected techniques in every domain. Ornamentalists such as Chenavard or Liénard, sculptors such as Feuchère, goldsmiths like Froment-Meurice played a leading role here. Sculptors were of particular importance, creating the taste for three-dimensional figurines and modeling. The return to the past brought about the revival of some neglected techniques such as niello, enamel and metal *repoussé* work.

292. Chinese Openwork Breakfast Set Belonging to Queen Marie-Amélie
Sèvres, Royal Porcelain Manufactory, 1840

Hard-paste porcelain, H 29.5 cm (11.6 in.); Ø 50 cm (19.7 in.)
Gift of M. and Mme Jean-Marie Rossi, 1987.
OA 11098–11111

The taste for exoticism which was widespread under Louis-Philippe is clear from this breakfast set, which is a free interpretation of Chinese models, adapted for Western purposes. One of the most remarkable aspects of this borrowing from China is the openwork with a double wall, where the outer wall is pierced to let in the light. The first complete Chinese openwork breakfast set, i.e., incorporating a tray, was shown in the exhibition of products from the royal manufactories in 1835. Queen Marie-Amélie seems to have been very taken with this type of breakfast set since she placed several orders for it. The set in the Louvre was presented to her on March 1, 1840.

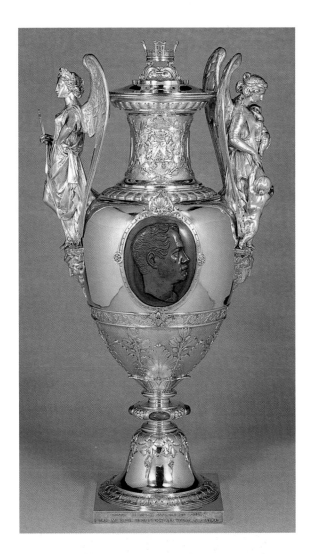

293. François-Désiré Froment-Meurice
1802–1855
Feuchères Vase
Paris, 1843

Silver-gilt, malachite. H 0.60 m (23.6 in.)
Gift of the baroness of Feuchères, 1891. OA 3253

In 1843 the city of Paris commissioned two large vases in silver-gilt from its master silversmith Froment-Meurice. The vase shown was presented to the general, baron of Feuchères, as a token of thanks for his generous gift to the civic hospices of Paris. The vase, an official commission,

is neoclassical in spirit, unlike the *Coupe des Vendanges*, exhibited alongside it at the 1844 exhibition. The contrast reveals the eclecticism of Froment-Meurice. Two figurines in finely chased cast silver—the spirit of War and Charity—serve as handles. A malachite medallion by the sculptor James Pradier, showing the baron in profile, decorates the belly of the vase.

Napoleon III's Apartments

Under the Second Empire the rooms now known as Napoleon III's Apartments were fitted out as reception rooms for the minister of state in the wing designed to join the palaces of the Louvre and the Tuileries together. The architect Hector Lefuel (1810–1882) who had succeeded Visconti in working on the building of the new wing, designed the interior of the rooms under Achille Fould's watchful supervision. Major building works began in 1857 and the decoration was only completed in 1861. Louis XIV in style, the interior decoration is opulent: painted ceilings, decorative paintwork (in imitation Boulle marquetry in the two dining rooms), decor sculpted with cupids, trophies, garlands, and gilding almost to excess. Maréchal the Younger painted the pictures in the Grand Salon. The four vaults illustrate stages in the building of the Louvre under Francis I, Catherine de' Medici, Henry IV and Louis XIV; the ceiling is the crowning achievement of this group with an allegorical representation of Napoleon III and Eugénie joining the Louvre and the Tuileries together. The ceiling exults in the glory of the emperor, with pennons highlighting his military, economic and social deeds. These apartments have the rare privilege of having kept their original furniture—also in Louis XIV style—in perfect harmony with the surroundings: in walnut for the great antechamber, in darkened wood for the dining rooms and in gilt wood for the other rooms. After the Commune the rooms were assigned to the Ministry of Finance.

The entrance gallery

The Grand Salon

The small dining room

Sculpture

Romanesque France

Gothic France

Renaissance France

17th Century France

18th Century France

France in the First Half of the 19th Century

Italy

Germanic Countries

Low Countries

Introduction

When the Museum first opened, the only two examples of "modern" sculpture were Michelangelo's *Slaves* (no. 350) in the Galerie d'Apollon. Not until 1824 did the Galerie d'Angoulême, on the ground floor of the Cour Carrée, exhibit sculptures from the Renaissance to the contemporary period. The collections were inherited from the royal palaces, the French Academy of Painting and Sculpture and the Musée des Monuments Français (Museum of French Monuments) set up under the Revolution by Alexandre Lenoir.

From the palaces, the Louvre received what remained of park statuary, such as that at Marly, and collections of bronzes. From the Academy it acquired the wonderful series of *morceaux de réception* (masterpieces presented by artists in support of their application to become academicians), which give us a complete picture of the evolution of French sculpture from Louis XIV to the Revolution. Finally, from the Monuments Français, came statues and, in particular, monumental tomb sculpture which had been saved from churches and squares during the revolutionary upheavals.

Gradually, the rooms took shape. Commissions from artists in the early 19th century provided the basis for the neoclassical and romantic collections. While the Musée du Luxembourg exhibited the work of living sculptors, this work was usually earmarked for the Louvre after their death. But the first medieval statue was not acquired until 1850 and the first Italian work (door of the Stanga Palace) arrived in 1876. In 1871 the Department of Sculpture became entirely independent of the Department of Decorative Arts.

Generous donations from Campana, Davillier, Piot, Arconati-Visconti, Schlichting and Zoubaloff swelled the sculpture collection. In addition the department had an active acquisitions policy, and it also received works on loan from major institutions such as the Château de Versailles, Monuments Historiques and the École des Beaux-Arts. The move to the Pavillon des États in 1932 enabled works from the Middle Ages to the 17th century to be exhibited. But not until 1969 and 1971 could the majority of works (over a thousand) be displayed with the refurbishment of the Pavillon de Flore. In November 1993, French sculpture was moved to the new Richelieu Wing and a totally new display was set up. Around two glass-covered courtyards housing the grand open-air statuary there is a chronological itinerary going from the 7th century to 1850. Italian sculpture has been exhibited since October 1994 in the Mollien Wing (reached through the Pavillon Denon) in two large galleries on the mezzanine and ground floors. The works by North European sculptors (The Netherlands, Germany and England) are shown in the same wing around the corner from the Italian section.

Romanesque France

The French sculpture display begins with several examples of Merovingian art, but it is the panorama of work from the various Romanesque workshops that dominates the first two rooms. A major revival in sculpture followed a general cultural rebirth. This coincided with the emergence of royal power, feudal reorganization, and religious fervor following the Gregorian reform, along with the growth of trade networks, the bringing of land into cultivation, the establishment of new villages, and with communal organization. The religious revival was under the protection of authority as can be seen in the reconstruction and embellishment of the great abbeys and pilgrimage shrines; Conques, Autun, Vézelay, Toulouse, Saint-Gilles. The influence of workshops spread widely from these centers to priories and parishes. Romanesque sculpture, essentially religious in nature, is on the whole architectural in function. Vast historiated tympanums welcomed the pilgrim; naves and cloisters were decorated with capitals and reliefs. Isolated statues are, in contrast, rare, having been made of precious materials or polychromed woods that have seldom survived the passage of time. Unable to match the great centers of Romanesque art, the Department of Sculpture provides us with a quick survey.

294. Daniel in the Lions' Den
Paris, 6th and end of the 11th century

Marble capital. H 49,5 cm (19.5 in.);
W 53,4 cm (21 in.); D 51 cm (20,1 in.)
Church St. Genevieve, Paris. Entered the Louvre
in 1881. RF 457

This capital testifies to a long period of Parisian history. On the reverse are acanthus leaves from a Corinthian capital, carved for the Basilica of the Holy Apostles, founded by Clovis and Clotilde after the victory at Vouillé (507). After this church was destroyed, this capital was re-used in the new church dedicated to St. Genevieve at the time of its reconstruction, which coincided with the spread of Romanesque art. The architectonic structure of the capital is much in evidence, emphasized by the volutes at the corners of the corbel. The composition, showing the prophet Daniel seated meditatively between two lions, follows a compositional canon with his head framed beneath the central rosette, and the lions' heads under the volutes. The linearity of the folds and curled manes is juxtaposed with the skillfully rendered volumes of the main figure who stands out boldly from the concave ground.

295. Descent from the Cross

Burgundy, second quarter of the 12th century

Statue in wood with traces of gilding and polychromy. H 1.55 m (61 in.); W 1.68 m (66.1 in.); D 30 cm (11.8 in.)

Gift of Louis Courajod, 1895. RF 1082

Romanesque polychromed woodcarving is rare in France. But by comparing it with examples in Catalonia and Italy, one may assume that this dead Christ, with his right hand unnailed from the cross, figured in a Descent from the Cross surrounded by a sizeable group of figures. The style is typical of Burgundian Romanesque art. While the face recalls the Christ in Judgement on the Vézelay tympanum, the markedly linear folds are close to sculptures in Saint-Lazare d'Autun. The belt is remarkably complex, knotted at the top of the *perizonium* (loin-cloth). Note the fine pleating which falls in a pattern of concentric semicircles over the legs to increase the sense of volume outlining the knees.

296. Virgin and Child
Auvergne, second half of the
12th century

Reliquary statue, woodcarving with traces
of polychromy. H 84 cm (33.1 in.);
W 27 cm (10.6 in.); D 36 cm (14,2 in.)
Acq. 1894. RF 987

As Romanesque art developed,
a popular theme proved to be the
Virgin in majesty, seated on a throne
and holding the Christ-Child on her
knees. Assimilated to the throne
of the new Solomon, she represents
the throne of divine wisdom (*Sedes*
Sapientae). Some examples were made
of precious materials, such as one,
since destroyed, from Clermont
cathedral. Most of the free-standing
Virgins in majesty that have been
preserved, are carved and painted
in lifelike colors. Similar hieratic
images with frontal poses can be seen
on the tympanums of the earliest
Gothic portals. The graphic linearity
of Romanesque art, expressed in the
pleating of drapery in concentric
ripples, is allied to a bold and
simplified treatment of volumes.

297. Monk Martin (attributed to)
Head of St. Peter
Burgundy, second third of the
12th century

Fragment of statue, stone. H 21 cm (8.3 in.);
W 14.3 cm (5.6 in.); D 18.5 cm (7.3 in.)
Acq. 1923. RF 1783

The pilgrim's shrine dedicated
to St. Lazarus in Autun contained
a highly decorated architectural
aedicula, fragments of which survive
in the Musée d'Autun. Inside it,
a series of under lifesize stone statues
was arranged, as if on a stage,
to illustrate the raising of Lazarus,
surrounded by Sts. Peter, Andrew,
Martha and Magdalen. An inscription
stated that the stone for the

mausoleum had been cut by the
monk Martin under the episcopacy
of Etienne, probably Etienne II
(1170–1189). But several sculptors
seemed to have worked on this
ambitious mausoleum. The head
of St. Peter and the famous free-
standing statue of St. Andrew
(Musée d'Autun) are rare examples
of a monumental art which remains
linear in spirit, as reflected in the
parallel curls of Peter's fringe, with
all the locks falling from the same
point. This late Romanesque style
can be associated with works from
Provence and the Rhôneland.

Gothic France

While the south of France remained faithful to Romanesque art for some time, a new form appeared in the Ile-de-France to which the classicizing purists of the 18th century gave the derisive name of Gothic, stemming from the "barbarian" Goths. The flowering of the Gothic style accompanied urban, economic and political (communal) developments, alongside a growing role for the universities. The new master builders applied the Gothic technique of combining rib-vaulting and pointed arches first to Saint-Denis and then to the cathedrals in the Ile-de-France. Where sculpture is concerned, however, the frontier is less clear-cut between Romanesque forms and the more naturalistic freedom of the Gothic style. The *Altar-Piece of Carrières-Saint-Denis* (no. 298) is visibly situated at the confluence of the two styles. The 13th century was the golden age of equilibrium of which architecture with its grand projects at Chartres, Reims, Amiens, Bourges, was inextricably a part. The Louvre can only offer a glimpse of this classic monumental style removed from its context like *King Childebert* (no. 300) or through pieces coming from Parisian churches.

The collection is, however, rich in sculpture from the 14th century, that age of contrasts, of plague (in 1348), of war (the Hundred Years), but also of increasing royal power, princely patronage and the beginnings of humanism. Two contradictory styles developed in sculpture. There was a naturalistic tendency, at the wellspring of portraiture, which led to the demonstrative strength of Burgundian art revitalized by Claus Sluter. On the other hand, there was a search for sophistication in delineation of form and stylization. Early in the 15th century, this stylistic evolution flowed on uninterruptedly in centers under the control of the dukes of Berry and of Burgundy. There is a marked change of pace in the middle of the century when, with peace restored after the long Hundred Years' War, the process of rebuilding the kingdom began again. This moment of "relaxation" is reflected in new centers like the Languedoc, Burgundy and above all in the Loire valley. *The Education of the Holy Child* (no. 307) from Longvé, statues by Chantelle, *St. John on Calvary* (no. 306) from Loché, and works by Michel Colombe exemplify this art of the Loire valley, sharp and tender by turns, in which late Gothic becomes infused with a new humanism.

298. Altar-Piece from the Church of Carrières-Saint-Denis
Ile-de-France, third quarter of the 12th century

High relief, stone with traces of polychromy.
H 90.6 cm (35.7 in.); W 1.84 m (72.4 in.);
D 19.5 cm (7.7 in.)
Acq. 1915. RF 1612

The theme of the Virgin in majesty reappears at the center of one of the oldest altar-pieces preserved in France. The structure of this highly architectonic work is organized around two scenes from the Gospel, the Annunciation and the Baptism of Christ. The tall, thin silhouettes are separated from the central figure by little columns decorated with chevrons. While the base and sides are covered in a scrollwork pattern populated with figures, the upper part of the altar-piece is decorated with an architectural system of multiple arching bays, like those found on Romanesque capitals and on the royal portal at Chartres. The vaulted design is adapted to the figures it glorifies. But some of the scenic details such as the waters of Jordan and the Archangel Gabriel's wings overlap the borders. The overall style in this church, which was a dependent of the Abbey of Saint-Denis, is typical of the Ile-de-France at that delicate point of transition from Romanesque to Gothic. The altar-piece is still recognizably Romanesque in its elongated forms and linear treatment of drapery.

299. The Angel Dictating to St. Matthew the Evangelist
Chartres, second quarter of the 13th century

High relief, stone. H 64.5 cm (25.4 in.);
W 50 cm (19.7 in.); D 15 cm (5.9 in.)
Acq. 1905. RF 1388

This is a fragment of the rood-screen which divided choir from nave at Chartres cathedral until its removal in 1763. Comprising several columns of narrative reliefs, some large reliefs remain, illustrating the Childhood of Christ (in the treasury of Chartres cathedral), and small reliefs from the Last Judgement to which the figure of Matthew the Evangelist, as narrator, was attached. The serene figure here reflects something of the monumental scope developing at the transept portals of the cathedral. St. Matthew is wrapped in a cloak with broken folds which give it volume, in contrast to the close-knit pleats which were the norm until then. With its bold, flattened planes, the style of this piece is linked to the sculpture on the western front of Notre-Dame in Paris.

300. King Childebert
Ile-de-France, c. 1239–1244

Statue, stone with traces of polychromy. H 1.91 m
(75.2 in.); W 53 cm (20.9 in.); D 55 cm (21.6 in.)
Seized in the Revolution, entered the Louvre
in 1851. ML 93

This retrospective statue of the
Merovingian King Childebert, who
died in 558, was affixed between
1239 and 1244 to the central pillar
of the portal leading to the refectory
of the abbey at St. Germain-des-Prés.
He was the founder of the original
abbey, dedicated to the Holy Cross
and to St. Vincent. With its expressive
smile, the statue is characteristic
of a monumental classical style, with
soft but severe drapery. Naturalistic
detail, such as the metalwork belt
girding the waist, is of a piece with
the animated frontality of the arms
and slight turn of the hips swiveling
the torso gently out of alignment
with the plane of the feet.

301. Virgin and Child
Ile-de-France, second quarter of the
14th century

Statue, marble. H 1.05 m (41.3 in.);
W 24.5 cm (9.6 in.); D 24 cm (9.4 in.)
Gift of the marchioness Arconati-Visconti, 1916.
RF 1632

In the 14th century the Marian cult
prompted wealthy donors and
humble laborers to offer images
of the Virgin and Child to the
churches. These numerous statues
in stone, polychromed wood
or in marble (in the case of the
wealthy) have many features
in common. Iconographic constraints
imposed the floral-patterned crown

over a veil framing the Virgin's face
and a large draped mantle, which
sometimes rises apron-like over the
dress. The striving for refinement
dictated a somewhat unnatural
posture, which is often turned at the
hips, arched, and undulating.
At the same time interest in line
is seen in complex folds falling
in scrolls and arabesque shapes. The
statue shown here belongs to a group
of Virgins preserved in the
Ile-de-France; the sculptor has gone
beyond the mere quest for virtuosity
to stress the intimate nature
of maternal love. The eyes of Virgin
and Child—who holds an apple and
a bird—meet in an expression
of tender trust.

302. Evrard d'Orléans (attributed to)
known from 1292 to his death in 1357
Angel with Cruets
Ile-de-France, c. 1340

Wall statuette, marble. H 52.7 cm (20.7 in.);
W 14 cm (5.5 in.); D 8.3 cm (3.3 in.)
Gift of the Société des Amis du Louvre, 1904.
RF 1438

Alongside the development of the
single, devotional statue, the sculpted
altar-piece proved remarkably
popular. It often consisted of narrative
reliefs in white marble applied
to a black marble ground. The altar-
piece in the Chapelle Saint-Paul
et Sainte-Catherine, founded in 1340
by Jeanne d'Evreux, Queen of France

in the Royal Abbey of Maubuisson,
was one of the most prestigious
ensembles. It featured, among other
scenes, a large representation of the
Last Supper (now in the Carmelite
church), and a narrower one of the
Communion of St. Denis, with a row
of prophets and the angel with the
cruets holding the wine and water
as a reminder of the altar-piece's
overall Eucharistic meaning.
This angel, which has been ascribed
to an important sculptor from the
royal court, is not stylized in any
way, and stems rather from a calm
and serene aesthetic emphasizing the
monumentality of the masses treated.

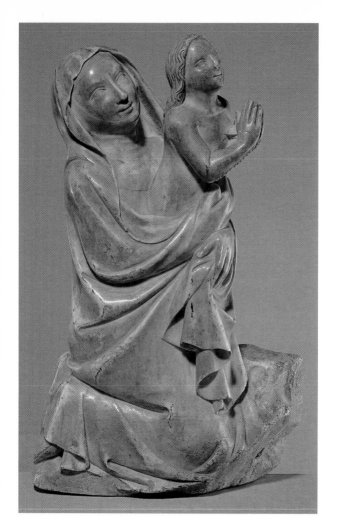

**303. Resurrection of a Girl from
l'Isle-sur-la-Sorgue,** fragment from
the **Tomb of Elzear de Sabran**
Comtat Venaissin, c. 1370–1373

Bas-relief, alabaster. H 34 cm (13.4 in.);
W 21.4 cm (8.4 in.); D 10 cm (3.9 in.)
Gift of Maurice Sulzbach, 1919. RF 1676

Elzear de Sabran, a young Provençal
nobleman who had followed the
fortunes of the Angevins as far
as Naples, took vows of chastity and
prayer. A tertiary in the Order
of St. Francis, he was buried in the
Gray Friars' Church (Eglise des
Cordeliers) in Apt. Miracles occurring
during his lifetime, on his funeral
procession and at his tomb led to his
canonization in 1371. A magnificent
ciborium, on the model of that for
St. John Lateran, was created to hold
his relics. The decoration, composed
of reliefs illustrating the miracles
of the saint, is now dispersed.
The fragment in the Louvre shows
a drowned girl coming back to life
in the arms of her mother before the
saint's coffin. The sculpture is typical
of art from Avignon, enriched
by every stylistic current through the
presence of the papal court.

304. Charles V, King of France
Ile-de-France, last third of the
14th century

Statue, stone. H 1.95 m (76.8 in.);
W 71 cm (27.9 in.); D 40 cm (15.7 in.)
Former Salle des Antiques at the Louvre,
17th–18th century. Entered the Louvre in 1904,
RF 1377

This image of King Charles V who
reigned from 1364 to 1380, and its
pendant, the statue of Queen Jeanne
de Bourbon, were long thought
to have come from the portal of the
Parisian hospice the Quinze-Vingt,
or from the Parisian Abbey of the
Celestines and to have represented
St. Louis and his wife with the

features of the reigning monarchs.
In fact they may have come from
the Palais du Louvre, which was
extended and embellished
by Charles V. Although the hands
are restored, the king's face
is a striking portrait, firm and
sardonic; the drapery, which
is gathered round and then falls
in a generous movement, is also
treated with vigor. The king's
profoundly human expression
coincides with the development
of the art of portraiture in the middle
of the 14th century.

305. Tomb of Philippe Pot
Burgundy, last quarter of the
15th century

Painted stone. H 1.80 m (70.9 in.);
W 2.65 m (104.3 in.)
Abbey Church of Cîteaux. Acq. 1889. RF 795

This haunting funerary monument
was commissioned by the powerful
lord of La Roche-Pot, Philippe, who
died in 1494. He was seneschal
(steward) to the duke of Burgundy,
then chamberlain to Louis XI,
rallying to his side on the death
of Charles the Bold. The quality
of the sculpture owes more to its
extraordinary, monumental and
expressive composition than to any
stylistic refinement. The dead knight
is borne on a slab by eight hooded
official mourners.
This funerary cortège evokes the
grandiose and spectacular funeral
processions of the time, and recalls
the figurines of mourners on the
great tombs at the end of the Middle
Ages. It differs from them in its
monumental size, the lack
of individualization, and the almost

dynastic significance of the
emblazoned shields carried
by the mourners and representing
the eight noble quarterings of the
dead man.

306. St. John on Calvary
Loire Valley, third quarter of the 15th
century

Statue, walnut. H 1.40 m (55.1 in.);
W 46 cm (18.1 in.); D 39 cm (15.3 in.)
Acq. 1904. RF 1363

With his arms crossed, and bowed
in his grief, this sculpture of St. John,
and its pendant the *Virgin* (now
in the Metropolitan Museum of Art,
New York) were part of a Calvary
group, at the feet of Christ on the
cross. These groups were frequently
placed at the entrance to the Choir,
high up on a so-called "beam

307. The Education of the Holy Child

Bourbonnais, end of the 15th century

Group, stone with traces of polychromy. H 85 cm
(33.5 in.); W 59 cm (23.2 in.); D 46 cm (18.1 in.)
Acq. 1955, RF 2763

The "relaxation" of the Gothic style
was most apparent in the Loire valley.
This work, which was kept for
a long period in the private chapel
in the hamlet of Longvé, not far
from Bressolles (Allier), is a good
example. The group depicts the
education of the Holy Child, who
plays in his mother's lap, idly turning
the leaves of an open book.
The composition is concentrated and
serenely pyramidal in outline,
enlivened by voluminous folds
breaking at the base into deep planes.
The Virgin has a delicately absent
expression below a wide curving
brow, her eyes languidly peer from
under lowered eyelids; her mouth
is small and fleshy and her cheeks
full. This striving for a simplified
purity, which is compact and
all-encompassing, is in keeping with
the refined aesthetic which reigned
at the court of the dukes of Bourbon
at Moulins with artists such as the
Master of Moulins, Jean de Chartres
and Michel Colombe.

of glory." In the 19th century this
work was kept in the little Church
of Loché in the Touraine; it is typical
of the austere grandeur of art from
the Loire valley. The pure volumes
of the face, which recall the style
of Jean Fouquet, the master of Tours,
and the voluminous drapery with its
broken folds contribute to an expression of quiet sadness. Any picturesque
detail that might detract from this
striving for the inner meaning
has been banished. Other examples
of this can be seen in the art
of Touraine wood-carvers.

Renaissance France

Little by little French art abandoned Gothic forms. New inspiration came from Renaissance Italy, which French knights eagerly discovered during the wars with Italy. The desire for novelty led first to the adoption of a Lombard style of ornamentation employing grotesques, candelabra, scrollwork and volutes. This "Early Renaissance," centered round the royal and aristocratic houses in the Loire valley and the Château de Gaillon in Normandy, was accompanied by the arrival of Italian sculptors, like the Giusti family, who were responsible for the tomb of Louis XII at Saint-Denis. Great French sculptors, like Michel Colombe and his nephew Guillaume Regnault, imbued the "relaxed" Gothic style with a new feeling of humanity and a concern for clarity of expression and composition.

Under Francis I, after the troubled years that followed the defeat at Pavia and the captivity of the king at Madrid, the palace of Fontainebleau was fairly bustling with Italian artists who came with Rosso and Primaticcio. The name of the Château itself came to designate the mannerist school. After Italian sculptors like Domenico Fiorentino—who sculpted the tomb of Claude de Lorraine—and Benvenuto Cellini, who during his brief sojourn executed the *Nymph of Fontainebleau* (no. 351), the French took over. Among them we should mention François Marchand, creator of the reliefs on the rood-screen at the Church of St. Père at Chartres, and Pierre Bontemps. We should add Jean Goujon who gave new flow to the bas-relief by filling out the conceptual spiraling line with "wet" drapery to emphasize volumes. We should also remember Barthélemy Prieur and cite Germain Pilon who adopted the elongated female figure characteristic of mannerist art, linking it successfully to the realism of portraiture and the expressive strength of a new religious fervor—that of the Counter-Reformation.

After years of civil war, during which only Pilon managed to sustain his art, the accession of Henry IV heralded a revival of mannerist art. Known as the "Second School of Fontainebleau," a group of sculptors—Pierre Biard, Pierre Francqueville and Mathieu Jacquet—gave new life to the turbulent mannerist style.

308. Michel Colombe
c. 1430–after 1511
Saint George and the Dragon
Tours, 1508–1509

Relief, marble. H with surround 1.75 m (68.9 in.);
W 2.735 m (107.7 in.) D 41.5 cm (16.3 in.)
From the chapel in the Château de Gaillon. Seized
during the Revolution. Entered the Louvre in 1818.
MR 1645

The venerable Gothic image-maker
of Tours, Michel Colombe, who
designed the tomb for Queen Anne
of Brittany's parents in Nantes
cathedral, was commissioned in 1508
to carve a marble altar-piece for the
high chapel in the Château
de Gaillon, palace of the Archbishop
of Rouen, Cardinal Georges
d'Amboise. It was in this center
of the early French Renaissance that
this minister of Louis XII—aided
by French and Italian artisans—
introduced Lombard ornamentation
into what was still a Gothic architectural setting. Michel Colombe gave
depth to a pictorial image of the
archbishop's patron saint, George,
shown as a contemporary knight
fighting the dragon which terrorized
the town of Trebizond (now
Trabzon), and freeing the captive
princess. This first large Italian-style
relief, in which the sculptor has not
quite mastered perspective, nor the
depiction of nature (a few meagre
clumps of trees), nor the myth (the
dragon is naive in style), nevertheless
exemplifies a drive for compositional
unity and clarity which heralds the
Renaissance. Italian ornamentalists,
probably under the Florentine,
Jérôme Pacherot (Girolamo
Pacchiarotti may have been his
original name), were responsible for
the surround which is typical
of decorations based on pilasters and
grotesques imported from Italy.

309. Louise de Savoie
Loire valley, beginning of the 16th century

Bust, terracotta. H 47 cm (18.5 in.);
W 53,4 cm (21 in.); D 23 cm (9.1 in.)
Gift of the Société des Amis du Louvre, 1949.
RF 2658

This intriguing bust was found in a niche in a small château in the Touraine, La Péraudière. Cut off at the shoulders and with a fullness of form, it is like the Italian busts which were widely known from Tuscany to Lombardy in the latter half of the 15th century but which were unknown in France. Comparison with a medallion has established it as a portrait of Louise of Savoy, mother of King Francis I (1476–1531). A concern for realism accentuates her features which are firm and powerful, like those found on the bust that is a pendant to this, which probably portrays Duprat, later chancellor to Francis I. Special techniques, such as the construction of the headdress, made from super-imposed layers of clay held together by brass pins, the iconography and its realism give this bold work its uniqueness.

311. Jean Goujon
c. 1510–c. 1565
Nymph and Putto
Paris, c. 1549

Relief, stone. H 74 cm (29.1 in.);
W 1.95 m (76.8 in.); D 13 cm (5.1 in.)
From the Fountain of the Innocents, Paris. Entered
the Louvre in 1818. MR 1738

310. Guillaume Regnault
(workshop of)
c. 1460–1532
Virgin and Child
Loire valley, c. 1510–1520

Statue, marble. H 1.83 m (72.1 in.);
W 60 cm (23.6 in.); D 41 cm (16.1 in.)
From the Château de Couasnon at Olivet near
Orleans. Acq. 1875. RF 202

This statue is a perfect example of the serene grandeur of art in the Loire after the death of Michel Colombe. With her two feet in rounded shoes firmly planted on the ground, and her drapery set within a rectangle, the Virgin is finely balanced and monumental. A fashionable detail, a scarf fixed with a monogrammed brooch, enlivens the costume. The celebration of the Virgin Mother for her serenity and grandeur is accompanied by idealized features: oval face, straight nose, small mouth, and heavy-lidded, almond-shaped eyes. The pride of the mother presenting her fine laughing child is mingled with a tender melancholy which presages the Passion.

The architect and sculptor Jean Goujon introduced a new form of bas-relief; his figures are perfectly contained within the frame and are autonomous. Without seeking to compete with painting they command their own illusory perspective within the thin slab of stone. Goujon sculpted lithe, slender figures contained within graceful spirals like these on the façade of the Louvre, or on the rood-screen in Saint-Germain-l'Auxerrois (fragments of which are in the Louvre), or again on the Fountain of the Innocents, where a section of the reliefs was dismantled and rearranged in the 18th century, with the rest going to the Louvre. His sense of the ideal is conveyed by the strong conceptual outline to the figures, which are further emphasized by the rippling draperies surrounding them.

312. Diana the Huntress
France, mid-16th century

Group, marble. H 2.11 m (83.1 in.); W 2.58 m
(101.6 in.); D 1.345 m (52.9 in.)
From the Château d'Anet. Seized during the
Revolution, entered the Louvre in 1823. MR 1581

Diana of Poitiers, mistress and
counsellor to Henry II, had
a monumental fountain built
by Philibert Delorme in a courtyard
of her Château d'Anet. It was
surmounted by a marble sculpture
of Diana caressing a large stag,
surrounded by her dogs. The
sculpture recalls Cellini's *Nymph
of Fontainebleau* (no. 351), which
figured in the portal of the Château
d'Anet. Diana recalls the royal
favorite although this is not a portrait.
Ascribed successively to Jean Goujon,
Pierre Bontemps, Benvenuto Cellini
and Germain Pilon, the work
displays the elaborate and high-
flown elegance characteristic of the
School of Fontainebleau. The chaste
goddess, who is distant yet gentle,
has a certain cold sensuality about
her which recalls the *Girl Pulling
Out a Thorn* by Ponce Jacquiot.

313. Pierre Bontemps
c. 1505–1568
Charles de Maigny
Paris, c. 1557

Funerary statue, stone.
H 1.45 m (57.1 in.); W 70 cm (27.6 in.);
D 42 cm (16.5 in.)
Church of the Celestines, Paris. Seized during the
Revolution, entered the Louvre in 1818.
MR 1729

With the Renaissance, tomb figures
which by tradition were recumbent
became more varied in posture,
leaning forward or kneeling
in prayer. In 1557 Pierre Bontemps,
responsible for the tomb sculpture
for Francis I, was commissioned
to sculpt the figure of Charles
de Maigny, captain of the King's
Guards. He was to be portrayed
sitting like a guard who has fallen
asleep at his post, before the king's
door. The massive body, slumping
against a heraldic stool, is brought
into relief by the fine carving of the
decorative elements.

314. Germain Pilon
c. 1528–1590
**Monument for the Heart of Henry II:
The Three Graces**
Paris, c. 1560–1566

Group, marble. H 1.50 m (59.1 in.);
W 75.5 cm (29.7 in.); D 75.5 cm (29.7 in.)
Church of the Celestines, Paris. Seized during the
Revolution, entered the Louvre in 1818. MR 1591

Working by turns on anti-naturalistic
themes and on realistic portraits,
Germain Pilon managed to reconcile
the contradictions of the mannerist
style. Commissioned by Catherine
de' Medici to execute the funerary
sculpture for Henry II, who died
following an accident in 1559, Pilon
decorated the tomb for his body
in the Abbey of Saint-Denis with
shapely figures of the Virtues.
To carry the casket containing the
king's heart he was commissioned
to sculpt the Three Graces in a circle,
standing on a pedestal decorated
by Domenico Fiorentino. He adapted
an engraving by Marco Antonio
Raimondi after Raphael, creating
a group of graceful caryatids holding
the heart casket on their heads.
While rejecting the exuberance and
the serpentine line of mannerism,
he retained its elongated forms,
which he clothed in crumpled
drapery, tumbling down at times
in graceful curves.

315. Barthélemy Prieur
1536–1611
Tomb of Christophe de Thou
Paris, 1583–1585

Statues, bronze; bust: H. 74 cm (29.1 in.), red and
white marbles; reliefs, marble.
Church of Saint-André-des-Arts, Paris. Seized
during the Revolution, entered the Louvre in 1824.
MR 1684, MR 1685, MR 2116, RF 4405, RF 4406

Barthélemy Prieur was a Protestant
who owed his fortune to the
protection of politicians anxious for
reconciliation to bring an end to
the wars of religion. The family of the
Constable of Montmorency, who was
a friend of Henry II, commissioned
two funerary monuments from
Prieur, which are now in the Louvre.
As for the politician de Thou,
he ordered two tombs to be sculpted,
one for his father and one for his
first wife. Prieur juxtaposed

a characterful, realistic bust with
two thin and tormented spirits,
inspired by Michelangelo's statues
(*The Times of Day*) on the Medici
tombs, in the New Sacristy, San
Lorenzo, Florence.

316. Germain Pilon
c. 1528–1590
Virgin of Sorrows
Paris, c. 1585

Statue, polychromed terracotta. H 1.59 m (62.6 in.);
W 1.19 m (46.8 in.); D 81.5 cm (32.1 in.)
From the Sainte-Chapelle, Paris. Seized during the
Revolution, entered the Louvre in 1890. RF 3147

317. Pierre Biard
1559–1609
Fame
Paris, 1597

Statue, bronze. H 1.77 m (69.7 in.);
W 1.20 m (47.2 in.)
From the chapel in the Château de Cadillac. Seized
during the Revolution, entered the Louvre in 1834.
LP 361

The other side to Pilon's art
is a refined but pointed and troubled
pathos which finds expression in the
reliefs depicting the Descent from
the Cross, on the pulpit in the Grands
Augustins and on the altar-piece
in Saint-Etienne-du-Mont. *The Virgin
of Sorrows*—unlike a Pietà in which
the Virgin holds Christ's body—
introduced a new mystical contemplation of sorrow and solitude which
corresponded to a revived Catholic
spirituality. Used as a model for
a statue in marble, now in the Paris
church of St. Paul and St. Louis,
it was designed to fit in with
an ensemble, the *Resurrection* (in the
Louvre) and *St. Francis* (in the church
of St. John and St. Francis), commissioned by Queen Catherine de'
Medici for Henry II's funerary
chapel in the Abbey of Saint-Denis.

The duke of Epernon, governor
of Gascony, embellished his Château
de Cadillac and had a tiered funerary
mausoleum, modeled on the royal
tombs in Saint-Denis, built in his
chapel. Surmounting this was the
statue of Fame holding the trumpet
of ill repute in one hand and blowing
into that of good repute. The same
iconography can be found later,
on certain great noble tombs in
Westminster Abbey. Commissioned
in 1597, the statue is a mannerist
figure balancing precariously on one
leg like Giambologna's *Mercury*.
The art of the second School
of Fontainebleau, less refined in its
attention to the hairstyle and
ornament than the first, concentrated
on the thrust of volumes turning
in space.

17th Century France

Several major movements affected French sculpture between 1600 and the death of Louis XIV (1715). A late mannerism lingered on under Henry IV and Louis XIII alongside the solid realism of sculptors of tomb effigies.

A new style appeared around 1640, dominated by figures like Simon Guillain, Jacques Sarazin and the Anguier brothers. Their training in Italy during the emergence of the baroque style brought them to scenic and dynamic forms. Contact with classical art disciplined them, however, and the combination of a classical ideal with a tempered baroque style gave rise to a classical, balanced and intellectually-based sculpture in France.

Art under Louis XIV was at the outset dominated by Colbert's administration (1665–1683), which supplied royal artists with the means of production. The establishment of the Royal Academy of Painting and Sculpture devoted both to training and theory, the setting up of the French Academy in Rome and the great building projects at the Louvre, Versailles, the Invalides and Marly, all called for a great deal of sculpture in keeping with the canons laid down by the Court painters.

Only Puget, in Provence, escaped Court interference and managed to create bold and passionate works. Under his influence, and under that of colorist painters, official art took a more dynamic turn, By 1700 or so, the "rocaille" style, or French rococo, an interpretation of the baroque, held sway, most spectacularly in the park at Marly.

318. Pierre Francqueville (Pietro Francavilla)
1548–1615
Francesco Bordoni
1580–1654
Four Captives in Chains
Paris, 1614–1618

Statues, bronze. Each: H 1.55 m (61 in.);
W 66 cm (26 in.); D 70 cm (27.6 in.)
From the equestrian monument of Henry IV on the
Pont Neuf. Seized during the Revolution, entered
the Louvre in 1817. MR 1668–1671

The arrival of Pierre Francqueville, who was already famous in Florence under the name Francavilla, with his son-in-law Bordoni, marked the arrival of Tuscan mannerism at the court of Henry IV. As official sculptor to the king, he was asked to collaborate on the equestrian statue of Henry IV, erected on the tip of the Ile de la Cité, by the Pont Neuf. While the statue itself, commissioned by Queen Marie de Médicis in Florence as early as 1604, was by Pietro Tacca, another pupil of Giambologna, the four slaves at each corner of the pedestal were cast by Bordoni in 1613 after models made by Francqueville before his death (1615). Symbolizing enchained passions, subjugated nations and the ages of man, these captives with their unstable postures are very agitated. The fine chiseling accentuates their tortured, suffering bodies.

319. Jacques Sarazin
1592–1660
Monument for the Heart of Louis XIII
Paris, c. 1645

Relief, marble. Each medaillon H 1.02 m (40.2 in.);
W 74 cm (29.1 in.)
From the church of St. Louis of the Jesuits, Paris.
Seized during the Revolution, entered the Louvre
in 1881. RF 607–610, RF 3052–3053

After a long period in Rome,
Jacques Sarazin was responsible for
introducing the new concepts
of Italian art into France. The
Louvre possesses a large selection
of his work, which is classical
in character though imbued with
a baroque warmth. From the joyful,
generous group, *Children Playing
with a Goat*, to the statue of the
founder of the Ordre de l'Oratoire,
Cardinal de Bérulle in Ecstasy,
including statuettes and reliefs for
private devotion, and the marble
St. Peter and Mary Magdalen, along
with the terracotta *Virgin and Child*,
the variety of materials and forms
allowed for a great liberty
of treatment.

The monument for the heart
of Louis XIII decorated an arch in the
choir of the Jesuits' church (now
St. Paul and St. Louis). From the
keystone hung two angels in vermeil,
melted down during the Empire
to make Chaudet's sculpture *Peace*.
On the jambs were epitaphs on a red
marble ground held out by weeping
cherubs, and in the ovals figured the
Cardinal Virtues in classicizing style.

320. François Anguier
1604–1669
Monument for the Heart of Henry, Duke of Longueville
Paris, c. 1661

Marble and gilt bronze. H 7.00 m (275.6 in.);
W 2.02 m (79.5 in.)
Church of the Celestines, Paris. Seized during the
Revolution, entered the Louvre in 1824.
MR 1749–1752, 2669–2672, 3373–3374

The Anguier brothers, François and Michel, went to Rome to study from the Antique, where they worked with Algardi, the leading light of Roman classicism. Back in France they evolved a taste for fine materials—marble and bronze—and for harmony within a reinterpretation of the Antique that strove for subtle mobility. Among the great funerary monuments by Anguier housed in the Louvre, like those for de Thou and de Souvré, the funerary "pyramid" which graced the monument for the heart of Henry, duke of Longueville is remarkable for its imposing stature. A high obelisk sculpted with the attributes of the arts and of high office, it stood in the church of the Celestines upon a high pedestal decorated with reliefs narrating victories of the duke at the side of Henry IV. Four statues of the Cardinal Virtues lean against it. Fortitude, helmeted with the Nemean lionskin and holding the club of Hercules, is a robust armored matron, whose sinuous bend at the hips comes from a marked *contrapposto* pose.

321. Pierre Puget
1620–1694
Milon of Croton
Provence, 1670–1682

Group, marble. H 2.70 m (106.3 in.);
W 1.40 m (55.1 in.); D 98 cm (38.6 in.)
Parc de Versailles (commissioned by Louis XIV).
Entered the Louvre in 1819. MR 2075

A native of Marseilles, Pierre Puget was taught the dynamic force of baroque art when in Rome and especially in Genoa. In 1670 Colbert commissioned from him three major works for Versailles, the *Milon of Croton*, *Alexander and Diogenes*, and *Perseus Freeing Andromeda*.

Puget sought a lyricism and ardor that was to alter ideas about French sculpture. Of the three great marbles at the Louvre, the statue of *Milon* showing a man with his hand caught in the cleft of a tree he was splitting being savaged by a lion, is a display of intense torment. This dying hero, vanquished by his own ebbing strength, caused the queen to exclaim in 1683: "poor man!"

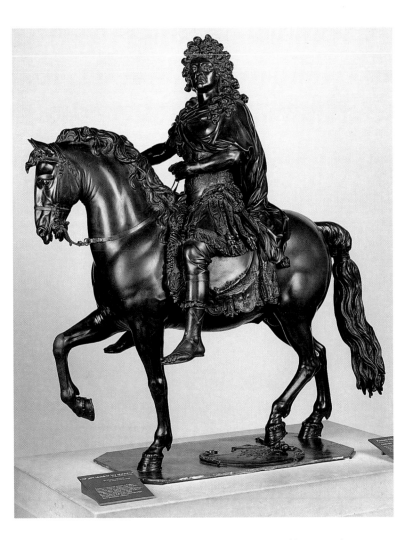

322. François Girardon
1628–1715
Louis XIV on Horseback
Paris, 1685–1692

Equestrian statuette, bronze. H 1.02 m (40.2 in.);
W 97 cm (38.2 in.); D 50 cm (19.7 in.)
Coll. of the French Crown since 1784. Seized
during the Revolution, entered the Louvre in 1818.
MR 3229

Of all the great equestrian monuments
raised to the glory of Louis XIV
in the towns of France—Paris, Lyons,
Dijon, Rennes and Montpellier—not
one royal figure escaped destruction.
But the fame of these works, which
exalted royal power, encouraged
sculptors to make small-scale copies.

This one, signed by Girardon,
reproduces the gigantic bronze, cast
in one piece by Jean-Balthazar
Keller in 1692, after Girardon's
model, and under the supervision
of Robert de Cotte, the architect.
Erected in 1699 in the Place
Vendôme, the new urban space
conceived by Louvois in Paris, the
equestrian statue was intended
as a sign of the sovereign's power,
shown here as a Roman Emperor
in the classical style.

323. Jean Arnould or **Regnaud**
known in 1685–1687
**The "Magnificent Buildings
of Versailles"**
Paris, 1686

Medallion, bronze, Ø 77.5 cm (30.5 in.)
From the Place des Victoires, Paris. Acq. 1980.
RF 3466

The Maréchal de La Feuillade,
Gascon warlord and courtier
at Versailles, undertook an ambitious
project in honor of Louis XIV: the
creation of a royal circus, the Place
des Victoires, in the heart of Paris.
The architecture, by Jules Hardouin-
Mansart, was completed by a statue
of the king standing, cast in gilt

bronze by the sculptor Desjardins.
The Louvre possesses fragments
which escaped destruction during
the Revolution; the four reliefs and
the two medallions from the plinth.
In addition, there are on display
eight bronze medallions executed
to decorate lamp-posts in the circus.
The ensemble illustrated the glorious
events of the reign. This one shows
the building of Versailles, presented
by a lissom nymph reclining in the
foreground before the château and
the aqueduct. The painter Pierre
Mignard executed the drawing for
the medallion, which was made by
Arnould and cast by Pierre Le Neer.

324. Antoine Coysevox
1640–1720
The Prince of Condé
Paris, 1688

Bust, bronze. H 75 cm (29.5 in.); W 68 cm (26.8 in.);
D 34 cm (13.4 in.)
Coll. of the Prince of Conti. Seized during the
Revolution. MR 3343

Under Louis XVI, the French bust
sculpted in marble or bronze,
expressed both the psychological
depth of the person depicted and the
importance of his function. While
Girardon worked within calm and
reasoned frameworks, Coysevox
aimed to capture the nervous tension
of his model, along with a certain
realist grandeur. The bust of Condé,
prince of the blood and victor at the
battle of Rocroy against the Spanish,
depicts a man of compelling ugliness,
with the thin, haughty profile
of a hawk. He is glorified by his
classical breast-plate, picked out with
griffons and with epaulettes in the
form of a lion's muzzle. Although
this portrait was posthumous,
destined for the Palace of the Prince
of Conti, it is akin to a terracotta
bust made by Coysevox during
Condé's lifetime.

325. Antoine Coysevox
1640–1720
Fame Riding Pegasus
Paris, 1699–1702

Group, marble. H 3.26 m (128.3 in.);
W 2.91 m (114.6 in.); D 1.28 m (50.4 in.)
From the ornamental horse-pond in Marly
(commissioned by Louis XIV). Entered the Louvre
in 1996. MR 1824

The ornamental sculpture for the park at Marly was the grand project at the end of Louis XIV's reign. The marble groups, which were dotted among the lakes and waterfalls, and the statues decorating the groves were all dispersed, first under the Regency, after 1715, then during the Revolution. Today, more than 40 pieces are in the Louvre and the Cour Marly has been specially laid out to display them. The most celebrated monumental groups were *Fame* and *Mercury*, each astride a winged horse. Originally they dominated the ornamental horse-pond at Marly; under the Regency they were transported to the entrance of the Tuileries. They were replaced by replicas when the originals were moved into the Louvre. That these gigantic marble monoliths should be completed in the space of two years is a tribute to the technical brilliance of Coysevox. Typical of official rhetoric glorifying the king's good name in the peace regained in the aftermath of war, these dynamic groups rearing above a trophy of arms are caught in mid-movement, and mark an early baroque inflection in court art.

18th Century France

Rococo, a baroque art of contrasts, reached its peak at the beginning
of Louis XV's reign. At the Royal Academy, acceptance pieces (*morceaux
de réception*) took on a dramatic and violent tone. The room devoted
to sculpture at the Academy displays its development very clearly. At Court,
the *Marly Horses* by Coustou (no. 327) show an intense dynamism while portrait
sculpture and small statuary for connoisseurs are charming and seductive.
Around 1750 a reaction set in, signaled by a return to nature and to the
Antique. Bouchardon, Pigalle and, at times, Falconet, gave new expression
to the familiar classical themes. But they had to cater to the intellectual
or wordly tastes of art lovers whose influence became increasingly significant.
An authentic neoclassical style took root around 1770. The cult of the great
appeared with the series of statues commissioned by the royal administration
(Bâtiments du Roi) for the future Museum. Houdon, Pajou, Clodion, and
Julien among others, sought a simplicity of volume which was often enlivened
by a deep sensuality. Much in favor at this time were statuettes (collected
by connoisseurs) and portraits expressing the sentiments and individuality
held in honor by contemporary philosophers. Caffieri and Houdon were
leaders in this art of portrait sculpture.

326. Jean Thierry
1669–1739
Leda and the Swan
Paris, 1717

Group, marble. H 81 cm (31.9 in.);
W 40 cm (15.7 in.); D 44 cm (17.3 in.)
Coll. of the Academy. Entered the Louvre in 1849.
MR 2100

When Thierry was received into the
Royal Academy, the painter Coypel
provided him with the subject for
his acceptance piece, which was
submitted in 1717: Leda, Queen
of Sparta, adored by Zeus who meets
her on the riverbank in the shape
of a swan. This elegant and
voluptuous theme is treated with
a sense of flow characteristic
of rococo. Later, Thierry worked
at the Court of Spain, where
he introduced the spirit of Versailles
quickened by a new baroque
inspiration.

327. Guillaume Coustou
1677–1746
Horse Restrained by a Groom, known
as **the Marly Horse**
Paris, 1739–1745

Group, marble. H 3.55 m (139.8 in.);
W 2.84 m (111.8 in.); D 1.15 m (45.3 in.)
Commissioned by Louis XV for the ornamental
horse-pond at Marly. Entered the Louvre in 1984.
MR 1803

The winged steeds by Coysevox
(no. 325) were removed from the

pond at the Château de Marly
during the Regency. Twenty years
later, Louis XV decided to furnish
the empty pedestals with groups
commissioned from Coysevox's
nephew, Guillaume Coustou.
Forsaking the constraints of official
iconography, the royal administration
ordered wild, rearing horses
to be sculpted, held back by naked
men whose faces or feathered hats

evoked various parts of the world.
They are homages to nature,
so difficult to tame, and recall the
classical Dioscuri. Horses and grooms
offer an image of vigor, exertion
and the unerring struggle of man
and beast. This dynamism sought
by a sculptor who wrote of "manes
standing on end" and the "light and
floating" tail, galvanizes groups that
are still baroque, but already

naturalistic since live models were
used. Their fame, which earned
them their place, from 1795, at the
entrance to the Champs-Élysées,
on an order from the painter David,
has remained constant. They have
been replaced by copies.

328. Edme Bouchardon
1698–1762
**Cupid Cutting a Bow out
of Hercules' Club**
Paris, 1739–1750

Statue, marble. H 1.73 m (68.1 in.);
W 75 cm (29.5 in.); D 75 cm (29.5 in.)
Commissioned by Louis XV. Entered the Louvre
before 1824. MR 1761

329. Jean-Baptiste Pigalle
1714–1785
**Mercury Attaching His
Winged Sandals**
Paris, 1744

Statuette, marble. H 59 cm (23.2 in.);
W 35 cm (13.8 in.); D 30 cm (11 8 in.)
Coll. of the Royal Academy. Entered the Louvre
c. 1848–1850. MR 1957

Bouchardon was a tireless draughts-man, finding inspiration from the Antique and from study of the human body. Moulds of the body and preparatory drawings led, after long deliberation, to this marble statue; the sketch was exhibited at the 1739 Salon, and the marble sculpted from 1747 to 1750. A long spiral shapes the body of the sardonic youth who has stolen the weapons of Mars and Hercules to fashion for himself a bow out of the club. Nevertheless, the Versailles court was shocked by the naturalness of the body, which seemed too real.

This is a youthful work by a sculptor who was to become the most significant figure in his field under Louis XV. This *Mercury* was a long time in the making; the sketch may have been made at Lyons in 1739, when Pigalle returned from Rome where he had studied at the French Academy. The model together with its pendant, *Venus Giving a Message*, were shown at the Salon of 1742. In 1744, Pigalle was asked by the Academicians to execute the sculpture in marble as his admission piece into the Academy. Although the work has an official aspect to it (later still it was reproduced on a larger scale for a gift by the king to Frederick II of Prussia), what is striking is the freedom in Mercury's turning movement. Guided by a knowledge of the *Belvedere Torso* or a composition by Jordaens, he worked with a true understanding of anatomy and with a light, subtle sense of movement.

330. Etienne-Maurice Falconet
1716–1791
Bather
Paris, 1757

Statuette, marble. H 80.5 cm (31.7 in.); W 25.7 cm (10.1 in.); D 29 cm (11.4 in.)
Coll. of Mme Du Barry. Seized during the Revolution, entered the Louvre before 1855.
MR 1846

A protégé of Madame de Pompadour, Falconet was torn between his desire to execute an ambitious, moralistic sculpture, and the requirements of a court which favored decorative elegance. This nymph stretching out her foot toward the water is a refined work. The elongated and graceful feminine figure, with sloping shoulders and small breasts is a constant feature of Falconet's art. He introduced a scarcely perceptible reserve into this candid face with lowered eyelids, thus avoiding any risk of vulgarity. The work, of which a copy was shown in the 1757 Salon, epitomizes the style of a sculptor which became widely known thanks to Sèvres unglazed porcelain figurines.

Bust, terracotta, H 34.5 cm (13.6 in.);
W 24.2 cm (9.5 in.); D 18 cm (7.1 in.)
Acq. 1898, RF 1197

Houdon is best known for his portraits; official marble busts such as *Madame Victoire*, more intimate terracottas, plasters and bronzes, as well as large marble statues such as Voltaire. Portraitist of men of letters and philosophers (Rousseau, Diderot, Buffon), he also depicted the aristocracy, and the early heroes of American Independence (Franklin, Washington). But it was in the close observation of his own family and friends that he captured his most tender, lively expressions. With the busts of his wife and of their daughters Sabine, Anne-Ange and Claudine, and the children of Brongniart the architect, the Louvre has fine examples of his realistic sculpture, full of a youthful freshness.

331. Jean-Antoine Houdon
1741–1828
Louise Brongniart, Aged Five Years
Paris, 1777

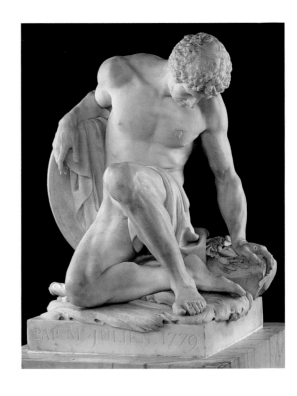

333. Claude Michel, known as Clodion
1738–1814
Venus and Cupid Bathing with Leda and the Swan
Paris, c. 1782

Relief, stone. H 1.03 m (40.5 in.);
W 3.23 m (127.2 in.); D 27 cm (10.6 in.)
From the Hôtel de Besenval, Paris. Acq. 1986.
RF 4103

332. Pierre Julien
1732–1804
Dying Gladiator
Paris, 1779

Statuette, marble. H 60.7 cm (23.9 in.); W 48.5 cm
(19.1 in.); D 42 cm (16.5 in.)
Coll. of the Royal Academy. Entered the Louvre
in 1855 FR 4623

The acceptance piece for the Royal Academy was a masterpiece in marble which the artist had to produce to be admitted to the Academy, and during the 18th century it was normally dramatic in content. After the energetic, baroque works of men like Adam or the Slodtz family, Julien, who was already a mature man, presented a resolutely neoclassical piece. He had copied numerous classical statues, and his work is a densely composed recollection of the *Dying Gladiator* on the Capitol. Silent and heroic, this is a stoic's death. The extoling of virtue and the serene balance of the work are the components of this new classical feeling.

Eighteenth-century collectors, who appreciated Clodion for his light touch and sensitive modeling, cast him in the role of the great neoclassical decorator. There are a number of exuberant terracottas by him, and a few austere marbles. The reliefs and vases which decorated the bathroom of the Baron of Besenval, general of the Swiss Guard—more courtier than warrior—are the remains of a major neoclassical interior conceived by Brongniart the architect. Clodion manages to give a poetic atmosphere to amusing scenes of startled bathers. The liveliness in the modeling and the concise, rapid treatment of the foliage are akin to Hellenistic art then being rediscovered.

334. Jean-Jacques Caffieri
1725–1792
Canon Alexandre-Gui Pingré
Paris, 1788

Bust, terracotta, H 67.5 cm (26.6 in.); W 51.5 cm
(20.3 in.); D 34.6 cm (13.6 in.)
Observatory, Paris. Entered the Louvre in 1909.
RF 1496

Houdon's rival in the art of portraiture, Caffieri, has managed
to convey the jovial wit of the Canon
Pingré (1711–1796) without
disguising his pendulous cheeks,
short, fat nose, thick greedy lips and
double chin. Yet this portrait of the
renowned astronomer, canon
of Sainte-Geneviève and freemason
was a wholly official work of which
the original plaster model was
exhibited at the 1789 Salon.

335. Jean-Antoine Houdon
1741–1828
Diana the Huntress
Paris, 1790

Statue, bronze. H 2.055 m (80.9 in.); W 79.5 m
(31.3 in.); D 93.5 cm (36.8 in.)
Acq. 1829. CC 204

Houdon's studies in France, and
then at the French Academy
in Rome, led him to value the
Antique and respect human anatomy.
His *Diana*, the plaster model for
which dates from 1776, the marble
from 1780, and this bronze cast
executed by the artist himself
in 1790, merges elegance of contour,
assured naturalism (the detail in her
nakedness was deemed shocking),
and a quest for suppleness and
balance which harks back
to mannerism but in a new simplicity.

336. Augustin Pajou
1730–1809
Psyche Abandoned
Paris, 1790

Statue, marble. H 1.77 m (69.7 in.);
W 86 cm (33.9 in.); D 86 cm (33.9 in.)
Commissioned by Louis XVI. Entered the Louvre
in 1829. MR Sup 82

Official sculptor to Louis XV at the close of his reign, then to Louis XVI and a survivor of the Revolution, Augustin Pajou tried his hand at many genres, portraits, architectural decoration and monumental sculpture. The royal administration (Bâtiments du roi) commissioned this *Psyche* from him in 1783, designed as a pendant to Bouchardon's *Cupid* (no. 328). The original plaster cast, shown at the 1785 Salon, created a *succès de scandale* for its portrayal of naked beauty in all its naturalness and sensuality. But the treatment in marble, executed under the Revolution, stressed the neoclassical decoration of the furnishings.

France in the First Half of the 19ᵗʰ Century

The neoclassical style dominated French official art under Napoleon. Chaudet's silver sculpture *Peace*, and the statue of *Napoleon* by Ramey display a grand monumental rigor both sturdy and austere. But the portraits and sketches by Chinard, and the sculpture *Cupid* (no. 338) by Chaudet make way for something lighter and more flowing. This classical tradition continued under the Restoration with Pradier, Bosio, Jaley and Le Moyne Saint-Paul, but they came to terms with the romantic revolution as well. The animal sculptor Barye tirelessly pursued his image of a wild and lofty nature. There are two sculptors in particular who embody the contradictions of this period, torn between naturalism and Antiquity, between feeling and expression: one is Rude, the eclectic creator of the *Marseillaise* on the Arc de Triomphe, and the other is David d'Angers, who celebrated great men and grand causes.

337. Joseph Chinard
1756–1813
Young Harpist
Statuette, clay. H 28 cm (11 in.); W 25 cm (9.8 in.); D 12 cm (4.7 in.)
Acq. 1910. RF 1503

The sculptor Chinard from Lyons was best known for his bust and medallion portraits of revolutionary, and later imperial figures, such as the bust of Madame de Verninac in marble or that of the young woman in terracotta (both in the Louvre). But he was also a remarkable modeler, and a showcase displays designs and sketches of great freedom of execution. Some of them, such as the monument to General Desaix, are official commissions while others, like the one shown here, are more spontaneous expressions of elegant sentiment.

338. Antoine-Denis Chaudet
1763–1810
Cupid Playing with a Butterfly
Paris, 1802–1807

Statue, marble. H 89.5 cm (35.2 in.);
W 64 cm (25.2 in.); D 44 cm (17.3 in.)
Coll. of the French Crown. Entered the Louvre
before 1847. LL. 56

The neoclassical revival culminated
in the celebration of heroism and
of republican and imperial virtues,
alongside a graceful relaxation
of tension. Chaudet embodied the
first sentiment in his silver statue
Peace, his bust of Napoleon and the
group *Oedipus and Phorbas*. This
Cupid, on the other hand, is more
graceful. Holding a butterfly by its
wings, he is perhaps tormenting
a human soul, as the reliefs on the
plinth, illustrating the pangs and
pleasures of love, would suggest.
The philosophical allusion is a rich
one; however, the sculptor was
chiefly concerned with the dynamic
lines of a young body. Chaudet, who
made this model in 1802, died before
he could finish the marble. It was
Pierre Cartellier who completed
the work.

troubadours, he plays his part in the
dynastic propaganda of the
Restoration in search of its glorious
past. Following this example, statues
of famous children became a genre
of simple yet expressive charm.
The plaster model was shown in the
Salon of 1822, and numerous marble
or bronze copies were made of the
statue. This version, cast in silver
by Odiot the metalworker, and
wrought by Soyer, was the most
prestigious example and made for
the king.

339. François-Joseph Bosio
1768–1845
Henry of Navarre as a Boy
Paris, 1822–1825

Statue, silver. H 1.25 m (49.2 in.);
W 42 cm (16.5 in.); D 40 cm (15.7 in.)
Commissioned by Charles X. CC 37

Bosio of Monegasque birth worked
for Napoleon. At the inauguration
of the bronze quadriga which
surmounts the Arc du Carrousel
Louis XVIII appointed him as "First
Sculptor to the King." As official
sculptor—his *Louis XIV on Horseback*
is in the Place des Victoires in Paris,
and his *Nymph Salmacis* in the
Louvre—he was commissioned
to sculpt this retrospective statue
of Henry IV as a boy. With this
historical setting from the age of the

340. James Pradier
1790–1852
The Three Graces
Paris, 1829–1831

Group, marble. H 1.72 m (67.7 in.);
W 1.02 m (40.1 in.); D 45 cm (17.7 in.)
State Commission, 1831. Entered the Louvre
in 1928. LP 5

Originally from Geneva, Pradier
managed to establish himself in the
Parisian milieu. He received official

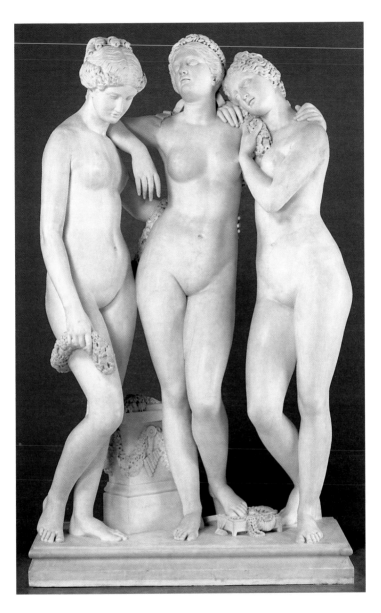

commissions under the Restoration (the monument of the duke of Berry) and under Louis-Philippe. He collaborated in the great political projects of the July Monarchy: working on the decorating of the Assemblée Nationale, the Arc de Triomphe, the Place de la Concorde, Napoleon's tomb, and the historical galleries in the museum at Versailles. His art is based on a classicism which is sometimes austere, and sometimes tinged with sensuality as in this group of *Graces*. Exhibited in the Salon of 1931, this reminder of the classical Borghese Graces and of Raphael's painting is warmed by a languor and a tenderness which Pradier was later to intensify, under the influence of romanticism, into a more passionate sensuality as seen in his group, *Satyr and Bacchante*.

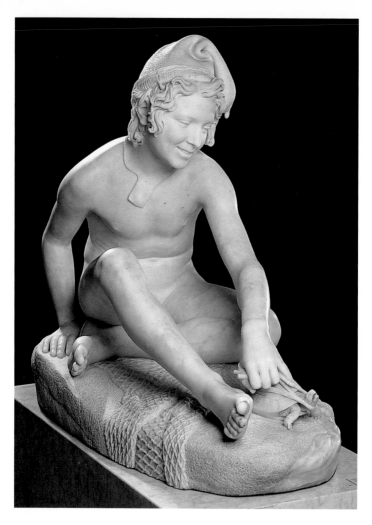

341. François Rude
1784–1855
**Young Neapolitan Fisherboy Playing
with a Tortoise**
Paris, 1831–1833

Statue, marble. H 82 cm (32.3 in.);
W 88 cm (34.6 in.); D 48 cm (18.9 in.)
Acq. by the civil list, 1823. Entered the Louvre
before 1863. LP 63

François Rude, native of Dijon and
creator of the famous *Marseillaise*,
offers here a genre scene in which
the classical style is overturned
by a new freedom. A young
Neapolitan fisherman, identified
by his cap, his net and his neck
band, plays with a tortoise which
he is restraining with a reed.
He is naked, like the mythological
heroes of the neoclassicists. But
in his striving for naturalness, this
life-loving sculptor has emphasized
movement and above all the
expression of joy in the boy's face, lit
up by a candid laugh which shows
his teeth. Rude made a preliminary
study of the subject while in Italy
in 1829; it was executed in plaster
in 1831 and in marble in 1833. The
sculpture inaugurated a romantic
taste for popular Italian subjects that
Carpeaux was to portray.

342. Jean-Bernard,
known as **Jehan Duseigneur**
1808–1866
Orlando Furioso
Paris, 1831–1867

Statue, bronze. H 1.30 m (51.2 in.);
W 1.40 m (55.1 in.); D 90 cm (35.4 in.)
Luxembourg Gardens. Entered the Louvre in 1900.
RF 2993

Nothing less than a romantic
manifesto at the 1831 Salon, *Orlando
Furioso* was cast in bronze in 1867.
In the rebellious attitude of Ariosto's
love-crazed hero, Roland, wrestling
to get free from his bonds, the
sculptor, who admired Victor Hugo,
sought to break away from the
classical formalities of neoclassicism.
Théophile Gautier who heaped
lavish praise on this "chivalrous
Roland who, foaming at the mouth,
rolls his wild and grim eyes about
beneath a knitted brow" was
a perfect spokesman for this rejection
of academicism in favor of lyrical
and even passionate expression.

343. Antoine-Louis Barye
1795–1875
Lion Crushing a Serpent
Paris, 1832–1835

Group, bronze. H 1.35 m (53.1 in.);
W 1.78 m (70.1 in.); D 96 cm (37.8 in.)
From the Tuileries Gardens (commissioned
by Louis-Philippe). Entered the Louvre in 1911.
LP 1184

Barye taught zoological drawing
at the Natural History Museum
in Paris, and was a regular visitor
to the Jardin des Plantes. He was
fascinated by animal sculpture.
He studied, drew, and sometimes
dissected and made casts from wild
animals. Using these studies
he would then execute statues and
statuettes which were calm and true
to life or else furiously romantic
in vein. A lover of the big cats, birds
of prey, and snakes, he was familiar
with the merciless struggles
of nature. Starting with a precise
knowledge of the muscles under the
pelt, he has depicted here the
ferocious expression of the king
of the beasts, vanquisher of its
enemies, in homage to Louis-Philippe
who became king in July 1830,
at the astrological conjunction
of Leo and Hydra.

344. Pierre-Jean David d'Angers
1788–1856
Child with a Bunch of Grapes
1837–1845

Statue, marble. H 1.31 m (51.6 in.);
W 55 cm (21.6 in.); D 48.5 cm (19.1 in.)
Robert David d'Angers coll. Jean-François Gigoux
bequest, 1896. RF 1118

There is an autobiographical origin
to this sculpture. Once on a walk,
the sculptor's young son Robert tried
to pick a bunch of grapes and
narrowly missed being bitten
by an adder, thanks to his father's
intervention. David d'Angers, who
was shaken by the incident and

who liked to philosophize and draw
morals, represented it as childhood
unaware of future menace. Here,
however, the snake, which still
featured in 1837 on the plaster model
in the Musée d'Angers, does not
appear. David endeavors to capture
the tender plumpness of the child's
body still with a fat tummy, and with
a good shock of hair on his head.
It is a surprisingly emotive work from
a sculptor who specialized in depicting the momentous and was the most
inspired portraitist of his time; his bust
of Lamartine and several medallions
by him can be seen in the Louvre.

Italy

While Pre-Romanesque art is represented by the ambo from the abbey
of Pomposa, Romanesque art is scarce in the Louvre. But for the 13th century,
several works from Pisa (*Virgin of the Annunciation*), Florence (monumental
statues from the Duomo in Florence), and Naples (*Cardinal Virtues* from
a tomb) convey an idea of an art in which classical traces, Roman stylization
and Gothic naturalism are reconciled. In the 14th century the Pisan
Annunciation carved in wood already possessed a monumental grandeur. The
art of the Quattrocento, synonymous with humanist harmony, is represented
in its most idealized Florentine form with such works as the *Beautiful
Florentine* or *Scipion Rattier*. These were the best-known works in the
19th century, but their success has been eclipsed in the collection today
by significant sculptures from the great Florentine revivalists Donatello and
Verrocchio, as well as by works from Mino da Fiesole, Agostino di Duccio,
Desiderio da Settignano and the Della Robbia family. But the piquancy
of Lombard art, rough-hewn in Mantegazza or delicately wrought in Amadeo
and Romano, the Ferraran anguish (*Dead Christ*), the Sienese vigor (Jacopo
Della Quercia, Francesco di Giorgio Martini) and the feeling of enigmatic
languor (*Female Bust* by Laurana) are not forgotten.

For the general public, the 16th century belongs to Michelangelo (*Slaves*,
no. 350). But the art of the portrait, especially in Venice with Vittoria, and
the classical revival in the north (Mosca) were accompanied by the birth
of mannerism, a movement which grew out of Michelangelo's grand style
to create an intellectual anti-naturalism marked by spirals and elongated
forms reflecting the anxieties of the period (Cellini, Pierino da Vinci,
Giambologna).

Until recently, however, the Louvre has turned its back on the Italian
baroque. Three pieces by Bernini, the revivalist of monumental sculpture,
were already in France during his lifetime (*Richelieu*, *Urban* VIII, and the
Christ Child). Subsequently only a few models have been added to the
collection. Collecting 18th century baroque work began only recently
(Mazzuoli, Corradini). The Italian collection closes with two masterpieces
by Canova and two newly acquired neoclassical marbles by Lorenzo Bartolini.

345. Descent from the Cross
Umbria or Latium, mid-13ᵗʰ century

Group, polychromed wood. Christ: H 1.83 m (72 in.);
W 1.23 m (48.4 in.); D 0.43 m (16.9 in.)
Acq. 1968. RF 2966–2969

The theme of the descent from the
Cross was illustrated in France
(no. 295), Spain and Italy by a certain
number of groups showing Christ
taken down from the Cross
by Nicodemus and Joseph
of Arimathaea, mourned by the
Virgin (absent here) and St. John.
Akin to the group in Tivoli cathedral,
the work shown still exhibits the
stylized, geometrical folds in Christ's
loincloth (*perizonium*) of the
Romanesque tradition.
But the three-dimensional figures
and the balance of masses look
forward to a more naturalistic spirit.

346. Jacopo Della Quercia
(attributed to)
c. 1371/1374–1438
Virgin and Child
Bologna? c. 1430–1435?

Statue, polychromed wood. H 1.78 m (70.1 in.)
Acq. 1898. RF 1112

The Sienese sculptor Jacopo Della
Quercia almost single-handedly
introduced a grandiose expressiveness
into sculpture. Master of relief
sculpture he strove less for individuality than for volume. Away from
the conflicts between Gothic and the
emerging Renaissance, he pursued
his research into form devoid of sen-
timentality and extraneous ornament.
The *Virgin* in the Louvre, like the
one on the tympanum of San Petronio
(Bologna), has a compactness
of volume and harmony, enlivened by
flowing draperies which enhance
the work's melancholic expressiveness.

347. Donato di Nicolo Bardi, known
as **Donatello**
1386–1466
Virgin and Child
Florence? c. 1440

Relief, polychromed terracotta. H 1.02 m (40.2 in.);
W 74 cm (29.1 in.); D 12 cm (4.7 in.)
Acq. 1898. RF 353

Donatello was the veritable
embodiment of Renaissance discovery
and invention with the monumental
grandeur of his statues, equestrian
works included, expressive
portraiture, perspectival depth
in reliefs, and incisive vigor of his
bronze chiseling. The Virgin and
Child reliefs by Donatello are often
expressions of the tragic, in which
the premonition of the Passion
outweighs the tenderness of the
subject. Here the profile of the Virgin
with her long neck and of the Child
who turns away from her, stand out
from a background drapery which
works with the chair in the
foreground to produce an illusion
of depth.

348. Mino da Fiesole
1429–1484
Dietisalvi Neroni
Florence, 1464

Marble bust. H 57 cm (22.4 in.); W 52 cm (20.5 in.);
D 34.5 cm (13.6 in.)
Gift of Gustave Dreyfus, 1919. RF 1669

Specializing in grand funerary
monuments (the Louvre houses
a fragment of one for Paul II from
the Vatican), and in the Florentine
tabernacle, Mino is now best known
for his busts. This one, of the
Florentine humanist Dietisalvi
Neroni, adviser to Piero de' Medici,
revives the Roman style of portraiture. Dressed in a kind of toga with
angular folds gathered in a knot
at the shoulder, his head is slightly
turned in an imperious movement.
The signs of age—he was 60—the
low forehead and the stooped neck
of the model are a clear indication
of the quest for truth in this
uncompromising art.

349. Agostino d'Antonio di Duccio
1418–1481
**Virgin and Child Surrounded
by Angels**
Florence, third quarter of the
15ᵗʰ century

Relief, marble. H 81 cm (31.9 in.);
W 77 cm (30.3 in.)
Acq. 1903. RF 1352

Often called the *Auvillers Madonna*,
after the name of the Picardy village
where it was kept during the
19th century, this relief still bears the
arms and diamantine ring which
identify Piero de' Medici (1416–1469)
as the original owner.
The style of Agostino, who created
the reliefs in the Malatesta Temple
in Rimini, is readily identifiable.
The convoluted drawing of folds
and hair, the linear elegance

of contours, the sybilline faces with
their heavy eyelids, the subtle
counterpoint set up between
the large smooth mandorla and the
elaborate draperies—all these
elements combine in an intellectual
exploration of ideal form.

350. Michelangiolo Buonarroti,
known as **Michelangelo**
1475–1564
Slaves
Rome, 1513–1515
Unfinished statues, marble. H 2.09 m (82.3 in.)
From the Châteaux of Ecouen, then Richelieu.
Seized during the Revolution, entered the Louvre
in 1794. MR 1589–1590

Through the sheer force of his genius,
Michelangelo is probably the most
famous of all sculptors, and his two
Slaves in the Louvre are the best
known works in the Department
of Sculpture. Their convoluted history
encapsulates one of Michelangelo's
greatest struggles. Conceived in 1505
as part of the first project for the
colossal funerary monument to Pope
Julius II, the sculptures were executed
for the second project (1513). They
were later set aside after the death
of the pope, when economic factors
altered plans for the tomb. Julius II,
who had dreamed of lying in
a detached mausoleum in St. Peter's
in Rome, was granted only a monumental vault in San Pietro in Vincoli,
the church in Rome which nevertheless houses Michelangelo's celebrated
Moses, contemporary with the *Slaves*.

Given by Michelangelo to the Florentine exile Roberto Strozzi, who in turn offered them as a token of homage to the king of France, the *Slaves* reached France during the sculptor's lifetime. Whether they represent subjugated provinces, the arts reduced to slavery by the death of the pope; whether, more simply, they share in the eternal triumph of the pontiff, or symbolize passions subdued, or, in Platonic vein, the human soul encumbered by its mortal coil, the *Slaves* were never finished. The same is true of the other four slaves at the Accademia in Florence, which were executed later, around 1531–1532. "Unfinished" works recur in Michelangelo's output as much because of the vagaries of his career as because of his unflagging quest for the absolute; but the master clearly considered these as works in their own right: he was ready to offer the *Slaves* as a gift, finished or not. Perhaps this was because the marks left in the marble by his tools stand eloquently for the struggle with matter which is the nature of sculpture.

351. Benvenuto Cellini
1500–1571
The Nymph of Fontainebleau
Paris, 1542–1543

High-relief, bronze. H 2.05 m (80.7 in.);
W 4.09 m (161 in.)
From the Château d'Anet. Seized during the
Revolution, entered the Louvre in 1797. MR 1708

idealizes form and adapts it to its surround. The smooth skin and sinuous line of the naked water-nymph of Fontainebleau stand out against a background of wild animals, overseen by a great stag evoking the forest setting.

In 1540, the silversmith Cellini moved to the court of Francis I where he made the famous saltcellar, now in the Kunsthistorisches Museum, Vienna. Wishing to try his hand at monumental statuary, he cast a gigantic bronze tympanum for the golden gate at the Château de Fontainebleau. The tympanum is held up by two satyrs and flanked by two spandrels decorated with two female personifications of Victory. The bronze was cast in Cellini's Parisian foundry and workshop, chiseled by French sculptors—among them Pierre Bontemps—and in fact placed in the porch of the Château d'Anet, the home of Diana of Poitiers, Henry II's favorite.

Even though the elongated female nude was modeled from nature—the capricious Catherine, then the shy, wild Jeanne—it is typical of a deco-rative anti-naturalism which

334

352. Pierino da Vinci
c. 1531–1554
River God
Pisa, c. 1548

Group, marble. H 1.35 m (53.1 in.);
W 48 cm (18.9 in.)
Schlichting bequest, 1915. RF 1623

This young river god was intended
for the collector Luca Martini who
gave it to the duchess of Tuscany,
Eleanor of Toledo. She in turn
offered it to her brother who placed
it in his Neapolitan garden. It was
destiny, in Vasari's opinion, that
marked Pierino for a short life and
to be nephew of the famous
Leonardo. In this work Pierino
is searching for a personal style,
wavering between classical echoes
and a fascination with Michelangelo.
He conveys the suppleness of the
youthful body with restrained
virtuosity and a pleasure tinged with
melancholy. The rhythm and curves
of this hedonistic piece make
it a forerunner of the mannerist
movement.

353. Gian Lorenzo Bernini
1598–1680
Angel with the Crown of Thorns
Rome, c. 1667

Model, terracotta. H 33 cm (13 in.);
W 13 cm (5.1 in.); D 19 cm (7.5 in.)
Acq. 1934. RF 2312

Bernini dominated the triumphant
period of Roman baroque. As stage-
manager of pontifical extravaganzas,
he breathed dynamic energy into all
his creations, and achieved an ambitious synthesis of all the arts.
Commissioned in 1667 to decorate
the Ponte Sant'Angelo, he devised
a triumphal way, flanked by colossal
statues of angels contemplating the
instruments of the Passion.

The model for the angel holding the
crown of thorns displays all the
vitality of Bernini's modeling—rapid,
expressive and over-elaborate.
To convey anguish, Bernini fashioned
the flowing, flame-like draperies
into a spiral which leads the eye
up to the expressive but schematized
face of the angel. Bernini himself
later carved the great marbles
depicting this angel and the one who
carries the *INRI* inscription. These
were deemed so excellent that they
were erected in Sant'Andrea delle
Frate in Rome, while the statues
installed on the bridge were carved
by sculptors in his circle following
his models.

354. Antonio Canova
1757–1822
Eros Awakening Psyche
Rome, 1793

Group, marble group. H 1.55 m (61 in.);
W 1.68 m (66 in.);D 1.01 m (39.8 in.)
Château de Villiers-la-Garenne. Entered the Louvre
before 1824. MR 1777

Canova revived classical art in Italy; schooled in Venice and active in Rome, he was in his time the dominating figure in European art. A master of marble, he sculpted great tombs such as Napoleon's in the classical style, but also created heroic Roman gods and delicate nymphs. This depiction of Eros awakening Psyche, who was put to sleep forever by inhaling a magic perfume, is as much an allusion to the legend of Psyche, the immortal soul of Platonic myth, as it is a hymn to love. Avoiding academicism, Canova constructs a pyramid out of the entwined bodies, animated by the delicate arrangement of limbs undulating in the light. The transparency of the white marble adds poetry to a group that was the fruit of long deliberation (the model dates from 1787), and then copied by Canova himself for Prince Youssoupov.

355. Lorenzo Bartolini
1777–1850
Nymph with Scorpion
Statue, marble. H 86 cm (33.8 in.);
W 1.253 m (49.3 in.); D 68.5 cm (27 in.)
From the Château d'Haroué. Gift of the Société
des Amis du Louvre, 1993. RF 4451

The Nymph sitting naked on the
ground is turning round to look
at her foot that has just been stung
by a scorpion. Her face expresses
anxiety and pain. But is she really
a nymph? The mythological title
is there to give an iconographic
meaning to this superb female
realistic nude, no doubt modeled
from life. The classical reference
is utterly subjugated by the
naturalism. Recorded in the
sculptor's studio in Florence as early
as 1837, the *Nymph* was bought
by the prince de Beauvau-Craon for
the gallery of contemporary art
he intended to make at his Château
d'Haroué in the Lorraine. It was
shown at the 1845 Salon where
it was very well received and
considered even by Baudelaire
as "the most important piece at the
Sculpture Salon."

Germanic Countries

With the exception of the fine 12th century *Christ on the Cross* from Bavaria, the Germanic sculpture collection in the Louvre is essentially of the 15th and 16th centuries and reflects the evolution of style from International Gothic through to the Renaissance.

At the beginning of the 15th century the so-called "Soft style" (*Weicher Stil*), characterized by smoothness and refinement was at its height; the Salzburg *Virgin and Child* is a good example of it. At the same time more acerbic tendencies were present, in which Rhineland mysticism expressed in angular lines the torment of the late Middle Ages. The enigmatic Master of the Rimini Altar-Piece, whose large pietà in alabaster is in the Louvre, exemplifies the subtle mixture of delicacy and harshness. Late Gothic (*Spätgotik*) was the name given to the stylistic renewal which mingled realist tendencies with an imaginative lyricism that brilliantly swelled and contracted forms at will. The Louvre boasts examples of this style from several regions: *The Virgin of Issenheim* (no. 356) from the Upper Rhine; the *Deacon* attributed to the Master of the Kefermarkt Altar-Piece from Austria; works by the great sculptor Riemenschneider from Franconia; and finally, from Swabia, the *Christ Praying on Mount of Olives*, the *Group of Prelates* from the workshop of Daniel Mauch and the famous *Magdalen* (no. 358) by Gregor Erhart.

356. Martin Hoffmann (attributed to)
Documented in Basle
from 1507–Basle, 1530/1531
Virgin and Child
Basle, c. 1510

Statue, limewood. H 1.72 m (67.7 in.);
L 69 cm (27.2 in.); D 49.5 cm (19.5 in.)
Commandery of the Antonites, Issenheim
(Haut-Rhin). Acq. 1924. RF1833

The crescent moon at the foot of the Madonna statue alludes to the Woman of the Apocalypse and to the belief in the Immaculate Conception. The handling of the tumultuous draperies, billowing out before the body and artificially falling into broken folds is characteristic of Germanic Late Gothic sculpture. The firmly modeled faces are indicative of the late Medieval wish to humanize representations of the Madonna and Child. The *Virgin and Child* of Issenheim is unmistakably linked stylistically to the known works of Martin Hoffmann.

357. Tilman Riemenschneider
c. 1460–1531
Virgin Annunciate
Würzburg, c. 1495

Statue, alabaster with highlights in polychromy.
H 53 cm (20.9 in.); W 40 cm (15.7 in.);
D 19 cm (7.5 in.)
From the church of Saint Peter, Erfurt, Thüringia.
Acq. 1904. RF 1384

Youthful and serene, the Virgin
is shown kneeling at her prie-dieu,
deep in meditation upon a holy text,
just as the archangel Gabriel appears
to her and announces that she will
give birth to the son of God. She has
stopped reading but remains
immobile, without turning toward
the heavenly messenger. The latter,
now lost, knelt to the Virgin's right
and the two figures belonged
to a small altar-piece. The Virgin
displays all the characteristics
of Tilman Riemenschneider's style
and of his idealized vision of female
beauty: the slim stature amplified
by drapery broken into myriad
facets, the delicate face, smoothly
modeled, the flat but gently wavy
hair, the eyes falling away toward
the temples and the tiny mouth with
a full lower lip. The fineness
of detail, the mannered gestures and
the subtle handling of the alabaster,
set off by highlights of gold or color
combine to give an expression
of supreme refinement. For several
decades Riemenschneider ran
a major workshop in Würzburg and
received numerous and illustrious
commissions: great altar-pieces
in limewood, sculptures in alabaster
or in sandstone, and tombs in marble.
The master imposed his own personal
style upon his fellow workers, a style
that enjoyed a prolonged success and
wide dissemination throughout
Franconia.

358. Gregor Erhart
Ulm, c. 1470–Augsburg, 1540
Mary Magdalen
Augsburg, c. 1515/1520

Statue, polychromed limewood. H 1.77 m (69.7 in.);
W 44 cm (17.3 in.); D 43 cm (16.9 in.)
Acq. 1902. RF 1338

According to legend, Mary Magdalen retired to the grotto of Sainte-Baume in Provence, where she lived without water or food, clad only in her own hair. Each day she was borne up to heaven to hear the music of the celestial choirs. Six sculptured angels, now lost, originally surrounded the statue. The conception of this daringly naked female body whose harmonious proportions evoke the work of Dürer, reveals a search for a sensual beauty that is quite specific to the Renaissance. It also conforms to the spiritual content of the religious image, in the Gothic tradition. The languishing pose and the contemplative expression betray mystic ecstasy; the idealized beauty and the glint of the golden locks, the radiance of sainthood. The original polychromy, still delicate and wan, emphasizes the subtle toolwork on the surface of the wood as well as the supreme delicacy in the modeling and in the anatomical details.

359. Attributed to Dietrich Schro
Known from 1545 to 1568
Ottoheinrich, Count and Elector Palatine
Mainz, c. 1556

Statuette, alabaster. H 15.5 cm (6.1 in.);
W 15.5 cm (6.1 in.); D 16 cm (6.3 in.)
Gift of C. Sauvageot, 1856. OA 204

This precious image of the patron and collector Ottoheinrich (1502–1559) conveys something of the power and character of the man who built the Renaissance wing of the castle at Heidelberg.

Low Countries

Two opposing tendencies of Gothic art predominated in the Low Countries. There was the anecdotal and picturesque style as in the altar-pieces, which are the best known and most represented pieces, and in contrast the bold and angular style to be seen in separate statues. Works from the southern Low Countries in the 15th and 16th centuries are the most abundant, often identified by makers' marks, with a mallet indicating Brussels, a hand indicating Antwerp, and three stakes indicating Mechelen. At the same time, certain works give us an idea of work in the northern Low Countries—the *Virgin and Child* attributed to Jan Nude, the relief of the *Nativity* and the imposing *St. Leonard* attributed to the Master of Elsloo. A more decorative Renaissance style succeeded this period, illustrated by the *Calvary* relief by Willem Van den Broek, and the gravestone by Jean de Coronmeus. Northern mannerism is represented only in the whirling group by Adriaen De Vries (no. 362), displayed in the Italian room, but the arrival of the baroque, brought back from Italy by traveling sculptors like Duquesnoy, Delcour, and Quellien and others, is well documented by the large busts by the Witsen family and by a suite of little terracotta models.

360. Calvary Virgin
Brabant, end of the 15th century

Statue, oak. H 1.63 m (64.2 in.); W 57 cm (22.4 in.);
D 38 cm (15 in.)
Probably from the rood-screen of the collegiate
church of Sainte-Gertrude de Nivelles.
Acq. 1880. RF 822

The wooden Calvary, composed of Christ on the cross, at the foot of which stand the Virgin and St. John, often surmount glory beams or rood-screens at the entrance to the choir in churches. Here the Virgin is in tears, her face half-hidden by a fringed veil; she crumples a handkerchief in her right hand. This expression of grief is comparable to the tragic, but restrained expression on altar-pieces painted by Flemish "Primitives." The considerable pathos is increased by the Virgin's static pose, and the steeply falling drapery with its folds breaking in sharp angles, but devoid of any gratuitous or decorative effect.

361. Altar-piece of the Passion
Antwerp, c. 1500/1510

Gilt and Polychromed oak. H 2.03 m (79.9 in.);
W 2.145 m (84.4 in.); D 26.5 cm (10.4 in.)
Church of Coligny (Marne). Acq. 1922. RF 1769

The altar-piece has lost its shutters, which folded over the central section. The iconography brings together the Passion of Christ, in the three main compartments, with the Nativity and the Adoration of the Magi in the lower central register, and with depictions of six of the sacraments around the Crucifixion. The mark of Antwerp workshops, a severed hand recalling a local legend, provides evidence that the altar-piece was made in Antwerp. Altar-pieces of this type were made in abundance at the beginning of the 16th century and were mostly for export. The compartmentation of the scenes made up of juxtaposed small reliefs, the speed of execution, the positive predilection for picturesque effects as well as the expressive poses are all distinguishing marks of this Antwerp art so eminently represented by the Coligny altar-piece.

Détail

362. Adriaen de Vries
1546–1626
Mercury and Psyche
Prague, 1593

Group, bronze. H 2.15 m (84.6 in.);
W 92 cm (36.2 in.); D 72 cm (28.3 in.)
Coll. of the French Crown. Entered the Louvre
c. 1877. MR 3270

At the end of 16th century and at the beginning of the 17th, the court of Emperor Rudolph II at Prague enjoyed a period of feverish artistic creativity thanks to the presence of some of the most famous European mannerists. The Dutchman Adriaen De Vries, who trained in Florence under Giambologna, executed two pendant groups for Prague Castle, one of Psyche carried by Cupids and this one, Psyche borne by Mercury to Olympus where she rejoined Eros. Seized as booty by Swedish troops in 1648, the first of these is now in Stockholm while the second, a diplomatic gift, entered the ministerial collections before embellishing the royal parks of Versailles and then Marly. The grand mannerist spiral animates the whirling group which owes its serpentine line and sense of space to the creations of Giambologna.

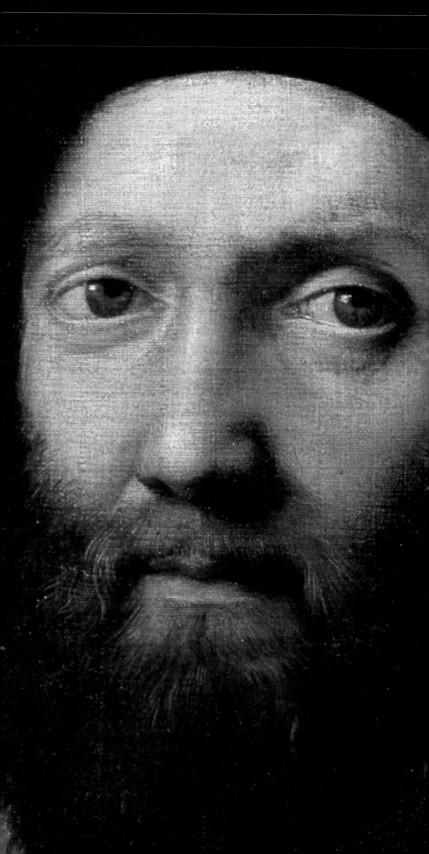

Paintings

France

Italy

Spain

Germany

Flanders and Holland

Great Britain

Introduction

There are over 6,000 European paintings in the Louvre, dating from the late 13th century to the mid-19th century. Despite the predominance of French paintings—almost two thirds of the collection—and some major gaps in foreign schools, the Louvre collections are unique for their uncompromising eclecticism. This was precisely the intention from around 1750, when the idea first emerged of giving the French nation the chance to see the Crown paintings which were scattered throughout royal residences or relegated to storage. The count of Angiviller, superintendent of buildings under Louis XVI, devoted much time to establishing the museum in the Grande Galerie of the Louvre. He also filled gaps in the royal collections which traditionally favored the French, Italian and Flemish schools—linked by history and geography—and acquired other works, Dutch for the most part. The Spanish school, which was barely represented, acquired its first jewel, *The Young Beggar* (no. 440) by Murillo. A few German masterpieces entering the royal collections during the 17th century completed the European panorama. Under the French Revolution, Louis XVI's project finally came to fruition and the museum was opened to the public in 1793. The bulk arrival of new paintings, the result of national requisitions and the spoils of war under the Convention and Empire, widened the diversity of the collection. Most of the works requisitioned from abroad were later returned, and French collections were shared out among the museums of France. But the experience impressed curators of the Louvre with the desire to reflect all the artistic developments of Europe and at the same time retain an exhaustive repository of French painting. The evolution of taste, the longlasting fascination among connoisseurs with Spain, and then with the early masters and English painting, not to mention the development of the discipline of art history, were all to contribute to the continuing comprehensive nature of the Department of Paintings, which as early as 1794, was organized into national schools for the benefit of visitors.

France

While the Louvre's collection of French paintings remains unsurpassed, interest in the origins of French art trailed behind later periods in the Louvre. The inclusion of French easel painting from its 14th century origins to the early 17th century is relatively recent. The makings of what now is the greatest collection of works of the French early masters or "Primitives" and the School of Fontainebleau began no earlier than the middle of the 19th century. The French school gained prominence with the Sun King, Louis XIV. He was an inveterate collector. Turning against his father whose patronage was sparse, he became the first king to develop a royal collection, proclaiming classicism as its aesthetic, with three artists, Poussin, Claude Gelée and Le Brun favored above all others. The king was well aware of Poussin's genius, which served as a model for the Academy that henceforth dominated artistic life.

He acquired 31 of the 39 Poussins now in the Louvre, no less than 10 paintings by Claude Gellée, and virtually all the work of Le Brun. Buying up the remaining contents of official painters' studios, the work of Lebrun (followed by Mignard) became the property of the monarchy, on their deaths.

Add to this the work of other contemporaries such as Perrier, Bourdon and Stella, and we can see how much French classicism owes to Louis XIV. Louis XVI was to finish the work he began. Under his reign, Le Sueur entered the royal collection with his two great cycles (for the Chartreuse in Paris, and the Hôtel Lambert), which set the pattern for the subtle and refined "Parisian Attic" paintings of the mid-17th century. Revolutionary requisitions, which brought most of the Champaignes to the Louvre, virtually completed this classical collection which was, even early on, unparalleled, and was only to increase with chance acquisitions. There was another side to 17th century painting, the painters of reality. It was rediscovered much later under the Second Empire, with a pioneering bequest of Le Nain paintings to the Louvre by La Caze who had a particular affection for this artist. The complex path from Le Nain to La Tour, via still-life painting, has been mapped by historians.

Unlike his contemporaries, Louis XV was no collector. There is not one Watteau or Fragonard at Versailles. Commissions by the Marquis of Marigny, from Chardin to Vernet (*Views of the French Ports*), history paintings ordered for the Gobelins and the decoration of royal residences (Boucher, Carle Van Loo) barely compensated for the uncommon indifference of the king. Acquisitions by the Madame de Pompadour, the dictator of rococo taste, were private and were dispersed at auction on the death of her heir, as were the collections of the most active patrons of the time. Despite its wealth of work by old Academicians (Watteau's *Pilgrimage to Cythera*, no. 383, Chardin's *The Skate*, no. 386), the 18th century owes its wide representation in the Louvre to a providential gift by the greatest French collector, La Caze. His bequest in 1869 brought most of the rococo masterpieces to the Louvre, principally a wonderful series of eight paintings by Watteau, the *Pierrot* (no. 384) amongst them, thirteen Chardins and nine Fragonards. The reign of Louis XVI, who showed little fondness for the art of his time, was marked by ambitious commissions from the superintendent of buildings, the Count of Angiviller, in an effort to revive history painting. The Louvre still possesses the most remarkable of the great Salon compositions, beginning with the *Oath of the Horatii* (no. 391) and David's *Brutus*. After a brief hiatus during the Revolution, this commission policy resumed under the Empire.

The huge history paintings of the Napoleonic legend are perfect examples, *Napoleon Bonaparte Visiting the Victims of the Plague at Jaffa* by Gros (no. 393) and *The Coronation of Napoleon* by David (no. 395) and those rooms where they are displayed in the Louvre are invaluable for a proper understanding of that period.

The Restoration brought the establishment in 1818 of the Musée du Luxembourg, the first museum of contemporary art, where most of the great classical paintings were displayed before entering the Louvre. Works by artists such as Girodet, Guérin, Gérard, Prud'hon, were bought regularly by Dominque-Vivant Denon and the count of Forbin until 1830. *The Raft of the Medusa* by Géricault (no. 397) was acquired, not without some difficulty, by the French museums in 1825, proof that, at least until the middle of the century, new trends could be followed and that there was room for the boldest painters, Delacroix above all. The task of completing this series of history paintings with portraits fell to contemporaries. Three large bequests early in the 20th century helped to make up for the deficiencies of a buying policy which had become increasingly obsessed by academic painting, and had disregarded Courbet, Millet and Daumier. Thomy Thiery (1902) introduced the Barbizon school, Moreau-Nélaton (1927) his Corots, and Chauchard (1909) brought Millet's *Angelus*. Courbet's *Studio* was acquired only in 1920 by public subscription. However, the two latter paintings now belong to the Musée d'Orsay where, with a few exceptions, works of artists born after 1820 are exhibited.

France, 14ᵗʰ–16ᵗʰ century

363. Portrait of John the Good
c. 1350

Wood. H 60 cm (23.6 in.); W 44.5 cm (17.5 in.)
On loan from the Bibliothèque Nationale
de France, 1925, RF 2490

364. Henri Bellechose
known from 1415 to his death
c. 1440/1444
The St. Denis Altar-Piece
1416

Wood transferred to canvas. H 1.62 m (63.8 in.);
W 2.11 m (83.1 in.)
From the Charteuse de Champmol. Gift of Frédéric
Reiset, 1863, MI 674

John II (1319–1364) became king
of France in 1350. His difficult reign
as the second king of the house
of Valois was marked by the defeat
of Poitiers, captivity in London, and
the revolt of Etienne Marcel and the
Jacquerie (so named from the *jacque*
or peasant's jerkin). His portrait has
a special place in the history of easel
painting. Believed to be one of the
oldest works of the French school,
it is also the earliest surviving
individual profile portrait known
in Europe. It may reflect an earlier
lost prototype by one of the great
Sienese masters working in Avignon,
Simone Martini or Matteo
Giovannetti.

To the left of the Trinity, St. Denis,
apostle to the Gauls, is taking the
last communion from the hand
of Christ; to the right, he undergoes
decapitation as a martyr, with his two
acolytes Rusticus and Eleutherius.
The picture was painted for the
Carthusian monastery of Champmol
in 1415–1416 by the last representative
of the "Franco-Flemish" school
which flourished between 1380 and
1420 at the court of the dukes
of Burgundy at Dijon. Against
a brilliant gold ground, the scenes
combine realism with the graceful
stylization of international Gothic.

365. Jean Fouquet
c.1420–1477/1481
Portrait of Charles VII
c. 1445–1450

Wood. H 86 cm (33.9 in.); W 71 cm (27.9 in.)
Acq. 1838, INV 9106

The inscription on the original frame of the painting records the fact that Charles VII, (1403–1461), king from 1422, "le très victorieux roy de France," liberated his country from occupation by the English. This is one of the earliest remaining works by Jean Fouquet, the great painter of 15th century France, who invented a new type of official portraiture with this lifesize, three-quarter-view half-lenght portrait. While the confined framing is still Gothic, the picture breaks permanently with tradition in the new fullness of form given to the king's body.

367. Jean Hey,
known as **the Master of Moulins**
**Presumed Portrait of Madeleine
de Bourgogne, Lady of Laage,
Presented by St. Mary Magdalen**
c. 1490

Wood. H 56 cm (22 in.); L 40 cm (15.7 in.)
Acq. 1904. RF 1521

366. Enguerrand Quarton
Active in Provence between 1444
and 1466
The Villeneuve-lès-Avignon Pietà
c. 1455

Wood. H 1.63 m (64.2 in.); L. 2.185 m (86 in.)
Gift of the Société des Amis du Louvre, 1906.
RF 1569

Nothing was known about this
picture other than its provenance
from Villeneuve-lès-Avignon. It has
now been attributed to the most
illustrious member of the 15th-century
school of Provence, author of the
no less celebrated *Coronation of the
Virgin* (Museum of Villeneuve-lès-
Avignon). Around the stiff body
of Christ, the praying donor and
St. John, the Virgin and Magdalen
have an austerity and monumentality
about them which belongs to the
French sculptural tradition,
interpreted by Quarton into the
clearly delineated, shadow-modeled,
stark forms of the school of Avignon.

Last remnant of a lost diptych
or triptych, this panel shows St. Mary
Magdalen and a donor wearing
a "tinder box" broach, a symbol of the
house of Burgundy. She is presumed
to be Madeleine de Bourgogne,
bastard daughter of Philip the Good,
who after her marriage resided
at the court of the dukes of Bourbon
at Moulins. This would have been
the most likely spot for her to have
been painted by this great late
15th century artist, working between
1480 and 1500 for the Bourbons and
the French Court. He was known
as the "Master of Moulins" from the
triptych in Moulins cathedral, and
is now thought to have been a painter
of Flemish origin, Jean Hey.

368. Diana the Huntress
School of Fontainebleau,
mid-16th century

Canvas. H 1.91 m (75.2 in.); W 1.32 m (52 in.)
Acq. 1840. INV 445

Of unknown authorship, *Diana the Huntress* is the archetype of the Fontainebleau ideal flourishing in 16th century France, under the influence of Italian masters summoned by Francis I to the Château de Fontainebleau from 1530 (Rosso, Primaticcio). Some have seen this as a metaphorical portrait of Diana of Poitiers (1499–1566), mistress of Henry II, during the flourishing period around 1500, when the Château d'Anet was being built. It exemplifies a taste for mythological nudes, where the primacy of design and the mannerist predilection for the elongated body and twisted pose predominate.

369. François Clouet
d. 1572
Portrait of Pierre Quthe
1562

Wood. H 91 cm (35.8 in.); W 70 cm (27.5 in.)
Gilt of the Société des Amis du Louvre, 1906.
RF 1719

François Clouet painted his apothecary friend Pierre Quthe (1519–after 1588) in 1562, at 43 years of age, as the Latin inscription indicates. It is one of the few works signed by the artist. Clouet concentrates on the psychological study of the man, but does not forget his social position, placing a herbal at his side, thereby alluding to the apothecary's garden of medicinal plants in Paris. The austere elegance of the pose suggests a knowledge of the Italian mannerists, and the controlled light and meticulous technique point to the Flemish masters. It was at the junction of these two influences that François Clouet, in the footsteps of his father Jean, developed the new ingredients of French portraiture.

France, 17th century

370. Valentin de Boulogne,
known as **Le Valentin**
1594–1632
Concert
c. 1628–1630?

Canvas. H 1.75 m (68.9 in.); W. 2.16 m (85 in.)
Coll of Louis XV. INV 8252

The concert theme and use of light and shade (*chiaroscuro*) are borrowed from Caravaggio, and this French artist was one of his most faithful followers in Rome. However, the master's harsh realism is filtered by the pupil's greater elegance, and there is a subtler use of color.

371. Lubin Baugin
c. 1612–1663
The Wafers
c. 1630–1635

Wood. H 41 cm (16.1 in.); W 52 cm (20.5 in.)
Acq. 1954. RF 1954-23

Four still-lifes signed Baugin, two of which are in the Louvre, offer the basis of what is known of the best 17th century French still-life painter now identified with the religious painter, Lubin Baugin. Only the subject itself derives from Flemish art. The simplicity and geometric arrangement of the composition reflect a current in French art under Louis XIII which is sober and austere and has occasionally been linked with Protestant ideas or Jansenism.

372. Simon Vouet
1590–1649
Allegorical Figure, known as **Wealth**
c. 1640

Canvas. H 1.70 m (66.9 in.); W 1.24 m (48.8 in.)
Coll. of Louis XIII. INV 8500

Vouet painted this clever allegory
for a royal château, possibly the
Château-Neuf of Saint-Germain-en-
Laye, whence come the Louvre's
Charity and *Virtue*. The subject,
related to temptation and a rejection
of worldly goods, is summed
up in its traditional title, *Wealth*.
With the generous forms of the
figures, the subtle arabesque
of drapery, and the brilliant color,
the picture is at the highpoint
of a lyrical and decorative style which
Vouet developed after abandoning
the Caravaggesque style he learnt
in Rome. When Louis XIII
summoned him back to France
in 1627, he imposed this new manner
on the French school.

373. Georges de La Tour
1593–1652
**Christ with St. Joseph
in the Carpenter's Shop**
c. 1640

Canvas. H 1.37 m (53.9 in.); W 1.02 m (40.2 in.)
Gift of Percy Moore Turner, 1948. RF 1948-27

Provincial painters in France continued working in a Caravaggesque
style until the middle of the
17th century. Born in Lunéville, La
Tour was appointed *peintre ordinaire*
to Louis XIII in 1639, and gave his
own very personal and pseudo-
archaic gloss to the style in a series
of "night scenes" with religious
themes, his mysticism expressing
itself in a simplified use of strongly
directed light. In this picture, with
its tightly-packed forms, the candle
flame lights a dramatic and humble
setting in which St. Joseph passes on
his worldly knowledge to the Infant
Jesus, with a painful premonition
in his eyes of the agony of the Cross.

374. Louis (or Antoine?) Le Nain
c. 1600/1610–1648
The Peasant Family
Canvas. H 1.13 m (44.5 in.); W 1.59 m (62.6 in.)
Acq. with Arthur Pernolet bequest, 1915. RF 2081

It is still not known precisely which of the three Le Nain brothers (most probably Louis or Antoine) was the author of a series of paintings with peasant subjects. The series is prominent among Western art of the genre, for its exceptional quality and solemnity. The picture's rigorous grid-like composition, its muted colors and the austere dignity of the figures, fixed in their watchful static poses give this homespun scene, the largest of the series, the universality of a classical text. Wine and bread are given emphasis as though steeped in symbolism.

375. Nicolas Poussin
1594–1665
The Rape of the Sabines
c. 1637–1638

Canvas. H 1.59 m (62.6 in.); W 2.08 m (81.9 in.)
Painted for Cardinal Omodei. Coll. of Louis XIV.
INV 7290

376. Claude Gellée,
known as **Claude Le Lorrain**
c. 1602–1682
The Disembarkation of Cleopatra at Tarsus
1642

Canvas. H 1.19 m (46.8 in.); W 1.68 m (66.1 in.)
Coll. of Louix XIV. INV 4716

Established in Rome in 1624, making only one stay in Paris from 1640 to 1642, Poussin posed as a master of the classical ideal, founded upon an erudite knowledge of the art and literature of the ancients. He concentrated on rigorous compositions in easel painting format for an avid circle of collectors. This picture is a powerful illustration of the phrygian mode that "vehement, furious, very severe form of expression" which Poussin thought befitted "the horrors of war." On the left we see Romulus, founder of Rome, overseeing the abduction of the Sabine women during a festival, in order to marry off his new citizens.

In an imaginary architecture suggestive of ancient splendors, Cleopatra disembarks at Tarsus intending to seduce Mark Anthony and, in so doing, submit him to the will of the Egyptians (41 B.C.). The moral portent of the picture is made explicit by a pendant, *The Consecration of David by Samuel* (Louvre), which contrasts the destiny of a humble boy crowned king, with the queen's ambition. Ancient history was not, however, much more than a pretext for this landscape painter from the Lorraine who moved to Rome; he uses it to animate a sun-drenched sea port in a perfect synthesis of the Bolognese classical ideal and the luminosity of the Italianizing Dutch school.

377. Eustache Le Sueur
1616–1655
Clio, Euterpe and Talia
c. 1652

Wood. H 1.30 m (51.2 in.); W 1.30 m (51.2 in.)
Painted for the Hôtel Lambert in Paris. Coll.
of Louis XVI. INV. 8057

No real idea of 17th century painting can be had without reference to the great ensembles which once decorated the walls of newly built Parisian *hôtels particuliers*. Although dismantled in 1776, the decorations Le Sueur painted for the Hôtel Lambert on the Ile Saint-Louis, Paris are one of the most complete ensembles to survive (13 paintings in the Louvre). This panel shows the Muses of History, Music and Comedy, which formed a Concert of nine Muses with four more panels, in the alcove of the bedroom of Mme Lambert de Thorigny.

378. Nicolas Poussin
1594–1665
Summer or **Ruth and Booz**
c. 1660–1664

Canvas. H 1.18 m (46.5 in.); W 1.60 m (63 in.)
Painted for the duke of Richelieu. Coll.
of Louis XIV. INV 7304

Summer is one of *The Four Seasons*
painted for the duke of Richelieu
between 1660 and 1664. Together
they mark the culmination of the
historical landscape genre.
The theme of the seasons is linked
with a biblical story, symbolizing
the ages of man, or great stages
in the history of the world. The
summer harvest in which Ruth and
Booz meet recalls Christ's union
with the Church and thus the
Christian era. But Poussin's message
to us, on the eve of his death,
consists above all of a timeless
meditation on relations between
man and nature, in this case
benificent, and in *Winter* or *The
Deluge*, hostile.

379. Philippe de Champaigne
1602–1674
The Ex-Voto of 1662
1662

H 1.65 m (65 in.); W 2.29 m (90.2 in.)
Given by the artist to the abbey of Port-Royal
in Paris. Seized during French Revolution. INV 1138

The *Ex-Voto* was painted as an act
of thanksgiving for the miraculous
healing of the artist's daughter,
Catherine, a nun in the Jansenist
convent of Port-Royal in Paris. She
recovered from a serious illness after
prayers held in the form of a novena
by the community. Champaigne has
depicted the moment when Mother
Agnès Arnauld, abbess of Port-Royal,
who is praying with the sick nun,
has a revelation of her imminent
healing. This double portrait stands
out from the enormous religious
output of this Brussels painter after
he moved to France in 1621 for its
austere, grandiloquent vision, well
served by an impeccable Flemish
technique.

380. Charles Le Brun
1619–1690
Entrance of Alexander into Babylon
1661–1665

Canvas. H 4.50 m (177.2 in.); W 7.07 m (275.3 in.)
Coll. of Louis XIV. INV 2898

Finished in 1665, this was the first of four huge canvases painted between 1661 and 1673 on the history of Alexander by the principal director of arts to Louis XIV (1638–1715), king of France from 1643. Standing on a chariot pulled by an elephant, Alexander makes his triumphal entrance into a magnificent Babylon, as the myth describes (the event occurred in 331 B.C.). With their skillful allusion to military glory and the virtues of monarchy, the four paintings, which had no specific destination, were a pretext for Le Brun to give expression to an epic vein of which he was the most brilliant exponent in France, long before he painted the Galerie des Glaces (Hall of Mirrors) at Versailles.

France, 18th century

381. Hyacinthe Rigaud
1659–1743
Portrait of Louis XIV
1701

Canvas. H 2.77 m (109 in.); W 1.84 m (72.4 in.)
Coll. of Louis XIV. INV 7492

Intended as a gift to Philip V, grandson of Louis XIV and king of Spain from 1700, this portrait of the Sun King was considered so fine at the court of Versailles that it remained in France. Thriving on his royal commissions, Rigaud had already caught the majestic and grandiloquent tone befitting a monarch who had become the symbol of absolute power. At sixty-three years of age, Louis XIV is shown in ceremonial robes with the instruments of his investiture: the ermine-lined mantle emblazoned with fleurs-de-lys, white stockings and slippers, the sword "Joyeuse" and his crown. The scepter and hand of justice belonged, however, to Henry IV. The head was painted from life, while costume and background were composed in the studio.

382. Nicolas de Largillière
1656–1746
Family Portrait

Canvas. H 1.49 m (58.7 in.); W 2.00 m (78.7 in.)
Dr. Louis La Caze bequest, 1869. MI 1085

An artistic battle of almost thirty years, duration ended around 1700, with the victory of the "Rubensians" who favored color, over the "Poussinists," the defenders of drawing. Established in Paris in 1682, Largillière along with Charles de la Fosse, put into practice the color theories of Roger de Piles. In this mature work, the copper gleam of the landscape, the tonal harmony and the reflections on the costumes are evidence of his debt to Van Dyck and Titian. This conscious influence is accompanied by a new conception of the portrait which is not so hieratic, with poses which are more relaxed and integrated into the setting. These qualities gave shape to French art under the Regency.

383. Jean-Antoine Watteau
1684–1721
The Pilgrimage to the Isle of Cythera
1717

Canvas. H 1.29 m (50.8 in.); W 1.94 m (76.4 in.)
Coll. of the Academy. INV 8525

Genre painting came back into
favor when the Academy admitted
Watteau to its ranks in 1717 on the
presentation of this work, the subject
of which was so novel that the term
fête galante was coined to describe
it. Drawing its inspiration from the
theater, the picture shows lovers
in party dress—some wearing the
pilgrim's hooded cape—coming
to seek love on the isle of Cythera,
under the statue of its goddess,
Venus. In an ephemeral landscape
which owes much to Venetian
painting, allegory is caught up in the
swirl of couples in a reverie; a new
and less learned interpretation
of Titian's elegiac mode.

384. Jean-Antoine Watteau
1684–1721
Pierrot, also known as **Gilles**
c. 1718–1719

Canvas. H 1.84 m (72.4 in.); W 1.49 m (58.7 in.)
Dr. Louis La Caze bequest, 1869. MI 1121

One of the few things we can be sure about in this famous but enigmatic work is the fact that Gilles is a Pierrot. Watteau may have painted the picture as a sign for the café run by the former actor, Belloni, who made his name as a Pierrot. But we do not know if it was a friend or an actor who modeled for Watteau. Standing with his arms dangling at his sides, with a dreamy, ingenuous look on his face, the moonstruck Pierrot stands out monumentally and idiosyncratically against a leafy Italianate background. At the foot of the mound, reminiscent of a fairground stage, four half-hidden figures—the Doctor on his ass, Léandre, Isabelle and the Captain—contribute to the singularity of the composition and the poetic drama.

385. François Lemoyne
1688–1737
Hercules and Omphale
1724

Canvas. H 1.84 m (72.4 in.); W 1.49 m (58.7 in.)
Dr. Louis La Caze bequest, 1869. MI 1086

Lemoyne was the most important
of the history painters working
during Louis XV's youth. Like
Watteau, his contemporary, he was
to die young, after the ambitious
decoration of the ceiling of Hercules
at Versailles, which earned him the
title of First Painter to the King
in 1736. His knowledge of Venetian
painting, completed by a trip to Italy
in 1723, where he painted *Hercules
and Omphale*, encouraged his use
of a lighter palette and richer
brushwork, appropriate to a celebration of the female nude, which after
his example became the favorite
theme of the generation of Boucher
and Carle Vanloo.

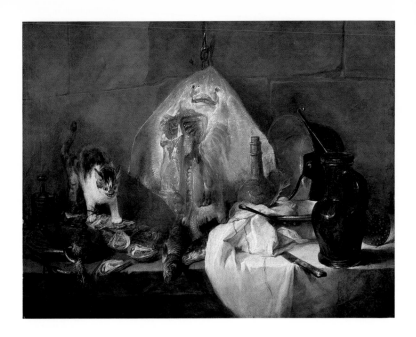

386. Jean-Siméon Chardin
1699–1779
The Skate
Before 1728

Canvas. H 1.14 m (44.9 in.); W 1.46 m (57.5 in.)
Coll. of the Academy. INV 3197

Despite a rigid hierarchy of genres
in which still-life held a very humble
position, Chardin earned a reputation
from an early age as a great artist,
with a technical "magic," which
excited Diderot's admiration. The
Academy was quick to recognize
him. Contrary to custom, Chardin
was made an associate and full
member on the same day in 1728
because both *The Skate*, which was
kept as an acceptance piece, and *The
Buffet*, matched the finest Flemish
examples of the genre (Jan Fyt for
example). A magnificent piece
of painting, the work in its rigorous
construction looks forward to the
small and more austere still-lifes
of his maturity (such as *The Smoking
Room, The Brioche*, and *The Silver
Goblet*).

387. François Boucher
1703–1770
Family Taking Breakfast
1739

Canvas. H 81.5 cm (32.1 in.); W 65.5 cm (25.8 in.)
Dr. Achille Malécot bequest, 1895. RF 926

For a brief period, between 1739 and
1746, this painter of mythical love
scenes extended his repertoire
to contemporary genre scenes,
influenced by 17th century Dutch
masters and more directly by Jean-
François de Troy. This picture
describes in detail, with a dazzlingly
fresh, graceful style, a scene of daily
life in a Parisian family—like that
of the painter himself, who was
at that time father of two small
sons—devoting themselves to the
new craze for coffee. The painter
of happiness has captured for
us an *art de vivre* that is more light-
hearted than Chardin's.

388.Jean-Baptiste Perronneau
1715–1783
Portrait of Madame de Sorquainville
1749

Canvas. H 1.01 m (39.8 in.); W 81 cm (31.9 in.)
Gift of D. David-Weill, 1937. RF 1937-8

The elegance of the costume and refined pose of the sitter recall the work of Nattier. However, what remains impressed upon us is the portrait's psychological insight typifying a current which developed in France during the mid-18th century with Maurice Quentin de la Tour and Perronneau, who were more interested in the sitter's character than in flattery. The artist has borrowed from his favorite technique of pastel, painting here in chalky tones with thinly-layered feathery brushwork and leaving some areas barely finished.

389. Jean-Honoré Fragonard
1732–1806
The Bathers

Canvas. H 64 cm (25.2 in.); W 80 cm (31.5 in.)
Dr. Louis La Caze bequest, 1869. MI 1055

The female nude was a constant
preoccupation of French rococo
painters. Unlike his master Boucher,
Fragonard needed no mythological
source as an excuse for painting this
gathering of blonde and Rubensian
beauties, when he returned from Italy
in 1761. Bodies, drapery and a lush
natural setting are intermingled
in a whirl of thick rapid brushstrokes.
These give the picture the dynamic
force of a sketch, a characteristic
quality of the most unconventional
artist of his time.

390. Jean-Baptiste Greuze
1725–1805
The Punished Son
1778

Canvas. H 1.30 m (51.2 in.); W 1.63 m (64.2 in.)
Acq. 1820. INV 5039

Together with its pendant *The
Father's Curse*, this picture illustrates
two scenes in a family drama
painted by Greuze in 1777 and 1778.
Here we see the son returning and
lamenting over the loss of his father
whose death he brought about
by leaving for the army. All the
resources of great history painting,
by Poussin in particular, were used
by this artist at the service of a new
genre combining contemporary
dress with a love of pathos. Greuze's
effusive, patriarchal and "pastoral"
moral didacticism described a new
bourgeois art in which the ideals
of the Age of Enlightenment
triumphed.

391. Louis David
1748–1825
The Oath of the Horatii
1784

Canvas. H 3.30 m (129.9 in.); W 4.25 m (167.3 in.)
Commissioned by Louis XVI. INV 3692

The three brothers, the Horatii, chosen by Rome to challenge the Curiatii, champions of the town of Alba, are taking an oath that they will win or die and are receiving weapons from their father. Like Corneille in his tragedy *Horace*, David contrasts the stoic resolution of the warriors, underlined by strict geometry and strident color, with the gentle delineation of the women which expresses their suffering. Shown in Paris in 1785, this painting earned David a European reputation as uncontested leader of the neoclassical movement.

392. Hubert Robert
1733–1808
The Pont du Gard
1787

Canvas. H 2.42 m (95.3 in.); W 2.42 m (95.3 in.)
Commissioned by Louis XVI. INV 7650

The fashion for archaeology in the 18th century redoubled with a new interest in national heritage when the Direction des Bâtiments commissioned Robert to paint for Louis XVI's appartments at Fontainebleau, four decorative paintings on the subject of antiquities in France. The famous aqueduct of Agrippa, built in 19 B.C. to bring water from the river Gard to Nîmes, featured prominently. A follower of Pannini and Piranesi, this indefatigable painter of ruins, whose success did not wane on his return from Rome in 1765, captures the picturesque details of the site without detracting from the harmonious color scheme and dynamic force of his composition.

France, 19th century

393. Antoine-Jean Gros
1772–1835
**Napoleon Bonaparte Visiting the
Victims of the Plague at Jaffa**
1804

Canvas. H 5.23 m (205.9 in.); W 7.15 m (281.5 in.)
Commissioned in 1804. INV 5064

Anticipating the huge canvases that
Gros, a pupil of David, devoted
to the Napoleonic epic, this picture
celebrates General Bonaparte's
courage and humanity, visiting the
sick without fear of contagion,
during the Syrian campaign
(March 11, 1799). The novelty of the
theme—a contemporary rather than
classical hero—is matched by Gros's
development of a style which from
1804 contained all the elements
of romantic painting. We see this
here in the strikingly naturalistic
bodies, the sense of color, and in the
cultural fascination with the Orient.

394. Pierre-Paul Prud'hon
1758–1823
The Empress Joséphine
1805

Canvas. H 2.44 m (96.1 in.); W 1.79 m (70.5 in.)
Coll. of Napoleon I. Entered the Louvre in 1879.
RF 270

A popular painter during the
French Empire, Prud'hon was fond
of shrouding his figures in mist
in the manner of Leonardo da Vinci
and Correggio. This adds to the
melancholic charm of his portraits,
usually set in the open air in the
English style. Born in Martinique
and widow of the general
Beauharnais, Joséphine Tascher
de la Pagerie(1763–1814), married
Bonaparte in 1796. When she did
not provide the Emperor with
an heir she was repudiated in 1809.
Prud'hon depicted her in the grounds
of her château at Malmaison in 1805,
a year after Napoleon's coronation.

395. Louis David
1748–1825
**The Coronation of Napoleon
in Notre-Dame**
1806–1807

Canvas. H 6.21 m (244.4 in.); W 9.79 m (385.4 in.)
Commissioned by Napoleon i, INV 3699

Appointed official painter to the
Emperor in December 1804, David
was given the task of commemorating
the coronation festivities in four
huge canvases, only two of which
were executed (*The Distribution of the
Eagle Standards* is at Versailles).
This ceremony took place in the
cathedral of Notre-Dame in Paris
on December 2, 1804. David chose
to show the episode following the
annointing: Napoleon is crowning
Josephine while Pope Pius VII gives
him his blessing. The action is only
a small part of a composition conceived as an enormous group portrait
containing over a hundred figures.

**396. Anne-Louis Girodet
de Roussy-Trioson**
1767–1824
The Burial of Atala
1808

Canvas. H 2.07 m (81.5 in.); W 2.67 m (105.1 in.)
Acq. 1819. INV 4958

With the help of Father Aubry, the
Indian Chactas is burying Atala,
a young Christian maiden who was
to take the veil, and who preferred
to poison herself rather than

succumb to carnal love. Girodet's
unusual talent, given to cavernous
gloom and spectral forms, was well
suited to illustrating Chateaubriand
whose novel *Atala* was published
in 1801 on his return from America.
There is a kindred meditative
feeling, a similar belief in savage
but beneficent nature and both men
were leading exponents of pre-
romantic sensibility.

397. Théodore Géricault
1791–1824
The Raft of the Medusa
1819

Canvas. H 4.91 m (193.3 in.); W 7.16 m (281.9 in.)
Acq. 1824. INV 488

Géricault was highly moved by the
real-life drama of 149 shipwrecked
sailors from the frigate *Medusa*,
abandoned for twelve days on a raft
off the Senegalese coast.
To illustrate it he chose the moment
on July 17, 1816 when the
15 survivors were overcome with
despair as the *Argus*, the ship that
eventually was to rescue them, sailed
off. This was the first time
a contemporary news item had been
made the subject for a painting
on such a large scale. The dark
subject, matched by the coloring and
the macabre though realistic
depiction of the dying, make what
was a controversial exhibit at the
1819 Salon, the first epic proclamation
of romanticism.

398. Eugène Delacroix
1798–1863
The Massacres at Chios
1824

Canvas. H 4.19 m (165 in.); W 3.54 m (139.4 in.)
Acq. 1824. INV 3823

The romantics, Byron especially,
ardently espoused the cause of the
Greeks under Turkish oppression.
The young Delacroix, whose *Dante
and Virgil* had caused a stir at the
1823 Salon, exhibited the following
year this cruel episode from the
Greek War of Independence,
illustrating the savage repression
of an uprising on the island of Chios
in 1822. Provoking bitter critical
divisions, it is a veritable manifesto
of romanticism. Though by no means
unimportant, the lavish colors and
exotic costumes are secondary to the
contemporary subject matter which
has political implications (the
liberation of peoples) and aesthetic
undertones (the freedom of form).

399. Eugène Delacroix
1798–1863
Liberty Leading the People
1830

Canvas. H 2.60 m (102.4 n.); W 3.25 m (127.9 in.)
Acq. 1831. RF 129

Delacroix was not actively involved
in the three days of July 1830,
known as the *Trois Glorieuses*, which
saw out the antiquated autocracy
of Charles X and brought in Louis-
Philippe's parliamentary monarchy.
But liberal and romantic as he was,
he was keen to celebrate the 28 July,
when Parisians took up arms in the
vain hope of restoring the Republic.
The allegorical figure of Liberty
waves the tricolor flag and storms
the corpse-ridden barricades with
a young combatant at her side.
Realism and epic vision work
together. Reviled by conservatives,
the work was bought by Louis-
Philippe at the 1831 Salon. Soon
after, it was hidden for fear
of inciting public unrest.

**400. Jean-Auguste-Dominique
Ingres**
1780–1867
Portrait of Louis-François Bertin
1832

Canvas. H 1.16 m (45.7 in.); W 95 cm (37.4 in.)
Acq. 1897. RF 1071

Founder of the *Journal des Débats*,
Ingres turned "Monsieur Bertin"
(1766–1841) into the epitome
of that triumphant bourgeoisie
of 1830 backed by his paper. The
secret of his success lies in the sitter's
forthright and commanding pose
which Ingres hit upon after much
searching, while his model was
conversing with a friend: "Come and
sit for me tomorrow," he told me,
"Your portrait's done." Finished
in under a month, this strikingly
vivid portrait which is meticulously
painted caused a public outcry at the
1833 Salon, but earned the admiration
of Baudelaire. Ingres was, in his
eyes, "the only man in France who
really made portraits."

401. Théodore Chassériau
1819–1856
Toilet of Esther
1841

Canvas. H 45.5 cm (17.9 in.); W 35.5 cm (14 in.)
Baron Arthur Chassériau bequest, 1934. RF 3900

By the time he painted *Esther*, this
precocious 22-year-old pupil
of Ingres had already exhibited
in five Salons and had visited Italy.
Keen to repeat the experience
of *Susanna Bathing* (Louvre), which
had earned him recognition in the
1839 Salon, Chassériau used the Old
Testament as a pretext for painting
the lavish color and sensuality
of an imaginary Orient. Learning
from Ingres' drawing and hieratic
models, and from Delacroix's
vibrant use of color in the middle
distance, he combined both their
approaches with subtlety, adding
a charm all his own with, among
other things, the nostalgic listlessness
of his figures.

402. Jean-Auguste-Dominique Ingres
1780–1867
The Turkish Bath
1862

Canvas on panel. H 1.10 m (43.3 in.);
W 1.10 m (43.3 in.)
Gift of the Société des Amis du Louvre, with
Maurice Fenaille, 1911. RF 1934

Completed when he was 82, this
composition was the result of many
studies which Ingres made from
1807 onward of female bathers,
a theme linking the female nude
with Ottoman exoticism.
His illustrations of the harem might
well have been inspired by the Lady
Montagu's *Letters* (1764), which
he had read forty years earlier.
The serpentine contours of the bodies
and his repeated use of the same
model add a note of abstraction
to the sensuality of this accumulation
of voluptuous flesh, a pure fantasy
of an erotic, perfumed Orient which
the western imagination had
perpetuated for over a century.

403. Camille Corot
1796–1875
The Church of Marissel near Beauvais
1866

Canvas. H 55 cm (21.6 in.); W 42 cm (16.5 in.)
Gift of Etienne Moreau-Nélaton, 1906. RF 1642

Familiar with the Beauvais countryside from visits to his painter friend Badin whom he had met in Italy, Corot shows the village of Marissel, on the banks of the Thérain, with its fortified church on the hill, which is still standing. Painted on the spot in nine morning sittings during the spring of 1866, the artist's intention was to combine the effects of perspective (the gap between the trees) with those of light (water reflections). The work owes a lot to the Dutch masters.

Corot enjoyed unwavering success during his lifetime. This picture, exhibited in the 1867 Salon, was admired by Queen Victoria and bought for the then substantial sum of 4,000 francs by a tailor called Richard.

Italy

Spurned by classicists, the "Primitives" or early Italian masters before Leonardo and Raphael were not rediscovered until the end of the 18th century. Paradoxically enough, this was due to the neoclassical movement.

Under Emperor Napoleon's orders, Dominique-Vivant Denon, Director of Museums, went to Italy and requisitioned altar-pieces by masters ranging from Cimabue to Fra Angelico, which went into the Louvre after 1815. But the French vogue for Italian Primitives dates from Napoleon III's acquisition of the marquis of Campana's collection. Leaving a number to go to the Musée du Petit Palais at Avignon, around a hundred pictures entered the Louvre including Paolo Uccello's *Battle* (no. 411) and Cosimo Tura's *Pietà* (no. 414). This formed the kernel of the collection, which was subsequently expanded with occasional acquisitions, ranging from Mantegna's *Saint Sebastian* to Piero della Francesca's *Portrait of Malatesta* (no. 410).

The Italian Renaissance, one of the Louvre's greatest treasures, owes its presence almost entirely to two kings: Francis I and Louis XIV. The former, a patron of the arts, protector of Leonardo da Vinci and founder of Fontainebleau, housed the most famous works of his time under one roof; among them, the *Mona Lisa* (no. 418) and the *Virgin of the Rocks* (no. 416) by Leonardo, the great *Holy Family* by Raphael and *Charity* (no. 423) by Andrea del Sarto. Louis XIV wisely purchased existing collections belonging to the Cardinal Mazarin and to the banker Jabach, which included works by Correggio, Raphael, Titian and Giulio Romano. The Renaissance was thus broadly represented when the Louvre was created in 1793.

The museum kept only a fraction, though significant one, of the immense gains from Napoleonic campaigns, including Veronese's *Wedding Feast at Cana* (no. 427). Isabella d'Este's collection in the Château de Richelieu was seized during the Revolution. The collection, admirable as it is, betrays its origins. Mannerism is not well represented; it was a period when even Renaissance art had to show evidence of a certain classical approach.

Taken with art in the "Grand Manner," Louis XIV was as interested in the great Italian painters as he was in the great French of his century.

His acquisition of Mazarin's and Jabach's collections, which came in turn from those of Charles I of England and the dukes of Mantua, brought Caravaggio and the Bolognese school into the royal collection. His efforts were completed a century later by the minister, Angiviller, who made purchases for Louis XVI with a view to making the future museum more comprehensive.

With the romantic perpetuation of the idyll of Venice, 19th century interest centered mainly on the 18th century Venetian school. However, 18th century Italian painting is poorly represented, despite an important collection of works by Pannini, and the cycle of *Venetian Festivals* (no. 434) by Guardi, seized during the Revolution. This collection has expanded since the Second World War and, alongside a few paintings by Tiepolo, now includes works by Piazzetta, Pellegrini, Sebastiano Ricci, Pietro Longhi, Canaletto and Crespi.

404. Cenni de Pepe,
known as **Cimabue**
c. 1240–after 1302
**Maestà. The Madonna and Child
in Majesty Surrounded by Angels**
c. 1270?
Wood. H 4.27 m (168.1 in.); W 2.80 m (110.2 in.)
Church of San Francesco, Pisa. Entered the Louvre
in 1813. INV 254

Drawing on Byzantine iconography,
the *Maestà*, an enthroned Virgin
on a gold ground, was a major
theme for the Tuscan masters, who
developed a new pictorial language
for Western art between the late
13th and the early 14th centuries.
First among them, Cimabue painted
his monumental *pala* for the church
of San Francesco at Pisa sometime
around 1270, which probably
precedes another *Maestà* by him,
along with two by Giotto and
Duccio in the Uffizi in Florence.
Cimabue substitutes delicate
modeling of skin tones and drapery
for the linear formalism of the
Byzantines.

405. Giotto di Bondone
c. 1267–1337
**St. Francis of Assisi Receiving
the Stigmata**

Wood. H 3.13 m (123.2 in.); W 1.63 m (64.2 in.)
Church of San Francesco, Pisa. Entered the Louvre
in 1813. INV 309

This altar-piece illustrates four
episodes in the life of the holy
founder of the mendicant order
of the Franciscans (1182–1226). With
some variants, the compositions are
drawn from frescoes executed
around 1290 by the young Giotto
in the upper Basilica of Assisi.
Signed along the lower edge of the
frame, the Louvre panel is a decisive
element in the attribution of the
Assisi cycle to Giotto, which was
once contested. He was the first
painter in the history of Western art
to set figures within a coherent space
and give them structural consistency.

406. Simone Martini
c. 1284–1344
The Carrying of the Cross
Wood. H 30 cm (11.8 in.); W 20 cm (7.9 in.)
Acq. 1834. INV 670 bis

The Carrying of the Cross is one of six panels of a portable polyptych which has now been dismantled (the other panels are in Antwerp and Berlin). It is thought to have been painted by this Sienese master a short while before his supposed arrival in 1336 at the papal court of Avignon. The tightly packed and agitated figures give drama to the scene. Its most salient features, however, are the clearly told narrative, jewel-like colors, stamped gold and a linear elegance, all of which mark the art of the most brilliant representative of Gothic painting in Italy.

407. Guido di Pietro,
known as **Fra Angelico**
Known from 1417–d. 1455
The Coronation of the Virgin
Before 1435

Wood. H 2.09 m (82.3 in.); W 2.06 m (81.1 in.)
Church of San Domenico, Fiesole. Entered the
Louvre in 1812. INV 314

A masterpiece of serene piety and
harmonious coloring, the *Coronation
of the Virgin* was painted for the
church of the Dominican convent
of Fiesole. The predella depicts the
entombment of Christ and six
episodes from the life of St. Dominic
who founded the order to which the
painter belonged. Clever use
of perspective and a skillful placing
of figures in space demonstrate that
despite his Medieval sensibility
Fra Angelico was one of the first
to make use of the architectonic
discoveries of Brunelleschi
and Masaccio who ushered in the
Florentine Renaissance.

408. Antonio Puccio,
known as **Pisanello**
Before 1395–1455?
Portrait of Ginevra d'Este
c. 1436–1438?

Wood. H 43 cm (16.9 in.); W 30 cm (11.8 in.)
Acq. 1893. RF 766

The sitter, who is wearing a sprig
of juniper on her bodice and the
Este family emblem (a two-handled
vase) on her robe, has been identified
as the princess Ginevra d'Este, first
wife of Sigismondo Malatesta, who

had her poisoned in 1440.
This portrait is one of the first
known examples of an independent
profile portrait in Italy, a type much
favored by Pisanello both in paintings
and medallions. Her barely modeled
face joins details of her dress
in a delicate web of arabesque lines.
This refinement, typical of international Gothic style, is enhanced
by the flowering branches behind.

409. Stefano di Giovanni,
known as **Sassetta**
1392?–1450
**The Madonna and Child Surrounded
by Six Angels, St. Anthony of Padua,
St. John the Evangelist**
c. 1437–1444

Wood. Central panel: H 2.07 m (81.5 in.); W 1.18 m
(46.5 in.) H. 1.95 m (76.8 in.); W 57 cm (22.4 in.);
Side panels: H 1.95 m (76.8 in.); W 57 cm (22.4 in.)
Acq. 1956. RF 1956-11

These three panels belong to the main
side of a now dismantled, immense
polyptych which was the most ambitious of its time, and was
executed for the main altar of the
church of San Francesco in Borgo
San Sepolcro. Two elements on the
predella, illustrating the legend
of the blessed Ranieri Rasini, who
died in this Tuscan town in 1304, are
also in the Louvre. The use of a gold
ground shows a respect for the
Medieval tradition, which
characterizes 15th century Sienese
art. Sassetta, its most brilliant
exponent, linked this to an infinitely
tender, mystical quality.

410. Piero della Francesca
c. 1422–1492
Portrait of Sigismondo Malatesta
c. 1450

Wood. H 44 cm (17.3 in.); W 34 cm (13.4 in.)
Acq. 1978. RF 1978-1

This portrait of the celebrated
condottiere and patron of Rimini,
Sigismund Malatesta (1417–1468)
was doubtless painted shortly before
the fresco of the *Tempio Malatestiano*
dated 1451, where Piero gives him
the same profile but shows him full
length and kneeling by his patron
saint, Sigismond. The formula of the
profile bust, borrowed from the
Gothic courtly tradition, is given
a strict rendition here. Piero brought
to it two new elements: the powerful
solid volume of the bust and the
flesh-tones enlivening the face,
the former deriving from Tuscan
art, the latter from the Flemish, and
combined them for the first time
in an Italian painting.

411. Paolo di Dono,
known as **Uccello**
1397–1475
The Battle of San Romano
c. 1455

Wood. H 1.82 m (71.65 in.); W 3.17 m (124.8 in.)
Compagna coll. Entered in 1863, MI 409

The victory by the Florentines over the Sienese at San Romano in 1432, is the theme of three panels painted by Uccello for the palace of Cosimo de' Medici at Florence (the other episodes are in Florence and London). The Louvre painting depicts the counterattack of Michelotto da Cotignola. The rhythm of lances and legs conveys a sense of commotion in the army which is described in a compact mass, with the artist making great use of masterly foreshortening. This exercise in pure geometry is enlivened by lavish costumes, which indicate that while Uccello took the theoretical experiments of the Florentine Renaissance to an extreme, he did not entirely forsake the florid forms of the Gothic tradition.

412. Andrea Mantegna
1431–1506
The Crucifixion
c. 1456–1460

Wood. H 76 cm (29.9 in.); W 96 cm (37.8 in.)
Church of San Zeno, Verona. Entered the Louvre
in 1798. INV 369

At Padua, where he was trained,
Mantegna made two parallel
discoveries: the art of antiquity and
the use of perspective as introduced
by Donatello and Uccello. Before
leaving for the court of Mantua
in 1459, he produced his first
masterpieces, including the altar-
piece for the church of San Zeno
at Verona. *The Crucifixion* is the
central panel of the predella which
was dismantled in the early
19th century (the side panels are in
the Musée de Tours). This tragic and
stony vision of Golgotha displays
a masterly command of space and
a meticulous attention to archaeological detail, which were the basis
of Mantegna's bold classicism.

413. Antonello da Messina
Known at Messina in 1456–d. 1479
Portrait of a Man,
known as **The Condottiere**
1475

Wood. H 36 cm (14.2 in.); W 30 cm (11.8 in.)
Acq. 1865. MI 693

In a southern Italy open to Flemish
influences, Antonello managed
in a unique way to combine the fluid
technique of Jan van Eyck with the
theory of the Tuscans and Piero
della Francesca. By the time he left
Sicily for a brief sojourn in Venice
in 1475–1476, his style was assured
and his visit had a decisive effect
on Venetian painters. Among the
masterpieces he produced, there
were several portraits, including
The Condottiere, where meticulous
Flemish observation blends with
a sober monumentality.

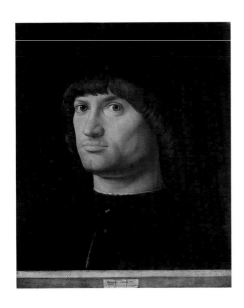

414. Cosimo Tura
Known in Ferrara from 1431 to 1495
Pietà
c. 1480

Wood. H 1.32 m (52 in.); W 2.68 m (105.5 in.)
Church of San Giorgio fuori le Mura, Ferrara.
Campana coll. Entered the Louvre in 1863. MII 485

Founder of the school of Ferrara,
Tura looked to the flourishing
Paduan school and, with Mantegna's
example, evolved an unusual style
combining monumentality with
linear incisiveness, geometric rigor
with a dry expressionism which may

have been borrowed from Rogier
van der Weyden. The anguished
Pietà once formed the upper lunette
of one of Tura's major works, the
polyptych painted for the Roverella
family in the church of San Giorgio
fuori le Mura at Ferrara (dismantled,
the central section is now in London).

415. Alessandro Filipepi,
known as **Botticelli**
c. 1445–1510
**Venus and the Graces Offering Gifts
to a Young Girl**
c. 1483

Fresco. H 2.11 m (83.1 in.); W 2.83 m (111.4 in.)
Villa Lemmi. Acq. 1882. RF 321

This fresco and its pendant came
from the Villa Lemmi near
Florence, which is thought to have
belonged to the Tornabuoni family,
who had links with the Medicis.
They are generally dated to around
1483, between the two great secular
paintings at the Uffizi, *Primavera*
and *The Birth of Venus*. The earthly
world, symbolized by the young girl,
on the right side, contrasts in its
simplicity with the flowing rhythms
of the celestial beauties, bearers
of that classical ideal, which Botticelli,
adopting the refined humanism
of Lorenzo the Magnificent, expresses
with complex linear rhythms and
soft colors.

416. Leonardo di ser Piero da Vinci, known as Leonardo da Vinci
1452–1519
Virgin of the Rocks
1483–1486

Arched-top canvas. H 1.99 m (78.3 in.);
W 1.22 m (48 in.)
Coll. of Francis I. INV 777

A universal genius in the sciences as well as the arts, Leonardo pursued a career that took him from Florence to Milan and Rome, before following Francis I to Amboise in 1517. First of the masterpieces painted at the Sforza's court, the *Virgin of the Rocks* was destined for the church of San Francesco Grande in Milan, then withdrawn after financial litigation (a second version is in London).
It is suffused with a gentle *sfumato*; that indicates a new approach to space which is no longer purely geometric in construction but is conveyed instead by a tonal gradation expressing the enveloping atmosphere.

417. Domenico di Tomaso Bigordi,
known as **Ghirlandaio**
1449–1494
The Visitation (with Mary Jacobi and Mary Salome)
1491
Wood. H 1.72 m (67.7 in.); W 1.65 m (65 in.)
Church of Santa Maria Maddelena dei Pazzi,
Florence. Entered the Louvre in 1812. INV 297

A contemporary of Botticelli, Ghirlandaio was head of the main Florentine workshop of the late 15th century. Some of his major works were executed for the Tornabuoni family; the cycle of the *Life of the Virgin* in the choir of Santa Maria Novella, and soon after, the Louvre *pala* which was commissioned by Lorenzo Tornabuoni for the chapel of the church of Cestello in Florence (Santa Maria Maddelena dei Pazzi) and completed, according to Vasari, by the artist's two brothers.

The figures, which combine linear grace with monumentality, stand out against a classical arch which opens onto a view of Rome.

418. Leonardo di ser Piero da Vinci, known as **Leonardo da Vinci**
1452–1519
Portrait of Lisa Gherardini, known as **The Mona Lisa** or **La Gioconda**
1503–1506
Wood. H 77 cm (30.3 in.); W 53 cm (20.9 in.)
Coll. of Francis I. INV 779

If Vasari is correct, the portrait which Leonardo took to France, and was acquired by Francis I, was of Lisa Gherardini (1479–d. before 1550) who in 1495 married Francesco di Bartolomeo di Zanoli del Giocondo. The title "La Gioconda" would thus derive from this notable Florentine's name. But in Italian *gioconda* also means a light-hearted woman. With a lasting effect on Italian art, this portrait stood for an ideal. The smile that gives her life is, however, a feature of many of Leonardo's figures. Several scholars have concluded that the portrait was worked on over a long period, starting around 1505–1506 in Florence, and that it was finished during Leonardo's peregrinations in Milan or Rome.

419. Raffaello Santi,
known as **Raphael**
1483–1520
**The Virgin and Child with St. John the
Baptist,** known as **La Belle Jardinière**
1507

Wood with arched top. H 1.22 m (48 in.);
W 80 cm (31.5 in.)
Coll. of Louis XIV. INV 602

This Virgin, which takes its nick-
name from the pastoral background,
is one of the most famous of Raphael's
Madonnas from his Florentine
period (1504–1508). The period was
an important one for the young
artist from Urbino, who forsook his
master Perugino's manner for
a classicism influenced by his study
of Leonardo, Michelangelo and
Fra Bartolomeo. The influence
of Leonardo is particularly apparent
here, and the latter left Florence
in 1506. However, drawing remains
Raphael's greatest concern here and
the serene atmosphere is quite remote
from the troubling complexities
of Leonardo.

420. Leonardo di ser Piero da Vinci,
known as **Leonardo da Vinci**
1452–1519
The Virgin and Child with St. Anne
c. 1510

Wood. H 1.68 m (66.1 in.); W 1.30 m (51.2 in.)
Coll. of Louis XIII. INV 776

Although quite rare, the depiction
of the Virgin in the lap of St. Anne
goes back to medieval times. This
version was painted in Milan around
1510, and was the fruit of much
deliberation, as drawings and

a cartoon indicate (the latter
is in London). Leonardo never quite
finished this panel, however, and
kept it with him until he died.
Painted in fine, translucent glazes
with the underdrawing showing
through in some areas, it represents
a culmination of his research into
aerial perspective, which Leonardo
codified in the draft of his *Treatise
on Painting*.

421. Vittore Carpaccio
c. 1450/1454–1525/1526
**The Sermon of St. Stephen
at Jerusalem**

Canvas. H 1.48 m (58.3 in.); W 1.94 m (76.4 in.)
Acq. as an exchange with the Brera, Milan, 1812.
INV 181

Carpaccio was the most brilliant
exponent of the narrative style
which developed in the frescoes
of the *Scuole* in Venice from the
second half of the 15th century. After
the monumental cycle of the *History
of St. Ursula* (Accademia, Venice)
and the frescoes which remain
in place in the Scuola di San Giorgio
degli Schiavoni, Carpaccio painted
six *Scenes from the Life of St. Stephen*
(Louvre, Brera, Stuttgart, Berlin)
between 1511 and 1520 for the
Scuola dei Lanieri at San Stefano.
This served as a pretext for
a depiction of a resplendent
Jerusalem, with Oriental costumes
and exoticism giving an added
richness to the classical ideal.

422. Raffaello Santi,
known as **Raphael**
1483–1520
Baltazar Castiglione
c. 1514–1515

Canvas. H 82 cm (32.3 in.); W 67 cm (26.4 in.)
Coll. of Louis XIV. INV 611

Papal patronage, which had attracted
all the most celebrated masters
to Rome from Giotto's time onward,
reached a peak with the elections
to the Holy See of Julius II and then
Leo X who from 1508 to 1520
patronized Bramante, Michelangelo
and Raphael. A valiant soldier and
man of letters, Baltazar Castiglione
(1478–1529) was the quintessence
of the Renaissance gentleman.
His *Book of the Courtier*, published
in 1528, reflects an ideal of aesthetic
and spiritual perfection which
is very close to Raphael's ideal
in painting. There could not
be a finer testimony of the friendship
between these two men than
this portrait, which combines
a magnificent costume with deep
psychological insight.

423. Andrea d'Agnolo di Francesco,
known as **Andrea del Sarto**
1486–1530
Charity
1518

Canvas. H 1.85 m (72.8 in.); W 1.37 m (53.9 in.)
Coll. of Francis I. INV 712

Andrea del Sarto gave Florentine classicism its last gleam before the spread of mannerism. Summoned to France by Francis I, he stayed there for less than a year (1518–1519). *Charity* is the only work known for certain to have been painted by the artist while in France. In a perfect pyramidal composition with great depth, it depicts the theological virtue of *Charity* surrounded by her customary attributes—three children—and a complex mesh of symbolic objects, such as the burning jar, an open pomegranate and nuts.

424. Antonio Allegri,
known as **Correggio**
1489?–1534
Venus and Cupid with a Satyr
c. 1525

Canvas. H 1.88 m (74 in.); W 1.25 m (49.2 in.)
Coll. of Louis XIV. INV 42

Born in Correggio, the artist moved
to nearby Palma in 1518, and in the
cupolas of the churches there
he developed a novel illusionism,
enriching the science of perspective
with luminous atmospheric effects.

In the *Sleep of Venus*, painted for the
Gonzagas at Mantua, possibly
as a pendant to *The School of Love*
(London), Correggio bathes bodies
in a uniformly glowing light, which
joins the soft forms and flowing
brushwork in a celebration of the
delicate sensuality of this Venus
in her abandonment, a symbol
of carnal love. Successors to this
picture can be seen in the voluptuous
mythological paintings of the
18th century.

425. Tiziano Vecellio,
known as **Titian**
1488/9–1576
The Entombment
c. 1525

Canvas. N 1.48 m (58.3 in.); W 2.12 m (83.5 in.)
Coll. of Louis XIV. INV 749

426. Giovanni Battista di Jacopo,
known as **Rosso Fiorentino**
1496–1540
Pietà
c. 1530–1535

Canvas. H 1.27 m (50 in.); W 1.63 m (64.2 in.)
Painted for the Constable Anne of Montmorency.
Chapel of the Château d'Ecouen. Seized during the
Revolution. INV 594

If the name of Venice is suggestive of the triumph of color in painting, it is thanks to Titian. After an early period under the influence of Giorgione, who painted the *Concert Champêtre* now in the Louvre, Titian reached maturity with a series of works in which classical rigor is allied to the effects of a "chromatic alchemy," which soon became paramount. The *Entombment* was painted for the Gonzagas at Mantua, and its composition was borrowed from Raphael. Titian heightens the drama with a warm-toned evening light which cuts across the figures, leaving the livid corpse of Christ half-hidden in shadow.

Rosso Fiorentino, thus known because of his red hair and Florentine birth, was summoned by Francis I to work on the Château de Fontainebleau in 1530. Of the numerous frescoes painted by this artist who was, along with Primaticcio, the leader of the School of Fontainebleau, all that remains are the frescoes in the Galerie de François I. Commissioned by Anne of Montmorency, whose arms it bears, this picture is unlike this mannerist master's usual ornamental inventions owing to its stern concentration on the drama. This is summed up in the pathos of the Virgin's gesture as she falters at the threshold of Christ's tomb.

427. Paolo Caliari, known as **Veronese**
1528–1588
The Wedding Feast at Cana
1562–1563

Canvas. H 6.66 m (262.2 in.); W 9.90 m (389.8 in.)
San Giorgio Maggiore, Venice. Entered the Louvre
in 1798. INV 142

Called to Venice in 1553, this painter
from Verona was an indefatigable
worker, making use of his exceptional
talent as a decorator, and a capacity
to cover huge surfaces combining
masterful stage sets, lavish contemporary costumes and resplendent

color. *The Wedding Feast at Cana*
once decorated the refectory that
Palladio built for the Benedictines
on the island of San Giorgio
Maggiore. Taking a sovereign liberty
with iconography, the sacred story
is transformed into the fashionable
splendor of a Venetian wedding.
If we are to believe a long-established
tradition, all the Venetian masters
are depicted here as musicians;
Titian, Jacopo Bassano, Tintoretto,
as well as Veronese himself dressed
in white.

428. Jacopo Robusti,
known as **Tintoretto**
1518–1594
Paradise

Canvas. H 1.43 m (56.3 in.); W 3.62 m (142.5 in.)
Entered the Louvre in 1798. INV 570

After the fire which ravaged the
Great Council room in the Doges'
Palace in 1577, a competition was
held to decorate the end wall with
a huge vision of *Paradise*. Veronese
and Bassano won the competition
but were unable to take up the

commission, and Tintoretto took
over, on Veronese's death in 1588.
More than the final work, executed
with his workshop, which is still
in situ, this preparatory sketch reveals
the visionary fervor of a man who
was at his artistic peak, painting the
cycle of the Scuola di San Rocco
at that same time. His vibrant
brushstroke, the convulsive bodies,
and circular rhythm of shadow-filled
clouds, express the turmoil that was
characteristic of mannerism.

429. Federico Barocci
c. 1535–1612
The Circumcision
1590

Canvas. H 3.56 m (140.2 in.); W 2.51 m (98.8 in.)
Entered the Louvre in 1798. MI 315

This work, which took a long time
to prepare with a series of drawings
and sketches, decorated the main
altar of the Nome di Gesù church
in Pesaro. The still life and the two
fine silhouettes of the shepherd and
officiating priest lead the eye into the
scene which is set towards the back
of a deep space constructed
in a perspective scheme typical
of late mannerism. The elongated
bodies, strident colors of the drapery
and pink and blue tones to the flesh
color are all stylistic elements
of mannerism.

430. Annibale Carracci
1560–1609
**The Virgin Appearing to St. Luke
and St. Catherine**
1592

Arched-top canvas. H 4.01 m (157.9 in.);
W 2.26 m (89 in.)
Entered the Louvre in 1797. INV 196

Painted for the cathedral of Reggio
Emilia, the work dates from the
painter's time in his native town
of Bologna, three years before he left
for Rome to lay down the foundations
of classicism. It illustrates the
preoccupations of the young Annibale
who, along with Luigi and Augustino
Carracci, founded a private academy
in Bologna with the aim of enriching
art with the combined study of nature
and the great Renaissance masters.
A synthesis of the art of Correggio
and that of Titian, this monumental
pala set both in a heavenly and
an earthly register epitomizes the
somewhat solemn eloquence of the
triumphant Counter-Reformation.

Italy, 17th century

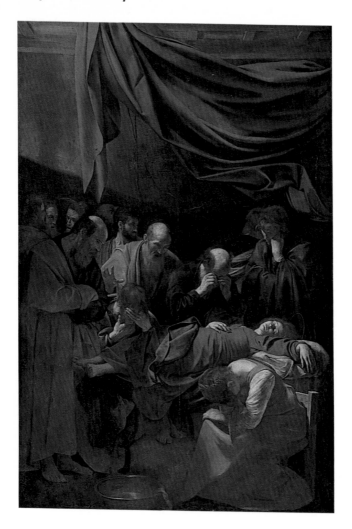

431. Michelangelo Merisi,
known as **Caravaggio**
c. 1571–1610
Death of the Virgin
1605–1606

Canvas. H 3.69 m (145.3 in.); W 2.45 m (96.5 in.)
Coll. of Louis XIV. INV 54

Painted for the church of Santa
Maria della Scala at Rome, the picture
was turned down for the very
reasons that made Caravaggio into
the artist who brought new life
to religious painting: the introduction
of the humblest everyday details into
a divine setting. Shocked by this
unorthodox realistic portrayal of the
Virgin, the clergy were oblivious
to the powerful effect of the human
message behind this corpse
of a young woman with swollen
ankles. Across the gloom of a barren
space, magnified by a large red
drape, a stroke of light gives depth
to the figures. This expressive use
of *chiaroscuro* was Caravaggio's
invention.

432. Guido Reni
1573–1642
Deianeira and the Centaur Nessus
1620–1621

Canvas. H 2.39 m (4.1 in.); W 1.93 m (76 in.)
Coll. of Louis XIV. INV 537

After twelve successful years in Rome
where he deepened his knowledge
of Raphael and antique sculpture,
Guido Reni returned to Bologna
where he settled in 1614.
His powerful and elegant classicism
came to the fore in four works
on the story of Hercules, painted
between 1617 and 1621 for the Villa
Favorita built by the duke Ferdinand
Gonzaga near Mantua. The action,
in which Hercules is relegated
to a minor role as a husband ready
to avenge Deianeira's abduction,
is centered on the foreground,
a magnificent celebration of bodies
set in a lithe rhythm of drapery and
gesture.

Italy, 18th century

433. Giovanni Paolo Pannini
1691–1765
Gallery of Views of Ancient Rome
1758

Canvas. H 2.31 m (90.9 in.); W 3.03 m (119.3 in.)
Princess Edmond de Polignac bequest, 1944.
RF 1944-21

This picture, which has as its
pendant a *Gallery of Views of Modern
Rome*, depicts an imaginary museum
made up of the main vestiges
of ancient Rome. Its architectural
monuments are conjured up by means
of a gallery of painting which is,
in some way, a catalogue of Pannini's
tireless studies of the Roman past.
Compelling for its perspectival
combinations and its cumulative
effect, the painting is eloquent
testimony to the archaeological
fervor in mid-18th century Europe
which followed upon the discoveries
of the buried cities of Herculaneum
and Pompeii.

434. Francesco Guardi
1712–1793
**The Doge on the Bucentaur
at the Venice Lido on Ascension Day**

Canvas. H 66 cm (26 in.); W 1.01 m (39.8 in.)
Seized during the Revolution. INV 20009

This picture belongs to a series
of 12 paintings (10 of which are
in the Louvre and 2 others in
Grenoble and Brussels) illustrating
Venetian festivities on the occasion
of the election of the Doge Alvise
Mocenigo in 1763. Painted around
ten years after the ceremonies, the
paintings were inspired by compositions engraved from Antonio
Caneletto, another master of the
veduta at Venice. Here we see
the Doge's galley, Bucentaur, setting
off towards the Lido, where each
year the Doge celebrated Venice's
marriage with the Adriatic.
For Guardi it was the perfect occasion
to paint a luminous and vibrant city
caught between sky and water, with
a lively brush and a novel sensitivity
to atmospheric effects.

Spain

With the exception of Murillo's *Young Beggar* (no. 440) acquired under Louis XVI, the Louvre did not, at the outset, take any great interest in the Spanish school. The change came with romanticism and the fashion for things Spanish, although the Napoleonic wars had already enabled collections to be amassed. Joseph Bonaparte and Maréchal Soult seized works from churches and convents, and the Musée Napoleon assembled of gains of war which Spain reclaimed when the Empire fell. The greatest promoter of Spanish painting was Louis-Philippe. Comprising hundreds of works by all the major masters, his collection was acquired in Spain by his emissary, the Baron Taylor, and was exhibited in the Louvre from 1838 to 1848. The Spanish gallery of Louis-Philippe, where Manet discovered Velásquez and Goya, had a profound effect on French art. However, the collection was sold at auction in London in 1853 and dispersed. Much later the Louvre recovered El Greco's *Christ on the Cross* (no. 437). The Maréchal Soult collection was also dispersed at that time, and the Louvre kept hold of a few masterpieces: Murillo's *Angels' Kitchen* and *The Birth of the Virgin* and Zurbarán's two *Scenes from the Life of St. Bonaventure* (no. 438) and *St. Apollonia*. It was private collectors who helped to complete the Louvre's presentation of the Golden Age of Spanish painting. The most famous example is La Caze's gift of Ribera's *The Crippled Child* (no. 439). The curators took it upon themselves to acquire a series of Goya portraits, later marked by two notable examples, the *Marquesa de la Solana* (no. 441), which was a gift, along with a gift in lieu of death duty, the *Marquesa de Santa Cruz*. This acquisition policy took on a pioneering role at the end of the 19th century, with its inclusion of early masters, forming an ensemble from Martorell (no. 435) to Huguet (no. 436), which, outside Spain, is virtually unsurpassed.

The Louvre has a Spanish collection which is small but representative. The Gothic artists of Catalonia and Castille, influenced by Italian and Flemish masters, are to be admired, along with the distinctive mannerism of El Greco, expressive of the mystical aspirations of the Counter-Reformation. The greatest names of the Golden Age can be seen, and there is Goya at his zenith as a portrait painter using color for psychological effect.

435. Bernardo Martorell
Known from 1427 to 1452
Judgement of St. George
c. 1430

Wood. H 1.07 m (42.1 in.); W 53 cm (20.9 in.)
Gift of the Société des Amis du Louvre, 1904.
RF 1570

Catalonia was the center of the
International Gothic style in the
Iberian peninsula, and had
in Martorell the most original artist
of the time. A masterpiece of the
painter's early period, the St. George
altar-piece (four panels of which are

in the Louvre, and the central panel
in Chicago) marks the artist's
progression toward a certain
narrative realism. The judgement
scene here illustrates this and,
conforming to Jacopo da Voragine's
Golden Legend, it depicts Dadianus
presiding over a secret tribunal and
condemning the saint to death
by decapitation after being paraded
through the town for his militant
faith.

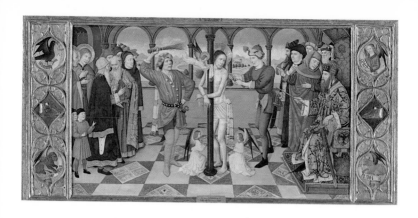

436. Jaume Huguet
c. 1415–1492
The Flagellation of Christ
c. 1450–1455

Wood. H 92 cm (36.2 in.); W 1.56 m (61.4 in.)
Chapel of St. Mark in Barcelona cathedral.
Acq. 1967 with help of Société des Amis
du Louvre. RF 1967-6

Close to the new developments
along the Mediterranean in Italy and
Provence, Huguet, who was
Martorell's successor in Barcelona,
led Catalan Gothic art towards
spatial unity and monumentality.
Once an altar front given to the
cathedral by the guild of shoemakers
(with the frame bearing their
emblem, the ankle-boot), this picture
shows the flagellation of Christ, set
within a rigorous geometry.
Arches open onto a luminous
landscape, which takes the place
of the traditional medieval gold
background.

437. Domenicos Theotocopoulos,
known as **El Greco**
1541–1614
**Christ on the Cross Adored by Two
Donors**
c. 1585–1590

Canvas. H 2.60 m (102.4 in.); W 1.71 m (67.3 in.)
Church of the Hieronymite nuns of La Reinsa,
Toledo. Louis-Philippe's Spanish gallery. Acq. 1900.
RF 1713

A Cretan by birth (hence the name), El Greco moved to Toledo in 1577, bringing with him a visionary language developed through contact with the mannerists in Italy. The Louvre *Christ on the Cross* is one of the finest and oldest known examples of a theme which recurs in his work. Contemporary with the *Burial of the Count of Orgaz* (Toledo), it belongs to his grandest period. His tormented style—thundery sky, elongated and twisted bodies, ecstatic faces—is tempered here by a rigorously symmetrical composition, with an austere color scheme and a sculptural depth to Christ's body.

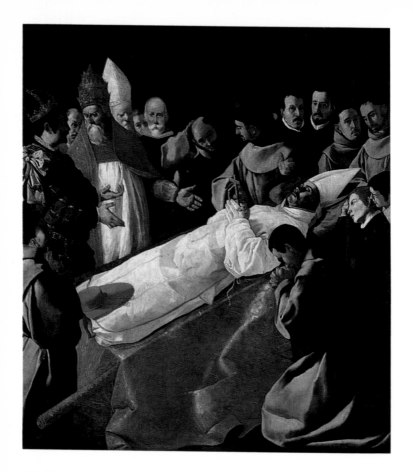

438. Francisco de Zurbarán
1598–1664
St. Bonaventura on his Deathbed
1629

Canvas. H 2.45 m (96.5 in.); W 2.20 m (86.6 in.)
Church of the College of Saint-Bonaventura,
Seville. Acq. 1858 from the heirs of Maréchal
Soult. MI 205

In 1629, a few years after his move
to Seville, Zurbarán supplied four
canvases (two are in the Louvre) to
complete the cycle of St. Bonaventura
begun by Herrera the Elder (two
also in the Louvre). Moral renovator
of the Franciscan order, the saint
died in 1274 at the Council of Lyons,
of which he was the moving spirit
and where he preached the Crusade
and church unification. Pope
Gregory X, the king of Aragon and

Franciscan monks are shown
mourning the prelate. The fervent
atmosphere, and simple composition,
bisected by the dazzling white of the
saint's vestments, offer ample
testimony to Zurbarán's skill, from
a young age, in interpreting
the monastic spirituality of the
Golden Age.

439. Jusepe de Ribera
1591–1652
The Crippled Child
1642

Canvas. H 1.64 m (64.6 in.); W 93 cm (36.6 in.)
Dr. Louis La Caze bequest, 1869. MI 893

With his crutch carried like a useless weapon and his begging note, "Give me alms for the love of God," suggesting he is dumb, with his crippled foot and gap-teeth, this young beggar apes the martial stance of a hidalgo; the cruel reverse-side to the Golden Age. Ribera has subordinated realism to social satire. By 1642, he had attained his full stature as an artist. He had broken free from the Caravaggesque shadows, at which he was a past master since his early period in Naples (1616) where he became official artist to the Spanish viceroys. And this bright painting, with its Flemish influence, peers out at the hollow gestures of the "Court of Miracles" with implacable acuity.

440. Bartolomé Esteban Murillo
1618–1682
The Young Beggar
c. 1650

Canvas. H 1.34 m (53.7 in.); W 1.00 m (39.4 in.)
Coll. of Louis XVI. INV 933

Along with many religious works,
Murillo has left us a striking image
of childhood in this lifesize picture
of a boy lousing himself.
Caravaggesque in inspiration,
it is an uncompromising portrayal
of a young and ragged Sevillian with
dirty feet in a barren rustic setting.
But the real *tour de force* here lies
in the slant of sunlight, boldly
expressing a concern for naturalism
which attracted the attention
of 19th century French painters, like
Edouard Manet, who were searching
for new ideas.

441. Francisco José de Goya y Lucientes
1746–1828
The Marquesa de la Solana
(1757–1795)

Canvas. H 1.81 m (71.3 in.); W 1.22 m (48 in.)
Gift of Carlos de Beistegui, 1942. Entered the Louvre in 1953. RF 1942-23

Painter to the king, and protégé of the nobility, Goya was, from the 1780s onward, the most fashionable portrait painter of Madrid society. "La Solana" (the countess of Carpio) was a friend of the duchess of Alba, another of Goya's famous models, and was a charitable, educated aristocrat who wrote plays and died prematurely in 1795 at the age of 38. Goya painted her in his usual society portrait manner: full length, against a neutral landscape, in an elegant, subtly-toned costume, adding a pink bow as the only luxury. The elegant brushwork does not detract from the psychological depth. The face is unusually grave, whether as a result of the model's illness or as a projection of the artist's mood. The picture is situated sometime after his illness of 1792–1793 which left him deaf.

Germany

The importance of this collection is unquestionable, despite the relatively
limited number of works it contains. The 15th century is dominated
by a collection of pictures of the school of Cologne which is unusual outside
German museums (Masters of the Holy Family, no. 442, of St Severinus,
of the Altar-Piece of St. Bartholomew, no. 443, and of the Legend of St. Ursula).
The collection's strong point remains the Renaissance, with Dürer's
Self-Portrait (no. 444), several Cranachs and Bruyns and above all the five
portraits by Hans Holbein the Younger; Erasmus, Warham (the Archbishop
of Canterbury), Kratzer (Henry VIII's astronomer) (no. 446), Anne of Cleves
(Henry VIII's fourth wife) and Sir Henry Wyatt (court counsellor). These
Holbeins have a notable origin; Louis XIV acquired them altogether in 1671
from the Cologne banker and collector Eberhardt Jabach. Alongside the
three great names, other artists testify to an artistic flowering in 16th century
Germany, such as Hans Baldung Grien, Hans Sebald Beham (work acquired
by Louis XIV from Mazarin's heirs), Mathias Gerung, Ulrich Apt, Hans
Maler and Wolf Huber. For subsequent periods, examples are more scattered
but no less significant; there are 17th century still-lifes (by Binoit, Flegel,
no. 447, and Gottfried von Wedig), portraits, mythological and religious
paintings from the 18th century (Denner, Seibold, Dietrich, Platzer,
Maulpertsch and Graff), neoclassicism (Angelica Kauffmann, Anton Krafft),
the Biedermeier period (Walmüller's portrait of a woman) and romanticism
(Friedrich, no. 448).

442. Master of the Holy Family
Active in Cologne from 1470/80
to 1515
Altar-Piece of the Seven Joys of Mary
c. 1480

Wood. H 1.27 m (50 in.); W 1.82 m (71.6 in.)
Benedictine convent of the Maccabeans, Cologne.
Acq. 1912, with contrib. from children of Jean
Dollfus. RF 2045

Divided into three scenes (*The Adoration of the Magi, The Presentation in the Temple, The Apparition of Christ to Mary*), this was the center of an altar-piece painted almost certainly around 1480 in Cologne. The two wings, each containing two scenes (*The Annunciation* and *The Nativity*, on the left, *The Ascension* and the *Assumption* on the right) are in Nuremberg. The Master of the Holy Family, so named after his mature masterpiece in the Wallraf Richartz Museum in Cologne, took his inspiration for the *Presentation in the Temple* from a composition of the same subject by the great painter of the Cologne School during the first half of the 15th century, Stephan Lochner, but the coloring and taste for rich fabrics and gilt is proof of his own genius.

Détail

443. Master of the Altar-Piece of St. Bartholomew
Active in Cologne c. 1480–1510
The Descent from the Cross
c. 1501–1505

Wood. H 2.275 m (89.6 in.) and 1.525 m (60 in.);
W 2.10 m (82.7 in.)
Church of the Val-de-Grâce. Seized during French
Revolution. INV 1445

The origin of this imposing altar-piece is not known; all we can be sure of is its 16th century location in the professed house of the Jesuits in Paris. St. Anthony's T-shaped cross and handbell decorating the *trompe-l'œil* frame indicate a possible connection with an Antonite community. Its author, very probably a Netherlander from Utrecht or Arnhem, so-named after his St. Bartholomew altar-piece from the Cologne church of the Holy Dove (Munich, Alte Pinakothek), who settled in Cologne around 1480, transposes Van der Weyden's famous *Descent from the Cross* (Madrid, Prado), into a late Gothic mannerist-like style. His interpretation is powerful and full of pathos; within a *trompe-l'œil* painted box, characters, like actors in a mystery play, are grouped in a complex interweaving of lines around Christ, who seems to leave the picture plane and enter our space.

444. Albrecht Dürer
1471–1528
Self-Portrait
1493

Parchment glued on to canvas. H 56.5 cm (22.2 in.);
W 45 cm (17.7 in.)
Acq. 1922. RF 2382

This is the only picture by Dürer
in France, and his first self-portrait,
preceeding those of 1498 (Madrid,
Prado) and 1500 (Munich, Alte
Pinakothek). It was painted during
his trip between Basle and Strasbourg
before his return to Nuremberg.
The painter shows himself as a serious
young man of 22, holding in his
right hand a branch of eryngo (a type
of thistle), the significance of which
has prompted much discussion.
Some see it as a symbol of conjugal
fidelity, with the picture destined for
his betrothed, Agnes Frey, whom
he married in 1494. For others
it is an allusion to Christ's Passion
(more specifically to the crown
of thorns), in connection with the
inscription on the picture: "Things
happen to me as ordained on high,"
in a mood looking forward to the
Self-Portrait of 1500 in which Dürer
appears as a "Salvator Mundi,"
surrounded by a God-given aura.

445. Lucas Cranach the Elder
1472–1553
Venus Standing in a Landscape
1529

Wood. H 38 cm (15 in.); W 25 cm (9.8 in.)
Entered the Louvre in 1806, from Germany.
INV 1180

Lucas Cranach was official painter to the prince electors of Saxony, painted Luther, and alongside Dürer and Holbein, was one of the three great painters of 16th century Germany. He excelled in mythological and allegorical painting, and devised a new iconographic image; a single woman in a landscape. The small Louvre painting, with its fine detail all by Cranach's own hand, shows a graceful Venus wearing a broad-brimmed hat, bejeweled necklace, and holding before her a diaphanous veil. The Gothic town in the background, reflected in the water, is evidence of his mastery of drawing and his deeply poetic sensitivity to landscape. The winged serpent holding a ring in its mouth is Cranach's seal and is skillfully merged into the stones on the ground.

446. Hans Holbein the Younger
1497/8–1543
Nicolas Kratzer
1528

Wood. H 83 cm (32.7 in.); W 67 cm (26.4 in.)
Coll. Eberhardt Jabach, acq. by Louis XIV in 1671.
INV 1343

The sitter's name and the date of the painting are indicated on the piece of paper on the left of the table. Kratzer (c. 1486–after 1550) was a compatriot of Holbein's, settled like him in England, and a correspondent of Dürer's. He became an important court figure as astronomer to Henry VIII. Holbein depicts him engaged in his principal task as "maker" of astronomical instruments. In one hand he holds a compass, and in the other a sundial which he is building. This dial and two others of different shapes, which can be seen in the background, are almost identical to those in the famous painting of the *Ambassadors* which Holbein painted in 1533 (National Gallery, London). In this portrait, which, like that of Warham painted in 1527 (also in the Louvre) dates from his first stay in London, Holbein displays his skills as an objective painter and his unparalleled craftsmanship in the painting of objects.

447. Georg Flegel
1566–1638
Still-Life with a Flask of Wine and Small Fish
1637

Wood. H 19 cm (7.5 in.); W 15 cm (5.9 in.)
Acq. 1981. RF 1981-21

Clearly influenced by Flemish artists who had settled in Germany, Georg Flegel, from Frankfurt, was one of the first German painters to give still-life a status of its own. Objects are skillfully arranged, linked to each other in an interplay of ovals and reflected color. The keenly observed fish are of species that once lived in the river Main. A *trompe-l'œil* effect, the insects—a fly and drone bee—are shown lifesize on the bread and edge of the plate. They are out of proportion as if they belonged not within the painting but to the world of the onlooker. They serve to remind us of the perishable nature of food and of worldly goods, and this contrasts with the religious significance behind the bread, wine and fish, which traditionally refer to the eucharistic meal that ensures the soul's eternal salvation.

448. Caspar David Friedrich
1774–1840
The Tree of Crows
c. 1822
Canvas. H 59 cm (23.2 in.); 73.7 cm (29 in.)
Acq. 1975. RF 1975-20

Far from being the simple depiction of a landscape, *The Tree of Crows* should be interpreted as a meditation on death, a major theme in German romantic painting of which Friedrich was the uncontested leader. The barren tree which appears to be rooted in a tumulus dating from the time of the Huns, symbolizes the vain aspiration of pagan heroes buried in such spots. Smilarly the few leaves clinging on the tree, and the crows evoke death and adversity. A glimmer of hope remains however: the distant light symbolizing eternal life. In the background, scholars have identified the town of Arkona and the chalk cliffs of the island of Rügen in the Baltic sea, the region where the artist was born.

Flanders and Holland

In the Louvre the northern schools of Flanders and Holland are combined here for convenience's sake, given their geographical and linguistic proximity and shared history up to the end of the 16th century. They are represented by no less than 1,200 pictures dating from the 15th to the early 20th century (everything post-1850 has now been transferred to the Musée d'Orsay). This amounts to more than the entire collection of Italian paintings (around 1,100) and to far more than the Spanish, German and English schools (amounting to a hundred or so works each), though is considerably less than the French school (between 3,000 and 4,000 paintings). This serves to indicate the relative importance of the Northern Schools in the collections, the kernel of which was brilliantly put together by Louis XIV—the Bril family, and, most notably, a large proportion of the work of Rubens and Van Dyck—and successfully expanded by Louis XVI thanks to an early acquisition policy which brought in the best Dutch masters (of the 17th century), including over 110 perfectly selected paintings (Ruisdael, Cuyp, Wouwerman, Berchem, Ter Borch, Dujardin, Dou, the Velde family, the Ostade family, Metsu and, among the Flemish, Rubens, Teniers, Jordaens etc.). Two centuries of museum history with its ups and downs (less than 15 or so Northern School acquisitions under Louis-Philippe and only 8 between 1959 and 1979…) reflect vicissitudes of taste and history. Over 130 Flemish and Dutch masters were presented during the Second Empire; Dr. La Caze in 1869 presented Frans Hals' *The Gypsy Girl* (no. 468), Rembrandt's *Bathsheba* (no. 466), 7 Rubens, and 19 Teniers, and there were bequests of 200 Dutch and Flemish paintings during the Third Republic. The museum and the unflagging support of its donors have thus continued the task the kings initiated so magnificently. For this reason the collection is at once varied and highly selective. To begin with it professes to be one of the best Rubens collections in the world, rivaling Munich and Vienna (because of the Galerie Médicis in particular), with 52 original works. Also considerable are the series of Van Dycks (over 20 works) and Rembrandts (a dozen certified works, including the unequaled *Bathsheba*), while the kernel of early 15th century masters (Primitives) includes all the great names up to Van der Goes (Van Eyck, Weyden, Bouts, Memling, Gerard David, Bosch, Geertgen tot Sint Jans, Joos van Gent, Sittow etc.) and *The Madonna of Chancellor Rolin* (no. 449) is a masterpiece of universal status. The 16th century is well represented and endowed with fine works from Metsys (*The Moneylender and His Wife*, no. 451) and Brueghel (*The Beggars*, no. 454), Hemessen and Floris, Lucas van Leyden, Van Cleve, Gossaert and Mor, Dalem and Barendsz, Sellaer, Jan van der Straet and Otto Veen, and more recently the museum has opened its doors to the troubled world of the mannerists (Spranger, Speeckaert, Wtewael, Cornelisz van Haarlem) who join their predecessors, Bloemaert and Goltzius. A golden age for painting, the 17th century is even richer. In Flanders there is on the one hand a lavish display of grand painting (mostly religious) following Rubens (Van Dyck, Jordaens, Van Mol, Crayer, Van Oost, Gerard Seghers and Thulden) and on the other, the whole delightful company of minor "realist" masters (a triumphant gathering of 40 paintings by Teniers,

7 by Francken, and works by Brouwer, Craesbeeck, Ryckaert and Vranck …) as well as a superb series of still-lifes (5 by Fyt, 8 by Snyders, and a Van Bouck) and animal paintings (16 by Pieter Boel). The collections of landscapes are no less remarkable (10 by Bril, 10 by Huysmans, and 5 by Momper) while Jan Breughel the Elder shines out, among others, with *The Battle of Arbela* and Daniel Seghers is notable for his crown of flowers surrounding Domenichino's *Triumph of Love*, again from Louis XIV.

Almost none of the Dutch of the great 17th century is missing, even though churches, marine paintings and still-lifes are somewhat rare and a single work often serves to illustrate a particular tendency (such as Terbrugghen's *The Duet*, bought in 1954, to illustrate the Caravaggesque tendency in Utrecht). The 4 Hals (including the *Gypsy Girl*, no. 464, and the *Buffoon with a Lute*), the 10 Van Goeyn, the Ruisdaels (6 by Salomon and 6 by Jacob) are a significant acquisition. But also present are fine examples of great names which are now scarce: Bosschaert and Saenredam, Sweerts and Hoogstraten (his admirable *Pair of Slippers* was long thought to be by Pieter der Hooch and later by Vermeer), Venne (*The Truce* of 1609) and Potter, Claesz and De Heem, Steen and Pieter de Hooch, Hobbema and Van der Heyden. Vermeer has pride of place with the *Lacemaker* (no. 471) and his *Astronomer*, which came to us in 1983, was the last Vermeer still in private hands.

449. Jan Van Eyck
d. 1441
The Madonna of Chancellor Rolin
c. 1435

Wood. H 66 cm (26 in.); W 62 cm (24.4 in.)
Collegiate church of Notre-Dame, Autun. Entered
the Louvre in 1800. INV 1271

The Chancellor of Burgundy, Nicolas
Rolin (1376–1462) commissioned this
picture of himself kneeling in prayer
before the Madonna, with Jesus
blessing him. He was a high dignitary
in the court of Philip the Good (one
of whose good deeds was to have
commissioned Van der Weyden
to paint the altar-piece of the *Last
Judgement* for the Beaune hospice).
The urban landscape in the
background does not, despite its
apparent precision, depict a real
town but is rather a juxtaposition
of several existing sites. All the
minutely rendered detail has
a precise religious significance.
Van Eyck conferred an intense
spiritual value upon the infinitely
small, with a perfect, almost
alchemical mastery of his technique.

Détail

450. Rogier Van der Weyden
1399/1400–1464
Braque Family Triptych
1450–1452

Wood. Central panel: H 41 cm (16.1 in.);
W 68 cm (26.8 in.); Wings: H 41 cm (16.1 in.);
W 34 cm (13.4 in.)
Acq. 1913 RF 2063

The central panel shows Christ the Redeemer between the Virgin Mary and St. John the Evangelist, the left wing St. John the Baptist and the right, St. Mary Magdalen. The arms painted on the reverse side belong to Jehan Braque and his wife, Catherine of Brabant from Tournai, suggesting that this portable triptych was painted either for their wedding in 1450–1451 or after Jehan Braque's death in 1452. In the latter case the skull and cross, which can also be seen, accompanied by inscriptions reminding us of the vanity of life on earth, would have had a particular poignancy. At that period, Van der Weyden had just returned from Italy, and Fra Angelico's influence can be felt in the choice of a rigorous symmetry, which is perfectly allied to the monumentality so natural to this master.

451. Quentin Metsys
1465/6–1530
The Moneylender and his Wife
1514

Wood. H 70.5 cm (27.7 in.); W 67 cm (26.4 in.)
Acq. 1806. INV 1444

Derived most probably from a lost work by Jan van Eyck dating from 1440, Metsys' picture is not a simple genre scene. A Latin inscription which figured on the frame during the 17th century, from Leviticus (Lev. 20:36), "Just balances, just weights […] shall ye have," would have explained the moral or even religious intention behind the work—the scales, which symbolize justice, also refer to the Last Judgement. The subject became very popular; the caricature of the usurer with his hands greedily clasping his gold, was generally the only focus of attention. This work is very different, however, and has a serene gravity about it. Also worthy of note is a motif which Van Eyck favored above all others: a mirror reflecting a man reading.

452. Jan Gossaert, known as **Mabuse**
c. 1478–1532
Carondelet Diptych
1517

Wood with arched top. Each panel: H 42.5 cm
(16.7 in.); W 27 cm (10.6 in.)
Acq. 1847. INV 1442–3

Jean Carondelet (1469–1545), dean
of the church of Besançon, counsellor
to Emperor Charles V and friend
of Erasmus, is shown praying opposite
the Madonna and Child. On the
back of one wing a skull is painted

in *trompe-l'œil*, in a niche, accompanied by a quotation from St. Jerome
inviting meditation on death.
Carondelet's face is skillfully modeled
and painted with a realism
accentuated by the confining frame,
and contrasts with the more timeless,
idealized image of the Virgin.
The finest element is the Vanitas,
an allegory to the transient nature
of the world, here it is a skull depicted
with terrifying; reality, deriving
impact from its formal intensity.

453. Frans Floris
1516–1570
**The Sacrifice of Christ Protecting
Humanity**
1562

Wood. H 1.65 m (65 in.); W 2.30 m (90.6 in.)
Church of St. Sulpice. Seized during French
Revolution. INV 20746

In a magnificently flowing style
using the elegant mannerist forms
which are the stamp of Floris (the
leading painter of mid-16th century
Antwerp, and true forerunner
of Rubens in his use of transparent
glazes), a complex religious metaphor
is transcribed, the literal nature
of which borders on boldness.
Indicated in the foreground
by St. John the Baptist in a fine red
robe, Christ (crucified on a symbolic
vine with great hen's wings) gathers
together all repentant sinners like
the mother hen of St. Luke's and
St. Matthew's Gospels: it is a sign
of perfect and all-encompassing
divine love. In the foreground a hen

is portrayed in fine realistic detail.
Meanwhile, an extraordinary
demon-bat hovers threateningly
on the right above a pope and some
Pharisees who, poor shepherds that
they are, turn believers onto
the wrong path. Opposite this
on the left, is the heavenly Jerusalem
indicated by Christ and his disciples
nearby. The whole work testifies
to an interestingly personal faith
(Floris and his wife are among the
people protected by God in the Holy
Trinity), on the borderline between
loyal Catholicism and new
Protestant Reform.

454. Pieter Brueghel the Elder
c. 1525–1569
The Cripples
1568

Wood. H 16.5 cm (6.5 in.); W. 21.5 cm (8.5 in.)
Gift of Paul Mantz, 1892. RF 730

The significance of this work
—the only Brueghel the Elder in the
Louvre—remains obscure, although
it has given rise to many interpreta-
tions. It may be an evocation
of human suffering, a political
allusion to Spanish domination
or a satirical description of different
classes of society. The fox-tails
attached to the cripples' clothing
have also given rise to much
speculation. But even without
explanation, the work, which was
painted at the very end of the artist's
career, is extremely powerful despite
its small size. Seen close up, the
absurd line-up is huddled together
with a highly skilled interplay
of forms.

455. Cornelis Van Haarlem
1562–1638
The Baptism of Christ
1588

Canvas. H 1.70 m (67 in.); W 2.06 m (81.1 in.)
Gift of the Société des Amis du Louvre, 1983.
RF 1983-25

A work of his youth—the artist was only 26 in 1588—*The Baptism of Christ* is one of the most successful works by a Haarlem mannerist. Here the new style is given its most eloquent expression. In a typical inversion of hierarchy, the subject of the work, Christ's baptism, is relegated to the background, while the foreground is occupied by those waiting to be baptized, a veritable lexicon of academic nudes in twisted poses and with expressive gestures. Fingers are clenched, muscles arched, and the painter is bold enough to show the bald naturalistic detail of the dirty sole of the foreground foot. The youthful, hotheaded brutality of this composition looks forward to Caravaggio's conquest of pictorial reality.

17th century, Flanders

456. Peter Paul Rubens
1577–1640
The Apotheosis of Henry IV and the Proclamation of the Regency of Marie de Médicis
1622–1625

Canvas. H 3.94 m (155.1 in.); W 7.27 m (286.2 in.)
Coll. of Louis XIV. INV 1779

The end wall of the great Galerie Médicis was painted by Rubens between 1622 and 1625 for the Palais du Luxembourg in Paris, at that time residence of the queen, Marie de Médicis (wife of Henry IV and mother of Louis XIII). This imposing production, of over 7 meters (23 feet) wide, is the focal point and thematic center of an immense decorative ensemble of 24 huge works painted in what was a record time for a single man. These 300 m² (over 3,225 square feet) of painting give us a good measure of Rubens' singular genius. The whole cycle is an epic account of the great deeds and sublime destiny of a powerful and royal woman, celebrated in the midst of, as well as because of, her misfortunes, and strengthened by adversity like a popular hero in 17th century literature. Here, in a lavish display of rich color and solid and

magnificent forms, the composition, skillfully organized in a system of huge, dynamic diagonals, balanced between two poles, draws attention to the dead king on the left, raised to heaven, a hero glorified, in a wonderful allegorical transposition of his tragic assassination in 1610. Meanwhile, to the right, the widowed queen, made regent from May 14 of the same year, receives the divine mission to be governor of state, and is acclaimed by the great of the kingdom.

457. Antoon Van Dyck (Sir Anthony)
1599–1641
**Venus Asking Vulcan for Arms
for Aeneas**
c. 1627–1632

Canvas. H 2.20 m (86.6 in.); W 1.45 m (57.1 in.)
Coll. of Louis XIV. INV 1234

Here we have a great mythological
subject to please cultivated
17th century minds brought up on the
classics and Virgil in particular, but
transposed by Van Dyck into the
timeless realm of aesthetics.
The beneficent influence of the Italian
Renaissance, examples of which
Van Dyck had recently seen in Italy
(Correggio the painter of female
flesh, Titian the sumptuous colorist)
and the grand baroque manner
of Rubens, Van Dyck's master
(ample, energetic forms) combine
with the artist's subtle colors and
febrile style in a composition that
is as eloquent as it is refined (c.f. the
contrast in skin tone of the white
goddess and Vulcan, the swarthy
forger). It is deliberately situated out
of time (there is no local color
or archaeological detail), devoid
of any prosaic realism, and set
within a suitably vertical format (the
bodies in their momentum seem
to burst out of their space).

458. Antoon Van Dyck (Sir Anthony)
1599–1641
Charles I at the Hunt
c. 1635

Canvas. H 2.66 m (104.7 in.); W 2.07 m (81.5 in.)
Coll. of Louis XVI. INV 1236

While not an official portrait
of Charles I (1600–1649) in the usual
sense (having been referred to by the
painter in a memoir written in French
around 1638 as "le roi alla ciasse"),
this is by far the most royal (or most
noble, thus most successful)
of portraits of the king, showing him
as a paragon among educated men.
He is distinguished and elegant, well
bred and charming as befitted
a twofold tradition, here effectively
combined, of the courtier
as an "honest man" and as a "prince"
among men; the individual matching
the persona. On the one hand there
are the servants, the cane standing
for government, clothes which are
almost too sumptuous for a hunt and
the proud stance; on the other,
a masterly isolation of the main
figure silhouetted against a pale
sky, and set subtly off-center,
as is emphasized by the sweep
of branches. His dignity is enhanced
by muted colors applied with a lively
and caressing brushstroke. From
antiquity, via Titian, comes the
culturally "ennobling" detail of the
horse scraping a deferential hoof.

459. Peter Paul Rubens
1577–1640
The Village Fair
c. 1635–1638

Wood. H 1.49 m (58.7 in.); W 2.61 m (102.7 in.)
Coll. of Louis XIV. INV 1797

Louis XIV could not have found a better or a more representative example of the genius of Rubens —the greatest painter of the century—when he bought this monumental panel from the artist's last years. With its sensual lyricism and vital exuberance—magnifying life in all its aspects whether animal or human—it conveys the sense of frenetic pleasure and irresistible energy that is allied to and fed by an old tradition of Flemish realism from Brueghel, though the moral tone is absent here. The swarming mass of bodies (a tumult cleverly organized in a beautiful succession of waves) contrasts with the deeply-felt still vastness of the landscape.

460. Peter Paul Rubens
1577–1640
Helena Fourment with a Carriage
c. 1639

Wood. H 1.95 m (76.8 in.); W 1.32 m (52 in.)
Marlborough coll., then Rothschild coll. Acq. 1977.
RF 1977-13

With its notable provenance, this large and ravishing "state" portrait is one of the Louvre's finest acquisitions since the Second World War. It is probably one of the last depictions of Rubens' second wife, Helena Fourment (married in 1630), who was a frequent model for the artist in his last years. She is accompanied by her young son Frans, born in 1663, and here about 6 or 7 years old. In a black costume of great distinction (but not of mourning!), adorned like a society lady, with the raised pompon hat then fashionable in the Low Countries, attached to a fine veil, she leaves her palatial residence to take her carriage (hence the brisk piece of landscape painting on the left). It represents a summit of Rubens' invention; a picture that displays ease and skill, triumphantly baroque in its spatial dynamism and superbly balanced relationship between forms, compelling for both its sentiment and painterliness, and a highpoint of the great tradition of humanistic and aristocratic portraiture that developed during the Renaissance.

461. Jacob Jordaens
1593–1678
Jesus Driving the Merchants from the Temple
c. 1650

Canvas. H 2.88 m (113.4 in.); W 4.36 m (171.6 in.)
Coll. of Louis XV. INV 1402

This superb royal purchase of 1751 presupposed the foundation of a museum in the Louvre, given that such a work with its eminently evangelical tone—Jesus purifying a sacred place of material and pagan corruption—could hardly serve as a palace decoration. The picture, sold by Charles Natoire, an artist protected by the king and a major figure in 18th century French rococo, bears witness to the impressive vigor of the great rival and successor to Rubens in Antwerp, who painted this huge canvas around 1650.

It is a masterfully organized pictorial tumult, a triumphal chain of full, dynamic forms within sumptuous and ponderous architecture beautifully depicted. Its rich tones and clear light combine knowledge with license, sculptural depth with pure painting. It is sheer delight to the eye: at the highpoint of baroque art.

462. Joachim Wtewael
1566–1638
Perseus and Andromeda
1611

Canvas. H 1.80 m (70.9 in.); W 1.50 m (19.7 in.)
Gift of the Société des Amis du Louvre, 1982.
RF 1982-51

Andromeda was the daughter of Cepheus (the king of Ethiopia). Her mother, Queen Cassiope, was rash enough to boast that Andromeda was more beautiful than the Nereids, the nymphs who live in sea. They chained Andromeda to a rock, leaving her at the mercy of a sea monster sent by Neptune. Perseus, mounted on Pegasus, rescued and took her for his wife. The subject was popular with mannerist painters. The Utrecht painter Wtewael interprets the story in an original way. It is really three pictures in one: the superb nude study, the rare detail of the blue-tinted entrancing landscape, and finally, in the foreground, an astonishing still-life of shells, a picture within a picture. *Perseus and Andromeda* is an excellent example of this artist's subdued mannerism, with the fresh elegance of the nude winning over the embittered style of his first period.

**463. Ambrosius Bosschaert
the Elder**
1573–1621
Bouquet of Flowers in an Arch
c. 1620

Copper. H 23 cm (9 in.); W 17 cm (6.7 in.)
Acq. with aid of Société des Amis du Louvre,
1984. RF 1984-150

The charm of this small picture,
which is nevertheless monumental
in feel, lies in Bosschaert's power
of invention. He was a protestant
from Antwerp who emigrated
to Holland. There are three aspects
to this still-life: the poignant contrast
between the infinite horizon and the
close precision of the flowers and
transparent glass; an intellectual
vision of a harmonious nature
linking flowers (all identifiable) that
bloom in fact in different seasons;
and the moral, quasi-religious
atmosphere suggested by half-eaten
leaves and the worn stone of the
niche, reminders of the vanity
of things and the fragile nature
of ephemeral reality. The little insect
(a kind of wasp known as a sphex)
on the right-hand border parodies
the painter's monogram AB.

464. Frans Hals
1581/5–1666
The Gypsy Girl
c. 1628–1630

Wood. H 58 cm (22.8 in.); W 52 cm (20.5 in.)
Dr. Louis La Caze bequest, 1869. MI 926

This is a picture of a courtesan in daring, if not provocative, décolleté rather than of a gypsy. The latter term usually denotes a fortuneteller. The realistic treatment of the subject links the picture to the limpid style painting of the Caravaggesque painters of Utrecht. Hals' contribution resides in the bravura of his varied brushwork: supple and soft across the face, the strokes become more animated, sharp and broken in the costume. The figure follows a line of "genre portraits" by Hals. One element giving added dynamism to the work is his somewhat atypical treatment of the background, consisting of an area of cloudy sky or rocky landscape, traversed by a brighter oblique strip giving it movement.

465. Harmensz. Rembrandt van Rijn
1606–1669
The Supper at Emmaus
1648

Wood. H 68 cm (26.8 in.); W 65 cm (25.6 in.)
Coll. of Louis XVI. INV 1739

The well-known subject of Christ
being recognized, during a meal
at Emmaus, by two of his disciples,
was much beloved of Rembrandt.
The interpretation he gave it in 1648
is full of solemn grandeur. Traditional
in its composition which draws
on recollections of High Renaissance
masters (Leonardo da Vinci, Titian
and Veronese), the picture is striking
for its iconographic intensity. The
figure of Christ, which is beautifully
displaced away from the central axis
of the composition, is poignantly
realistic. His pale, gaunt face is that
of the vanquisher of death.

The empty, overturned wineglass
and the lamb's skull broken in two
serve as reminders of this and are
symbols of the Passion of God made
Man, as revealed at the Last Supper.
Within one picture Rembrandt
renovates a whole tradition
of religious painting, giving it depth
and humanity.

466. Harmensz. Rembrandt van Rijn
1606–1669
Bathsheba
1654

Canvas. H 1.42 m (55.9 in.); W 1.42 m (55.9 in.)
Dr. Louis La Caze bequest, 1869. MI 957

Rembrandt chose to paint the episode most often illustrated by artists, in which King David catches a glimpse of Bathsheba while she is bathing, and summons her to the palace. A measure of Rembrandt's genius lies in the liberties he takes with traditional iconography. The king does not appear in the painting, and is represented only by the slightly crumpled letter of request that Bathsheba holds in her hand. The model is generally agreed to be Henrickje Stoffels, the artist's mistress. Quite "Venetian" in feeling, with its warm tonalities and emphasis on the lifesize nude figure, *Bathsheba* is, aside from any influence, an outstanding example of painterly bravura, visible in the superbly constructed white cloth, richly-worked layers of paint and highlights of glowing red brushstrokes.

467. Pieter de Hooch
1629–1684
A Young Woman Drinking
1658

Canvas. H 69 cm (27.2 in.); W 60 cm (23.6 in.)
Gift of Mme Piatigorsky, née Jacqueline
de Rothschild. RF 1974-29

Painted at Delft—notwithstanding
the map of Amsterdam visible
on the back wall—this is one of the
most flawless works of Pieter
de Hooch, from his best period
when he painted warmly-lit interiors
in a carefully arranged perspective.
Far from being an imitator
of Vermeer, this picture shows him
as a forerunner in the depiction
of quiet interior subjects.

The figures, which are intentionally
static as the result of a desire
to locate them in geometrical space,
have a story to tell. It is a study
of human behavior with moralizing
allusions to dissolute pleasures (the
figures are none other than
a courtesan, a procuress and suitors)
and to the vanity of sensual pleasures
such as drinking and smoking. The
picture of *Christ and the Adulteress*,
visible on the right, serves as a moral
and religious admonishment.

468. Gabriel Metsu
1629–1667
The Amsterdam Vegetable Market
c. 1660

Canvas. H 70 cm (27.6 in.); W 84.5 cm (33.3 in.)
Coll. of Louis XIV. INV 1460

The subject-matter—a genre scene set outside, rather than indoors—and the relatively large size of the painting are somewhat unusual in Metsu's work. Alongside a canal, a humble market is full swing and the protagonists—notably the housewife in the center and the young man in red at her side—are more occupied with the exchange of gallantries than goods. The lively colors of costumes and vegetables contrast with the softness and poetic stillness of the urban landscape, while the perfectly rendered still-life elements in the foreground display the artist's admirable pictorial command. Notice on the right the confrontation between dog and cockerel, at the foot of which lies a scrap of paper, dropped as if by chance and bearing the artist's signature.

469. Gerard Dou
1613–1675
The Dropsical Woman
1663

Wood. H 86 cm (33.9 in.); W 67.8 cm (26.7 in.)
Gift of Bertrand Clauzel, 1798. INV 1213

When he gave this picture to the Directoire, for the "Museum," the future Maréchal, Bertrand Clauzel, became the first donor to the Louvre. He obtained the picture from Charles Emmanuel IV of Savoy, king of Sardinia, a gift of distinction since it had been one of the glories of the royal gallery at Turin. The visit to the doctor is a choice subject of Dutch genre pictures. Gerard Dou gives it a masterly interpretation, putting his technique to good use, having a skillful and precise stroke which gives the scene a smooth, enameled appearance. The picture was once protected by two wings (also in the Louvre), upon which were painted in *trompe-l'œil* a silver ewer (alluding to the woman's illness) in an arched niche.

470. Jacob van Ruisdael
c. 1628/9–1682
The Ray of Sunlight
Canvas. H 83 cm (32.7 in.); W 99 cm (39 in.)
Coll. of Louis XVI. INV 1820

Using elements drawn from reality
—a windmill, the ruins of Brederode
castle near Haarlem, the hills
of Guelders and the banks of the
Rhine—Jacob van Ruisdael composed
a particularly grandiose imaginary
view. The almost architectural
cloudscape, underlined by the effects
of sunlight, plays an important part
in the dynamic construction of the
whole. The particularly fitting title
for the painting was given in the
19th century. While the reference
to Rembrandt landscapes is striking,
the pale tonalities in gray-blue and
green are the antithesis of that
master's warm and somber manner.
Most critics believe the figures are
by Philips Wouwerman,
in a collaboration that was very
common at that period.

471. Jan Vermeer
1632–1675
The Lacemaker
Canvas on wood. H 24 cm (9.4 in.);
W 21 cm (8.3 in.)
Acq. 1870. MI 1448

When this painting was acquired, Vermeer had only just been rediscovered by the critic Gustave Thoré, alias Bürger. Another hundred and thirteen years elapsed until, quite recently, another equally famous Vermeer, *The Astronomer*, entered the Louvre. The small size, tight composition and pale neutral ground all help to concentrate the spectator's attention on what the lacemaker is doing. The foreground (the tapestry and the red and white threads) is treated in a less precise manner, as if exaggeratedly large. This technique was much used by this artist, who played with optical effects like an artist-photographer.

Great Britain

The British school is, relatively-speaking, a recent one. It did not really attain definition and independence before the 18th century, which was the golden age of portraiture. British painting was likewise a latecomer to the Louvre. With the love of things English in France around 1900, a sustained interest developed, in which collectors (Bordeaux-Groult for example) and dealers played a decisive role. The Louvre acquired the great 18th century portrait painters: Lawrence, Romney, Raeburn, and Reynolds, with one of his most famous works, *Master Hare* (no. 473). But the other grand moment for the British collection only occurred after the Second World War when the first Gainsborough entered the Louvre. This was the portrait of *Lady Aston*, a fine example of his mature work. Tastes changed and the emphasis shifted from portraits to landscape. Bonington and Constable, founders of romantic landscape painting, were already in the Louvre in the 19th century. The famous *View of Salisbury*, acquired in 1952, is the best of the Constables, developing from the Dutch tradition of panoramic landscape. The most glaring gap in the museum was filled in 1967 with a picture by Turner (no. 474) in his final period, in which forms dissolve into a subtle interplay of patches of color. A new priority has emerged in recent years: narrative painting. The Louvre has added to its collections artists only just being rediscovered, like the great Fuseli, whose *Lady Macbeth,* painted at the same period as David's *Oath of the Horatii* is an exploration of the sublime, beloved of Burke, where horror predominated. There is the meditative Wright of Derby, whose *Lake Nemi* is much more than a view of the Roman countryside; and there is the elegant Zoffany, adept at the well-known genre of the "conversation piece," capturing a social elite in the act of being sociable. All the same, lacking a single Hogarth or Blake, the Louvre still has a long way to go to make up for its indifference to painting across the Channel.

472. Thomas Gainsborough
1727–1788
Conversation in a Park
c. 1746–1747

Canvas. H 73 cm (28.7 in.); W 68 cm (26.8 in.)
Gift of Pierre Bordeaux-Groult, 1952. RF 1952-16

This stiff couple are presumed
to be the artist himself with his wife
Margaret. Dating from the year
of their marriage (1746), the work has
a special value as a wedding souvenir.
The young Gainsborough, who was
barely twenty when he moved
to London, combined his two favorite
genres in this work: landscape,
ennobled by a folly, and portraiture,
with all the finesse of an engraving
by Gravelot, whose pupil he had
been. The bravura of the execution
adds to the charm of a genre which
flourished in 18th century England;
the "conversation piece," an intimate
society portrait executed in the genre
format.

473. Sir Joshua Reynolds
1723–1792
Master Hare
1788–1789

Canvas. H 77 cm (30.3 in.); W 63 cm (24.8 in.)
Verbal bequest by Baron Alphonse de Rothschild,
presented to the Louvre by his heirs, 1905.
RF 1580

At the end of a long, ambitious and
dogmatic career, Sir Joshua Reynolds
succumbed in this work to an English
love of the family, childhood and
compassion. Reproduced almost
immediately thereafter in an engraving entitled *Infancy*, this portrait
of Francis George Hare (1786–1842),
at two years of age, was painted for
the sitter's aunt. Loyal to his
convictions, Reynolds took care
to ennoble the subject-matter with
a gesture reminiscent of St. John the
Baptist in its religious connotation,
and with a handling of the autumn
landscape with a rich palette that
acknowledges his debt to Titian.

474. Joseph Mallord William Turner
1775–1851
**Landscape with a River and a Bay
in the Background**
c. 1845

Canvas. H 93 cm (36.6 in.); W 1.23 m (48.4 n.)
Acq. 1967. RF 1967-2

Of all the British artists to revive
European landscape painting,
Turner went furthest, pushing
the dissolution of forms in light to the
edge of abstraction. This painting
belongs to a group of unfinished
works composed around 1845, when
the elderly artist reprinted his *Liber
Studiorum*, a kind of sample book
of landscapes. One plate of this
anthology, inspired by Claude Gellée,
the *Confluence of the Severn and the
Wye* (1810), supplied the basis for
this composition, a flaming
"chimaera," in which romanticism
finds expression in a free technique,
close in its diaphanous effects to the
medium of watercolor.

Graphic Arts

France

Italy

Spain

Germany and Switzerland

The Netherlands and Flanders

Great Britain

Introduction

The Department of Graphic Arts, with holdings of some 130,000 items, is probably the least known in the Louvre because the fragile nature of the works and their sensitivity to light preclude permanent display. Created as the seventh department of the museum in 1988, it looks after the Cabinet des Dessins, the Chalcographie (Copper-Plate Prints) Section and the Edmond de Rothschild collection besides preserving the holdings of drawings from the Musée d'Orsay.

The Cabinet des Dessins

Housed from the very outset in the Louvre and installed since 1970 in the Flore Wing, the Cabinet des Dessins was instigated by Louis XIV and founded on the acquisition in 1671 of the collection of the Cologne banker, Eberhardt Jabach and augmented with those drawings found in the studio of First Painter to the King at his death. It was thus that the crown acquired the drawings of Charles Le Brun and his pupils in 1690, Pierre Mignard's drawings in 1695, and Antoine Coypel's in 1722. The acquisition policy was less well-defined in the 18th century. Nonetheless, the only major purchase, made at the sale of Pierre-Jean Mariette's renowned collection, brought in 1,051 drawings and albums of every school. At the French Revolution, the Cabinet Royal became the property of the Nation and the drawings, numbering 10,999 in 1792, were marked with the stamp of the National Museum. This number was doubled on the requisition of collections belonging to *émigrés*, including those of the count of Orsay and Charles Bourgevin Vialart de Saint-Morys. The arrival from Italy of the collection of the dukes of Modena in 1797 and the folios of drawings from Carlo Maratta's studio, found in the Low Countries, greatly enriched the Italian school. Further strengthening came with the acquisition in Florence, under Dominique-Vivant Denon's directorship, of albums containing almost 1,200 drawings assembled by the Florentine connoisseur Filippo Baldinucci. In the latter half of the 19th century when the Cabinet des Dessins was in the care of Frédéric Reiset, the collection was enriched still more, largely through various very important donations. Horace His de La Salle gave some 300 drawings in 1866 and 1878; the sculptor Jacques-Edouard Gateaux bequeathed 155 sheets in 1881, and there were several well-known acquisitions, among them items bought at the Wilhelm II of the Netherlands sale (1850), and the Codex Vallardi purchased in 1856.

Throughout the 20th century, the department continued to be the beneficiary of magnificent gifts. It was through the generosity of the painter Léon Bonnat (1912, 1919 and 1923), of Etienne Moreau-Nélaton (1907 and 1927), of Princess Louis de Croÿ (1930), of Baron Arthur Chassériau (1934), of Claude-Roger Marx and his daughter, Mme Paulette Asselain (1974 and 1978), that outstanding collections of work by artists of the 19th century (Michallon,

Delacroix, Corot, Chassériau, Millet, etc.) entered the Louvre. And through their munificence Félix Doistau (1919) and David David-Weill (1947) contributed to the growth of the miniature collection which had begun with works from the royal collections and from the academy. Nor should we forget the support of the Société des Amis du Louvre that has enabled major works of art to be acquired over the years (more than 400 since it was formed). Since 1797, when the first exhibition took place of 400 drawings in the Apollo Gallery, temporary exhibitions have been regularly put on to make the exceptional richness of the Louvre's holdings better known. Ever since the inventory and sorting undertaken by the first keeper of prints and drawings, Louis-Marie-Joseph Morel d'Arleux, and the follow-up work carried out by Frédéric Reiset from 1850 that led to the first scientific publications of the drawings, the collections have been systematically published, be it in the form of catalogues raisonnés issued from 1907 or in books tied in with temporary exhibitions. Today computerization of the collection enables any visitor to find out key information immediately on items in the collection. Furthermore, a reading room and a manuscript room provide direct access to the works of art to anybody who requests permission. Since 1991, moreover, there have been rolling displays of selections of works from the department at various locations in the museum linked to the paintings: cartoons and drawings of the French school of the 17th century (Sully Wing, second floor, rooms 20–23), tapestry cartoons from Italy of the 16th century (Denon Wing, first floor, rooms 8–10), pastels and miniatures (Sully Wing, second floor, rooms 41, 42 and 44), drawings from the Northern schools (Richelieu Wing, second floor, room 12).

Chalcographie (Copper-Plate Prints) Section

Set up under the Revolution alongside the Cabinet des Dessins, this section began with the plates of the Cabinet du Roi. Today there are 16,000 copper plates spanning the period from the Renaissance to modern times. Prints are sold by the Réunion des Musées Nationaux. This collection continues to grow through acquisitions and gifts.

The Edmond de Rothschild Collection

In accordance with Edmond de Rothschild's wishes, this collection was given to the Louvre in 1935 and is kept in the vicinity of the Cabinet des Dessins. Throughout his life Rothschild had built up a collection of prints where the greatest strengths were incunabula, niellos, works by Rembrandt and 18th century French prints. He amassed more than 40,000 prints, 3,000 drawings and 500 illustrated books.

The Musée d'Orsay Collection

Since 1977 drawings of the second half of the 19th century have been the responsibility of the Musée d'Orsay (artists born after 1820, bar a few exceptions such as Courbet, Daumier or Millet), but the department continues to handle the inventory and conservation aspects. Only pastels from the second half of the 19th century, and architectural and decorative art drawings have been transferred to the Musée d'Orsay where they are shown in a rolling display.

The Grande Salle of the Cabinet des Dessins

The Cabinet des Dessins was originally housed in the Hôtel de Gramont which once stood in what is now the Cour Napoléon and served as a repository of works of art. It has since been sited in several different locations in the palace. From 1970 it has been installed in the Flore Wing and the reading room was set up in the stairwell of the monumental stairway planned for the main apartments for guests of Emperor Napoleon III. The ceiling is by Cabanel. The bas-reliefs are by Eugène Guillaume and the statues in the niches are the work of Louis-Julien Franceschi. The collection may be consulted by anybody on request.

The Grande Salle of the Cabinet des Dessins

France

475. Jean Fouquet
c. 1420–1478/1481
Caesar Crossing the Rubicon
After 1470–1475

Miniature on parchment (H 45 cm (17.7 in.);
W 33 cm (13 in.)
Mrs H. Yates Thomson bequest, according to her
husband's wishes, 1946. RF 29493

This is one of four leaves at the Louvre that come from a missing manuscript, comprising two parts after ancient historical texts: *Ancient History until Caesar* and *Deeds of the Romans* taken from Orosius and Lucan. The *Crossing the Rubicon* as well as a second leaf, the *Flight of Pompey after Pharsalus*, come from the section in the second work concerned with the life of Caesar. These distinguished miniatures by the greatest painter and illuminator in 15th century France have been removed from the manuscript. They are remarkable for the way in which the figures fit within the space and for the intensity of the colors chosen according to the scenes portrayed. From the size of the miniatures we can guess what must have been the sumptuousness of the book, which probably dates from the end of Fouquet's career.

476. Nicolas Poussin
1590–1665
Venus at the Fountain
Verso of a letter written by the painter
A. Bouzonnet-Stella, addressed
to Poussin and dated 17 August 1657.
Pen and brown ink, brown and gray wash.
H 25.5 cm (10 in.); W 23.2 cm (9.1 in.)
Gift of His de la Salle, 1878. RF 762

This was drawn by the most
celebrated French artist of the
17th century, who worked chiefly
in Rome. The subject has poetic and
literary sources in classical Antiquity.
Leaning on a font, Venus is shown
doing her hair, with her right arm
raised over her head, and then
as an alternative, lowered
in contemplation of herself with
a mirror. At her feet, cherubs are
chasing a hare. A statue of Pan

in the background recalls pastoral
life, love and inebriation.
The drawing is in a shaky hand due
to an illness Poussin contracted
as an old man. In this period
he moved away from the rigorous
compositions of his maturity and
from the solemn and static
arrangements of his religious and
philosophical subjects.

456

477. Antoine Watteau
1684–1721
Six Studies of a Woman's Head and Two of a Youth
c. 1717

Three crayons with red chalk of several hues, traces of red chalk wash, white gouache and stumping on cream paper. H 22.5 cm (8.85 in.); W 34.8 cm (13.7 in.)
Gift of the Société des Amis du Louvre, 1997. RF 51760

This drawing was given to the museum by the Société des Amis du Louvre to mark its centenary. It is one of the most striking examples of the great talent of this master, reaching perfection in his quest for "truth" and the "natural," a quest he put above all else. In the freedom of positioning, these studies of the same woman's face and of a youth leave us guessing the order in which they were done, either dense and dark or else turning little by little into the light. These studies may be dated to the period when Watteau painted his acceptance piece for the painting academy, the *Pilgrimage to the Isle of Cythera* (no. 383). Although they do not have any precise link to the painting, they do nevertheless appear in the collections engraved after Watteau's death which brought together the drawings he had himself gathered into bound books that he called "thoughts."

His studies of heads are usually drawn with three crayons and the use of wash and of stumping are typical of his work of the period. It appears that Watteau himself invented this technique and it is often possible to detect his admiration for Rubens in the way he used it.

478. Jean-Baptiste Perronneau
1715-1783
Abraham Van Robais
1769

Pastel on gray-blue paper in two sheets over
stretchered canvas. Signed and dated in lead pencil
H 73.4 cm (28.9 in.); W 59.3 cm (23.3 in.)
Acq. 1912. RF 4146

If his correspondence is anything
to go by, Perronneau arrived
at Abbeville in 1769 to execute the
portrait of a local patrician.
The sitter, who is more than 70 years
old in this picture, belonged to a old
family of drapers, a flourishing
industry of the time. He was rich
and titled. Van Robais commissioned
no less than three pastel portraits
from the artist, who was forced
to seek his clientele in the provinces
in the face of the success of his arch
rival La Tour. The Louvre drawing
shows Perronneau at the height
of his powers in the way he com-
mingles realism and psychology.
It is a piquant indictment of the
arrogance of caste and the ravages
of age. In this, a meditative likeness
haunted by death, the haughtiness
of the old man merges with the
giddiness of introspection.

479. Jean-Auguste-Dominique Ingres
1780-1867
Madame Marcotte de Sainte-Marie
1826

Lead and graphite pencils. Signed. H 32.4 cm
(12.7 in.); W 24 cm (9.4 in.)
Acq. 1987. RF 41393

In 1810 while staying at the Villa
Medici, Ingres met Marcotte
d'Argenteuil, who was director
of Water and Forests in Napoleonic
Rome. The painter was introduced
to the Marcotte family and he received
commissions for portraits, an exercise
that he saw before all else as a source
of income. Back in France in 1824,
Ingres drew more than 20 portraits
for 14 members of the family,
including this one of Madame
Marcotte de Sainte-Marie, née
Salvaing de Boisseu, sister-in-law
of Marcotte d'Argenteuil.
The drawing is a study for the
Louvre painting, with the sitter
in very much the same pose. The
painting is similar to the study but
the back of the divan has disappeared
and the placing of the hands
is slightly different. The series
of portraits that Ingres executed
around 1824 to 1826 brilliantly
demonstrates his aggressive

classicism in diametric opposition
to the romantic tendency in vogue.
Primacy of form and tyranny of line
end up by eluding any kind
of psychology.

480. Théodore Géricault
1791–1824
The Freeing of the Prisoners of the Inquisition
c. 1820–1822

Black crayon and red chalk. H 41.9 cm (16.5 in.);
W 58.1 cm (22.9 in.)
Acq. 1991. RF 42989

On 9 March 1820, Madrid rose
up against Ferdinand VII, an absolute
monarch living in the wrong century.
The mob invaded the courts of the
Inquisition to release the unfortunate
prisoners languishing in the jails.
This monumental study whose
classical inspiration recalls Raphael
is undoubtedly linked to the Madrid
incident landed in France by the
liberal press, which had been scathing
about the Bourbons. The picture may
also be linked to the large drawing,
now in the Ecole des Beaux-Arts
in Paris, which Géricault executed
for his *African Slave Trade*. We do not
know for whom these two projects
were undertaken (it could be that
they were to be made into litho-
graphic prints), but they are among
the last works of the painter, who
was suffering from Pott's disease,
a cancer of the bone that ultimately
killed him in January 1824 at the
age of 33. They are political works
above all and attest to his liberal
commitment at the height of the
Restoration. Géricault reinvented
classicism with a didactic purpose
where idea triumphs over feeling.

481. Eugène Delacroix
1798–1863
Moroccan Notebook
1832

Album with boards, bound in dark-green paper,
containing 56 folios of sketches in lead pencil
or brown pen and ink, often heightened with
watercolor and accompanied by manuscript notes,
two endpapers in green paper. H. 10.5 cm (4.1 in.);
W. 9.8 cm (3.8 in.)
Delacroix studio sale, 1864 (sale stamp in red wax
on the top board). Acq. 1983. RF 39050

After the occupation of Algeria (1830),
King Louis-Philippe, anxious
to appease the sultan of Morocco,
ordered the count of Mornay
to undertake a peace-keeping
mission and Delacroix accompanied
him. The painter landed at Tangiers
on 24 January 1832 and stayed
in North Africa until June.
The Orient at that time was a legend
of light and color that haunted the
romantic world. For Delacroix, who
had already painted two masterpieces
of oriental inspiration, *The Massacres
of Chios* (1824 Salon) and *Death
of Sardanpale* (1827 Salon), both
in the Louvre, this mission was
an occasion to see for himself
a world about which he had only

dreamt. He came back with seven
albums of drawings executed from
life with written notes on life
in Morocco, the local customs, the
countryside and the architecture.
Of the seven albums only four have
survived, and three of them are
in the Louvre. In his Moroccan
notebook, put to use from the
moment he set foot in Tangiers,
words and lines, verbal expression
and drawing are the instruments
of a memory dazzled by the Orient:
"I am ... like a man who dreams
and who sees things that he fears
to see elude him," he wrote to Jean-
Baptiste Pierret on 25 January (letter
in the Louvre).

482. Jean-François Millet
1814–1875
Fishermen
Black crayon. H 32.8 cm (12.9 in.); W 49.2 cm
(19.4 in.)
Gift of Isaac de Camondo, 1911. Collection
of Musée d'Orsay. RF 4104

This scene of lobster fishing is set off
the coast of the Cotentin, the area
of Normandy where Millet was
born. The Louvre has a fine collection
of his drawings. The artist's
monumental style, based on the light
effects achieved by black crayon, his
favorite medium (one is reminded
of Seurat), attains an almost epic
realism here.
This work has been variously dated
to his maturity (1857–1860) and
to old age, around 1870–1871. His
noble vision does not detract from
the subversive strength of the
contents; this night fishing scene
is also the kind of direct depiction
of reality (the fishermen are
dropping their lobster pots) which
made Millet a social painter.

Italy

483. Antonio Pollaiuolo
1431/1432–1498
Nude Warriors in Combat
c. 1470–1475

Burin. H 40 cm (15.7 in.); W 60 cm (23.6 in.)
Edmond de Rothschild coll., bequeathed 1935.
INV 6813 LR

One of the greatest plates engraved
during the 15th century, both for its
size and breadth of composition,
the *Nude Warriors in Combat* is the
oldest Italian engraving bearing
the artist's full name: "Opus. Antonii.
Pollaioli. Florentini."
Art historians are divided about the
subject of the frieze-like scene but
it is doubtless simply a pretext for
depicting nudes in action, possibly
gladiators, against a decorative
backdrop of olive trees, millet and
vines. Pollaiuolo, who also worked
in enamel inlay, adopts zigzag lines,
long parallel cuts and crosshatching
to convey something of the style
of pen drawings of his time.

484. Leonardo di ser Piero da Vinci,
known as **Leonardo da Vinci**
1452–1519
Drapery for a Seated Figure

Brush and gray-brown tempera with white
heightening, on gray prepared canvas.
H 22 cm (8.7 in.); W 13.9 cm (5.5 in.)
Gift of Jean-Louis Marquis of Ganay and his
brothers, 1989. RF 41905

Two studies of drapery from the
hand of Leonardo da Vinci entered
the Louvre in 1989 where four other
drawings using the same treatment
were already conserved. Altogether
they are the most beautiful group
known today of small monochromatic
paintings drawn with the tip of the
brush on fine canvas. How the group
came about and what part these
pictures played in Leonardo's early
years may be induced from what
Giorgio Vasari wrote in his *Lives*,
1550. He describes Leonardo's work
in Andrea Verrocchio's workshop
thus: "… he studied much in drawing
from nature and he would sometimes
make models in clay over which
he would lay lengths of soft cloth
dipped in clay. He would then set
himself patiently to draw them
on very fine cloth or prepared linen.
In that way he was able to obtain
wonderful effects in black and white
with the point of his brush."

485. Antonio Allegri,
known as **Correggio**
1489?–1534
Allegory of Vices
c. 1529–1530

Tempera on canvas. H 1.42 m (55.9 in.);
W 85 cm (33.5 in.)
Coll. of the French Crown. INV 5927

Although there is no record
of the commission of this allegory
or the *Allegory of Virtues*, both pictures
hung in the *studiolo* of Isabella

d'Este at the Palazzo Ducale
in Mantua. The subject-matter
is disputed. It may depict
a mythological story (Apollo and
Marsyas) or an allegory of Pleasures,
Vices or Evil. The technique
of tempera, which by 1530 had
become something of an anachronism,
was probably chosen to harmonize
with other works in the room
by older artists (Mantegna, Costa
and Perugino). The grouping
of figures is an interpretation of the
Laocoön, a Hellenistic sculpture
found in Rome in 1506. It is in the
sculptural manner of Giulio
Romano, the great Mantuan painter
of the period. But the softened line
and flowing style, the delicate
coloring, the fluid highlights and
shadows are Correggio's own
contribution to the Italian
Renaissance.

486. Giovanni da Udine
1487–1561 or 1564
Pigeon Flying Toward the Left

Pen and brown ink, gray and brown wash, water color, white heightening (on verso: a pigeon perching, three-quarter view to the right). H 29.6 cm (11.6 in.); W 19.6 cm (7.7 in.)
Gift of the Société des Amis du Louvre, 1994.
RF 43394

Trained in the Veneto under Martino da Udine and Giorgione, Giovanni da Udine used his talents as stuccoer, ornamentalist and painter of animals in his work for Raphael and his pupils in Rome between 1515 and 1527. Since the middle of the 16th century, biographers have taken pleasure in reminding us that "he loved above all things to draw birds and [that] he soon filled a notebook with such variety and beauty that Raphael was delighted" (Vasari). The page reproduced here well exemplifies this naturalistic art of animal representation that was part of the great Venetian tradition. Although following a practice by then a century old, this drawing also shows a new freedom in the handling of the washes and colors.

487. Annibale Carracci
1560–1609
Polyphemus

Black chalk, white heightening, gray-blue paper (below right, study for right hand of Polyphemus). H 52.1 cm (20.5 in.); W 38.5 cm (15.2 in.)
Coll. of the French Crown. Cabinet des Dessins du Roi. INV 7319

This sketch is a study for the face of the cyclops, Polyphemus, who was in love with Galatea, a marine goddess enamoured of Acis, and who was rejected by her. The alterations to be seen on the head of the giant show how the painter hesitated over the representation of a face with only one eye. This masterly study is a preparation for the fresco at the Galleria Farnese in the Palazzo Farnese, Rome. Begun in 1597, this was the most ambitious undertaking of Annibale's career. It played a very important part in the development of decorative painting in the 17th century. The majority of preparatory drawings for the Farnese cycle, coming directly from Annibale's studio, are conserved in the Cabinet des Dessins.

488. Andrea Appiani
1754–1817
The Apotheosis of the Emperor Napoleon

Black chalk with white heightening. H 2.73 m
(107.5 in.); W 4.80 m (189 in.)
Acq. from artist's family, 1881. MI 754

The greatest work by Appiani,
master of Lombardian neoclassicism,
was the decoration of the Milan
royal palace in 1808, devoted to the
magnificence of the empire.
This cartoon is a preparation for the
monumental fresco which decorated
the vaulting of the throne room. The
required note of flattery is couched
in allegorical abstractions, a language
revived by the imitation of antiquity
according to Winckelmann. Four
Victories hold up the throne where
the emperor sits in majesty, amid the
diverse attributes of immortality.
Escaping the bombing of 1943 which
destroyed its setting, the fresco
is now at the Villa Carlotta
at Tremezzo. The Louvre has
a unique collection of more than
200 artists' cartoons.

Spain

of 16th century Spain. The drawing, which has enabled other pictures in the reserve collection at the Louvre to be identified, shows the influence of the masters of the Italian Renaissance, especially Michelangelo, when Berruguete stayed in Rome (and no doubt Florence also) between 1507 and 1517.

489. Alonso Berruguete
1486–1561
Study of a Seated Man
1540–1550

Pen and brown ink on buff paper, inscribed in pen and brown ink, center right: "de mano de beruge."
H 26.5 cm (10.4 in.); W 15 cm (5.9 in.)
Acq., 1995. RF 44343

The ancient inscription confirms the attribution of this recently acquired sheet which we can now recognize as one of the very rare drawings of Berruguete, an artist who worked in Toledo and Granada. The Graphic Arts Department was particularly keen to complement its collection of works from the Spanish school with this major work. The taut line and fine hatching confer a sense of movement to this supple figure within the space on the sheet. It should be compared to this artist's paintings and sculptures and sheds some valuable light on the still incomplete survey we have

490. Francisco José de Goya y Lucientes
1746–1828
The Street-Porter
1815–1820

Brush and sepia wash, lined with pink paper.
H 20.3 cm (8 in.); W 14.3 cm (5.6 in.)
Album F (numbered 92 in the hand of Goya and 66 in another hand). Gift in lieu of death duty, 1982.
RF 38976

After his series *Disasters of War*, recalling the winter of 1811–1812, Goya worked on Album F, executing a series of drawings without captions which exposed the rigid character of Spanish society. The street-porter

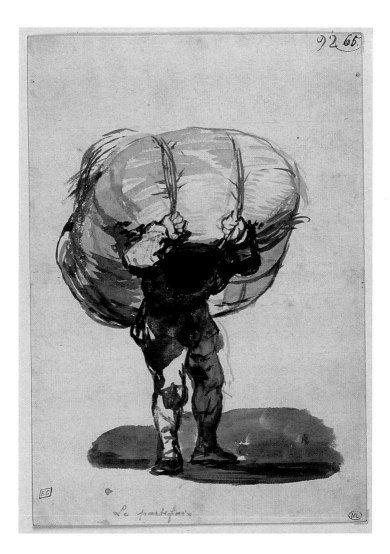

Le portefaix

theme depicting the roughest
of work is broached for the first time
on folio 60 where two heavily laden
porters are shown from behind.
Here the street-porter is facing us,
but we cannot discern his face masked
as it is by suffering and drowned in
brown wash. Only his hands bound
up with twine from the bale and his
legs bent with exertion stand out
against the rest of his body utterly
swallowed up by the shadow of his
own burden. It is an expressionless
face, and his silent body yields
us nothing unless maybe anticipating
a rupture: for his body is already
bent low and something is snapping
in his stomach. But what is this
burden? What is this man carrying?
It seems that through the porter's
isolation and dejection Goya has
been able to endow this simple scene
with the violence and dramatic
tension of the *Disasters of War*.
Is it the world that weighs so heavily
on his shoulders? Goya has
transformed the street-porter into
a latterday Atlas and contemplates
with us the anguish of the human
condition.

Germany and Switzerland

491. Albrecht Dürer
1471–1528
Livonian Lady
1521

Pen and sepia ink, watercolor. H 28.2 cm (11.1 in.);
W 18.8 cm (7.4 in.)
Edmond de Rothschild coll., bequeathed 1935.
INV 19 DR

492. Hans Baldung Grien
1484/1485–1545
The Witches
1510

Monochrome print, two blocks (gray and black).
H 37.8 cm (14.9 in.); W 25.8 cm (10.2 in.)
Edmond de Rothschild coll., bequeathed 1935.
INV 784 LR

The series of three drawings showing
women of Livonia is one of the
jewels of the Edmond de Rothschild
collection. These watercolors served
as models for the wood engravings
by Jost Amman, illustrating the
work entitled *Habitus præcipuorum
populorum* edited by Hans Weigel
at Nuremberg in 1577. It is possible
that the famous Nuremberg artist
saw these Livonian costumes
at Antwerp (a flourishing cosmopolitan town at that time), during his
trip to the Netherlands (1520–1521).
This richly dressed woman is a good
illustration of Dürer's ethnographical
interest; he noted down carefully
everything odd or out of the ordinary
he saw in his *Journal*.

This pupil of Dürer was interested
in the camaïeu printing technique,
a wood engraving which imitated
highlighted drawings on tinted
paper. It was while in Strasbourg,
between 1509 and 1512, that
Baldung was particularly preoccupied
with the theme of witches and
death. This nocturnal sabbath is one
of his most well-known works and
perhaps his first as an independent
master at Strasbourg. The figures,
shown on a large scale within
a precise composition, are geometri-
cally arranged in a pyramidal group
with diagonals fanning out from the
center. Hatching is skillfully used
to create light effects.

493. Johan Heinrich Füssli,
known as **Henry Fuseli**
1741–1825
Ezzelin and Meduna (?)
c. 1780

Pen and black ink over pencil lines. H 19.3 cm
(7.6 in.); W 27.7 cm (10.9 in.)
Gift of the Société des Amis du Louvre, 1992.
RF 43254

Fuseli drawings are rare in the
Louvre and this one is something
of a mystery since we still do not
know the subject of the dramatic
scene. The most convincing
hypothesis is that it is an imaginary
episode referred to by the artist
in his correspondence. In a sad epic
tale, Ezzelin, a medieval lord, kills
his wife, Meduna, on his return
from the Crusade because she has
broken her chastity belt, which
is taken as overwhelming proof
of her betrayal. The anecdote
encapsulates some of the painter's
favorite themes: sex and tragedy,
pathos and the sublime. When
he came back from Rome after

a long sojourn there from 1770
to 1778, fascinated by the classical
world and Michelangelo, the Swiss
Fuseli set himself up in London.
There he devoted a number
of works to his Gothic fantasy
in which his striving for expression
through rugged drawing flouted the
ideals of classicism. This aesthetic
of ugliness is not out of keeping with
the convulsive linework.

The Netherlands and Flanders

494. Apocalypsis Johannis
Netherlands, c. 1440

2nd edition. Woodcut. H 26.2 cm (10.3 in.);
W 19.8 cm (7.8 in.)
Edmond de Rothschild coll., bequeathed 1935.
INV L 51 LR

The left-hand folio of the woodcut
book, the *Apocalypse* of St. John
(presaging the destruction of Rome
which will give place to the new
Jerusalem, symbol of the kingdom
of God), illustrates the Opening
of the Third and Fourth Seals.
The third horseman, Famine upon
a black horse has a pair of balances
in his hand; the fourth, emerging
from the mouth of Hell, is named
Death or more precisely the Plague.
He sits astride a pale horse holding
a bowl from which flames dart. The
error in the coloring of the horses
was corrected after the first three
editions. This incunabulum takes its
inspiration from French and Anglo-
Norman manuscripts as well as from
the tapestry of the *Apocalypse*
at Angers, made in the last quarter
of the 14th century.

495. Georg Hoefnagel
1552–1600
White Ram and Black Sheep
1575–1582

Watercolor and gouache on vellum, oval frame
with gilded edge, numbered and inscribed in pen
with ink and gold. H. 14.5 cm (5.7 in.);
L. 18.6 cm (7.3 in.)
Acq. 1982. RF38986

Georg Hoefnagel, the son of a rich
Antwerp diamond merchant, left his
native city probably following
the Spanish insurrection, to enter the
service of the dukes Albert V and
William V of Bavaria. In 1582
he illuminated a missal for Archduke
Ferdinand of Tyrol and in 1590
entered the court of Emperor
Rudolph II, where he mostly
produced miniatures. This work
belongs to a set of four volumes
forming a bestiary and was executed
between 1575 and 1582. Rudolph II
acquired it not long after the artist's
arrival in Prague. The choice
of subject and the painstaking
draughtsmanship bear witness
to Dürer's influence. Each of the 227
drawings in this set has a saying.
This sheet, oval in shape, depicts
a ram in profile and a sheep lying
on its side facing each other, and
is surrounded by a two inscriptions
in Latin. The lower one may
be translated thus: "The ram repays
the cost of its food by butting with
its horns," and the upper one reads:
"Sheep are useless if the shepherd
is away." This second saying may
be an allusion to the image of the
Good Shepherd relayed in the New
Testament by that of Christ guiding
the faithful.

470

OVIVM NVLLVS VSVS SI PASTOR ABSIT .

XXVIII .

496. Antoon Van Dyck (Sir Anthony)
1599–1641
The Arrest of Christ
c. 1620

Brush, bistre wash, squared in black chalk.
H 24.6 cm (9.7 in.); W 21.2 cm (8.3 in.)
Saint-Morys coll. Seized during the French
Revolution, entered the Louvre in 1796. Inv. 19909

In 1620 Van Dyck left Rubens'
workshop for England, then several
months later, went to Antwerp where
he began work on a series of paintings
on the theme of the arrest of Christ.
This squared-up drawing is linked
directly to this important corpus
of works that includes three paintings
and seven preparatory drawings.
The composition, inspired by Dürer
and Marten de Vos, changes little
throughout the series. Certain details,
however, do differ: the two apostles
strangely asleep at the foot of the
tree disappear in the other versions
and are replaced in the Minneapolis
version by Malchus, a slave of one
of the high priests, who lies on the
ground after being smitten by one
of Christ's disciples (John 18:10).
The study brilliantly demonstrates the
survival of mannerist rhetoric in the
young Van Dyck's work. The mob
is frenzied, even fanatical, the curves,
lines and scrolls commingle with
violence in a maelstrom of spears and
swords. Only the serenity of Christ
contrasts with this savage affray.
He stands with arms outstretched
looking at Judas who has given him
his betraying kiss; the latter's face
in shadow as though overwhelmed
by the gravity of his deed.

Erasmus Rotterdamus

Ant. van Dyck fecit aqua forti.

497. Antoon Van Dyck (Sir Anthony)
1599–1641
Erasmus of Rotterdam

Aquatint and burin on copper, fifth state with the
address of the publisher Gillis Hendrickx (effaced).
H 24 cm (9.4 in.); W 15 cm (5.9 in.)
Copper-plate section, catalogue no. 2303

Returning from Italy after 1627,
Van Dyck undertook a monumental
work entitled *Iconography* which
he published himself and which may
be said to exemplify the tradition
of depicting galleries of illustrious
men, a tradition that attained
perfection in the 17th century.
Van Dyck's *Iconography* brings
together 80 plates, intermingling
portraits of princes with those
of learned men and artists, both
contemporary and from earlier
times. Such is the portrait of Erasmus,
inspired by Hans Holbein's painting
that Van Dyck may have seen
in London in 1620 in the collection
of the earl of Arundel. The lightness
of the point grazing the varnish,
along with the stippling, gives
contemplative strength to the face,
to the fullness of his robes and to the
fineness of his hands resting on an
open book. The *Iconography* was
published in Antwerp in 1641,
republished in 1646 with 20 further
pictures of which 15 were aquatints
signed by Van Dyck himself. The
whole collection is kept in a bound
volume in the Edmond de Rothschild
collection.

498. Harmensz. van Rijn Rembrandt
1606–1669
Jacob's Dream

Pen and brown ink, brown wash, corrections
in white gouache, inscribed in black chalk.
H 24.9 cm (9.8 in.); W 20.7 cm (8.1 in.)
Acq. 1775. INV 22881

Rembrandt's drawings, where his
use of *chiaroscuro* tends to turn the
image into a vision, display a rare
inwardness of feeling in his Bible
illustrations. Striving for depth
rather than description, the artist
often diverges from traditional
iconography. In *Jacob's Dream*,
which belonged to the renowned
collector Pierre-Jean Mariette,
he puts forward an intimist reading
of the celebrated passage in Genesis
(Gen. 28:10–16). On the road
to Haran Jacob lay down to sleep,
placing his head on a stone; above
a ladder set up between heaven
and earth on which angels ascend
and descend, God appears to him and
tells him that his descendants shall
be numerous and powerful. Here
the ladder in fact disappears: the
fusion of the real and the supernatural
is achieved through the presence
of two angels with outspread wings
who study Jacob almost affectionately.
The ellipsis of line and the shadows
surrounding the sleeper intensify the
light of the angels and reinforce his
nearness to God.

Great Britain

499. Lucas Hornebolte or **Horenbaut**
c. 1490–1544
Henry VIII
c. 1526–1527

Miniature on vellum. D 5.6 cm (2.2 in.)
Gift of the Société des Amis du Louvre, 1994.
RF 44315

Son of a famous illuminator from around Ghent and Bruges, Lucas Hornebolte went to England in 1524 and took up the enviable position of painter to King Henry VIII (1491–1547). He left seven portraits of the sovereign including this one, which in spite of its tiny diameter is the greatest in the series. He returns here to a style of composition first created in France by another painter from the Low Countries, Jean Clouet, where the bust is depicted against a neutral background within a medallion. Hornebolte belongs to the earliest stirrings of that much estimed genre of the 16th and 17th centuries, the portrait miniature. Judging by the king's face, this portrait pre-dates by ten years the famous likenesses of Henry VIII by Holbein and Joos van Cleve.

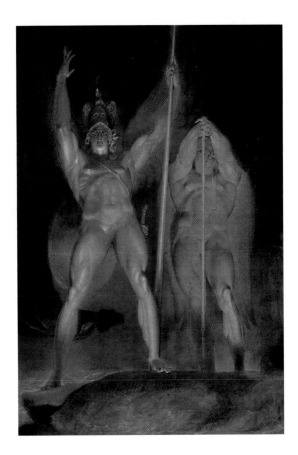

500. Sir Thomas Lawrence
1769–1830
Satan and Beelzebub
1795

Black chalk, with white heightening on buff paper
(on two sheets joined toward the middle widthwise).
H 1,270 m (50 in.); L 71 cm (27.9 in.)
Acq. 1980. RF 38363

Haunted by his obsession with the "grand style" which he had acquired from his master Reynolds, the young Lawrence, fashionable portrait painter, painter to the king and member of the Royal Academy, London, took up historical genre painting. In 1795, the optimism of the Enlightenment was already tempered by the taste for irrationality. Milton's *Paradise Lost* crystalized artists' interest. Lawrence took his subject from the first book of the epic where Satan assumes possession of Hell and harangues his legions: "Awake, arise or be forever fallen!" And the diabolical army of fallen angels gathers at his command "on the bare strand." The drawing in the Louvre is the most complete of the eight studies for the painting exhibited in 1797. The critics' reception was restrained: Satan was deemed to be colossal and very badly drawn with his body out of proportion and the color false. In fact Lawrence's work does not correspond to the canon of the classical conception of the "sublime" (Longin), rather it is in keeping with Burke's more modern one where the quintessence of beauty is now in the dread of the night and in "gloomy pomp."

Index of Artists

Abaquesne, Masséot 251
Agostino di Duccio 349
Andrea del Sarto (Andrea d'Agnolo
    di Francesco) 423
Anguier, François 320
Antonello da Messina 413
Appiani, Andrea 488
Arnould, Jean 323
Auguste, Robert-Joseph 282

Baldung Grien, Hans 492
Balzac, Edme-Pierre 278
Bapst, Evrard 290
Barocci, Federico 429
Bartolini, Lorenzo 355
Barye, Antoine-Louis 343
Baugin, Lubin 371
Bellano, Bartolomeo 244
Bellechose, Henri 364
Bernini, Gian Lorenzo 353
Berruguete, Alonso 489
Biard, Pierre 317
Biennais, Martin-Guillaume 288
Bontemps, Pierre 313
Bordoni, Francesco 318
Bosio, François-Joseph 339
Bosschaert, Ambrosius, the Elder 463
Botticelli (Alessandro Filipepi) 415
Bouchardon, Edme 328
Boucher, François 280, 387
Boulle, André-Charles 266
Boulogne, Jean (Giambologna) 248
Boulogne, Valentin de (Le Valentin) 370
Brueghel, Pieter, the Elder 454
Brygus, 161

Caffieri, Jean-Jacques 334
Canova, Antonio 354
Caravaggio (Michelangelo Merisi) 431
Carpaccio, Vittore 421
Carracci, Annibale 430, 487
Cellini, Benvenuto 351
Champaigne, Philippe de 379
Chardin, Jean-Siméon 386
Chassériau, Théodore 401
Chaudet, Antoine-Denis 338

Chinard, Joseph 337
Cimabue (Cenni di Pepo) 404
Clodion (Claude, Michel) 333
Clouet, François 369
Colombe, Michel 308
Corot, Camille 403
Correggio (Antonio Allegri) 424, 485
Cousinet, Henri-Nicolas 270
Coustou, Guillaume 327
Coysevox, Antoine 324, 325
Cranach the Elder, Lucas 445
Cressent, Charles 272

Da Fiesole, Mino 348
Da Urbino, Nicola 246
David, Louis 391, 395
David d'Angers, Pierre-Jean 344
Da Vinci, Leonardo, 416, 418, 420
Da Vinci, Pierino, 352
De Hooch, Pieter 467
Delacroix, Eugène 398, 399, 481
Della Francesca, Piero 410
Della Quercia, Jacopo 346
Del Sarto, Andrea (Andrea d'Agnolo
    di Francesco) 423
De Vries, Adriaan 362
Donatello (Donato di Niccolo Bardi)
    347
Dou, Gerrit 469
Dubois, Jacques 274
Duccio, Agostino d'Antonio di 349
Dürer, Albrecht 444, 491
Duseigneur, Jehan (Jean-Bernard) 342

El Greco (Domenicos Theotocopoulos)
    437
Erhart, Gregor 358
Euphronius, 157, 158
Evrard d'Orléans 302
Exekias 154

Falconet, Etienne-Maurice 330
Fiesole, Mino Da 348
Flegel, Georg 447
Floris, Frans 453
Fouquet, Jean 241, 365, 475
Fra Angelico (Guido di Pietro) 407
Fragonard, Jean-Honoré 389

Francavilla, Pietro 318
Francesca, Piero della 410
Francqueville, Pierre 318
Friedrich, Caspar David 448
Froment-Meurice, François-Désiré 293
Fuseli, Henry 493
Füssli, Johan Heinrich 493

Gainsborough, Thomas 472
Gellée, Claude (Le Lorrain) 376
Géricault, Théodore 397, 480
Germain, François-Thomas 276, 277
Ghirlandaio (Domenico di Tomaso
    Bigordi) 417
Giambologna (Jean Boulogne) 248
Giotto di Bondone 405
Girardon, François 322
Girodet de Roussy-Trioson, Anne-Louis
    396
Gossaert, Jan (Mabuse) 452
Gouers, Daniel 269
Goujon, Jean 311
Govaers, Daniel 269
Goya y Lucientes, Francesco José de
    441, 490
Greco, El (Domenicos Theotocopoulos)
    437
Greuze, Jean-Baptiste 390
Grien, Hans Baldung 492
Gros, Antoine-Jean 393
Guardi, Francesco 434

Hals, Frans 464
Hey, Jean (The Master of Moulins)
    367
Hoefnagel, Georg 495
Hoffmann, Martin 356
Holbein, Hans, the Younger 446
Hooch, Pieter de 467
Horenbaut, Lucas 499
Hornebolte, Lucas 499
Houdon, Jean-Antoine 331, 335
Huguet, Jaume 436

Ingres, Jean-Auguste-Dominique
    400, 402, 479

Jacob, Georges 283, 286

Jacob-Desmalter, François-Honoré-
    Georges 287
Jordaens, Jacob 461
Julien, Pierre 332

Largillière, Nicolas de 382
La Tour, Georges de 373
Lawrence, Sir Thomas 500
Le Brun, Charles 380
Leleu, Jean-François 281
Le Lorrain (Claude Gellée) 376
Lemoyne, François 385
Le Nain, Antoine 374
Le Nain, Louis 374
Leonardo da Vinci 416, 418, 420, 484
Le Sueur, Eustache 377
Le Valentin (Valentin de Boulogne) 370
Limousin, Léonard 249, 250

Mabuse (Jan Gossaert) 452
Mantegna, Andrea 412
Martin, Monk 297
Martini, Simone 406
Martorell, Bernardo 435
Master of the Altar-Piece
    of St. Bartholomew 443
Master of the Holy Family 442
Master of Moulins, The (Jean Hey) 367
Menière, Paul-Nicolas 290
Messina, Antonello da 413
Metsu, Gabriel 468
Metsys, Quentin 451
Michelangelo (Michelangiolo Buonarroti)
    350
Millet, Jean-François 482
Mino da Fiesole 348
Miseroni, Ottavio 258
Murillo, Bartolomé Esteban 440

Nicola da Urbino 246

Onesimos 155
Orléans, Evrard d' 302
Orley, Bernard van 256
Ouizille Charles 285

Painter of Ixion 173
Painter of the Niobides 167

Pajou, Augustin 336
Palissy, Bernard 252
Pannini, Giovanni Paolo 433
Perronneau, Jean-Baptiste 388, 478
Pierino da Vinci 352
Piero della Francesca 410
Pigalle, Jean-Baptiste 329
Pilon, Germain 314, 316
Pisanello (Antonio Puccio) 408
Pollaiuolo, Antonio 483
Poussin, Nicolas 375, 378, 476
Pradier, James 340
Praxiteles 171
Prieur, Barthélemy 257, 315
Prud'hon, Pierre-Paul 394
Puget, Pierre 321

Quarton, Enguerrand 366
Quercia, Jacopo Della 346

Raphael (Raffaello Santi) 419, 422
Regnaud, Jean 323
Regnault, Guillaume 310
Rembrandt Harmensz. van Rijn 465,
    466, 498
Reni, Guido 432
Reymond, Pierre 253
Reynolds, Sir Joshua 473
Ribera, Jusepe de 439
Riccio (Andrea Briosco) 245
Riemenschneider, Tilman 357
Rigaud, Hyacinthe 381
Robert, Hubert 392
Romain, Jules 264
Rosso Fiorentino (Giovanni Battista
    di Jacopo) 426
Rubens, Peter Paul 456, 459, 460
Rude, François 341
Ruisdael, Jacob van 470

Sarazin, Jacques 319
Sassetta (Stefano di Giovanni) 409
Schro, Dietrich 359

Thierry, Jean 326
Tintoretto (Jacopo Robusti) 428
Titian (Tiziano Vecellio) 425
Tura, Cosimo (Cosimè) 414

Turner, Joseph Mallord William 474

Uccello (Paolo di Dono) 411
Udine, Giovanni da 486
Urbino, Nicola da 246

Valentin de Boulogne (Le Valentin) 370
Van der Weyden, Rogier 450
Van Dyck, Antoon (Sir Anthony) 457,
    458, 496, 497
Van Eyck, Jan 449
Van Haarlem, Cornelis 455
Van Orley, Bernard 256
Vermeer, Johannes (Jan) 471
Veronese (Paolo Caliari) 427
Vinci, Leonardo da 416, 418, 420, 484
Vinci, Pierino da 352
Vouet, Simon 260, 372
Vries, Adriaen de 362
Watteau, Jean-Antoine 383, 384,
477Weisweiler, Adam 284
Wtewael, Joachim 462

Zurbarán, Francisco de 438

Photography:
Réunion des musées nationaux,
photographic dept.

Produced by the Publishing Dept.
Béatrice Foulon (Director)

Editorial Coordinator:
Marie-Claude Bianchini

Translation:
John Adamson
Frédéric Morvan

Graphic design:
Philippe Apeloig

Layout:
Vincent Grousson

Production:
Jacques Venelli

Photoengraving:
Haudressy, Paris

Printed and bound in september 1999
by Mame in Tours, France.

Premier dépôt légal: septembre 1999
Dépôt légal: janvier 2002
ISBN: 2-7118-3871-4
GG 20 3871